Christianities in the Tr

Series Edit(
Crawford Gril ₋₋ₗ
Department of History
Queen's University Belfast
Belfast, UK

Scott Spurlock
Department of Theology and Religious Studies
University of Glasgow
Glasgow, UK

Building upon the recent recovery of interest in religion in the early modern trans-Atlantic world, this series offers fresh, lively and inter-disciplinary perspectives on the broad view of its subject. Books in the series will work strategically and systematically to address major but under-studied or overly simplified themes in the religious and cultural history of the trans-Atlantic.

More information about this series at
http://www.palgrave.com/gp/series/14892

Timothy C. F. Stunt

The Life and Times of Samuel Prideaux Tregelles

A Forgotten Scholar

Timothy C. F. Stunt
Naples, FL, USA

Christianities in the Trans-Atlantic World
ISBN 978-3-030-32268-7   ISBN 978-3-030-32266-3   (eBook)
https://doi.org/10.1007/978-3-030-32266-3

Andrew Walls
Pignus amicitiae et gratiarum

PREFACE

This book has been some sixty years in the making.

When, as a schoolboy, I began my far from successful efforts to wrestle with classical Greek, my father who was an elder in the local assembly of Plymouth Brethren, where we worshiped as a family, was delighted. Being an earnest student of scripture, he reckoned that his son would now be able to read the New Testament in its original language. In 1955, for Christmas, he gave me a copy of Bagster's interlinear *Greek New Testament* with its apparatus detailing the variant readings of the seven principle printed editions, which succeeded the Erasmian text reproduced by Stephanus in 1550. In the book's introduction, I became acquainted with six strange editorial names of which I had previously never heard and which ever since have had for me something of a magic ring about them: Elzevir, Griesbach, Lachmann, Tischendorf, Tregelles and Alford.

My subsequent investigation of these exotic names uncovered something even more momentous for a boy whose family had been Plymouth Brethren for three generations. At my father's suggestion, I visited the Marylebone Public Library to consult the *Dictionary of National Biography* and learnt that for some fifteen years one of these scholarly editors, Samuel Prideaux Tregelles, had been a Plymouth Brother, a discovery that led me to wonder (with possibly a sigh of relief!) whether perhaps we (Brethren) were not quite so peculiar after all! It was a moment of instant bonding! I can no longer call myself a Plymouth Brother, but the discovery, over sixty years ago, that a scholar like

Tregelles had been numbered among us, set in motion the seemingly endless search for what came to be known in my family as 'Timothy's *Tregelliana*'.

In recent years, the focus of my long-standing interest in this remarkable man has been sharpened by the Cambridge University Library's readiness to pay over a million pounds to secure ownership of the sixth-century Codex Zacynthius—a palimpsest of St Luke's gospel that was first transcribed and edited by Tregelles more than a hundred and fifty years ago. In the words of Lord Williams, the former Archbishop of Canterbury, 'The discovery and identification of the undertext' of this Codex is 'a fascinating detective story', and because Tregelles contributed so much to our understanding of that text, his life must similarly, I feel, be worthy of investigation.

The quest for *Tregelliana* has been complicated and frustrating. In spite of extensive local searches in Cornish and Devonian archives, my findings relating to his early life in Falmouth have been sadly minimal, and if 'the child is father of the man', my account of his development has inevitably been hampered by this dearth of material.

By way of contrast, in the early 1960s I found well over a hundred of Tregelles's letters and other relevant materials in the private collection of the late Mr. C.E. Fry of Newport, Isle of Wight, who encouraged me to study them closely and authorized me to quote from them. Providentially, I transcribed (in those far off pre-Xerox days) many of these letters and I was later able to photocopy the remainder. Elsewhere, I have briefly described this unusual collection and some of its travails in the years before Mr. Fry consigned it to the safe keeping of the Christian Brethren Archive [CBA], in the John Rylands University Library of Manchester, but here I shall simply say that the laborious transcriptions of my youth have proved to be invaluable as during the intervening years several items in the collection were 'lost', although the new location of some of them has recently become apparent.[1]

A major challenge faced by biographers is to elucidate the context in which their subjects found themselves. Being a man of unbounded curiosity, Tregelles interacted with several cultural spheres, which were often

---

[1]For details of the Fry Collection, see my *From Awakening to Secession* (Edinburgh, 2000), 313–14. I shall indicate in footnotes if the original MS is now accessible in the CBA or elsewhere, or whether I have been dependent on one of my fifty-year-old transcriptions or a photocopy.

practically unknown to one another. Pioneers of the nineteenth-century Welsh renaissance could be forgiven for knowing nothing of evangelically minded folk in Tuscany, just as Anglican textual scholars in Cambridge were liable to have a very limited understanding of the fastidious morality of traditional Quakers or the theological peculiarities of the Plymouth Brethren. Tregelles engaged with all of these people and it is my hope that readers unfamiliar with one or more of these worlds with which, at different stages, he was involved, will bear with details that are necessary if we are to understand, not just the life of Tregelles but also the times in which he lived.

Two further preliminary caveats are needed. The verbosity of much Victorian writing can in any case be wearisome without having it further confused with religious jargon. As one who struggled in his youth to avoid what the French call 'le patois de Canaan'[2] I trust that my readers will forgive me if I stress that although such language may be tedious in the twenty-first century, those who used it (as Tregelles did sometimes) were not necessarily hypocrites but merely prisoners of their cultural circumstances. (In fact, it was something of an achievement to have extricated himself from the peculiarities of Quaker speech in which people as well as the deity were always addressed as 'thou' and 'thee'.) Their earnest and wordy expressions of religious sentiment may engender impatience but perhaps may also remind us of their less hurried world.

My second clarification is more specific. The maiden name of Tregelles's mother was Prideaux and not only was this, his second given name, but it was the name by which his family addressed him. Further to complicate matters, he married his maternal cousin Sarah Anna Prideaux. The frequent use of this name in these pages would inevitably leave room for confusion, and to avoid this I have sometimes used his full name or just his surname, but often I have simply used his initials 'SPT'—an identification, which also has the merit of brevity and ease of speech in the possessive form.[3] In a similar simplification, having to mention with some frequency the seven volumes of his *Edition of the Greek Text of the New Testament*, I have often referred to it as his *magnum opus*. Others of his works have a reasonable claim to greatness, but SPT's

---

[2]A mode of speech for which an English equivalent could be *bibledygook*.

[3]Perhaps, I should also make clear that my use of 'SPT' as his name is *not* a concession to the somewhat quaint practice of the early Plymouth Brethren whose authors frequently opted for the pseudo-anonymity of their initials (as in JND[arby] and BWN[ewton]).

Greek New Testament is truly a monument to one man's careful exactitude and incomparable endurance.

As will become apparent, the principle concern in Tregelles's life was the original Greek text of the New Testament. The manuscript transmission of ancient texts and their preservation in monastic and other libraries have an allure all of their own, and therefore, they have been an integral part of my quest for Tregelles. In all honesty to my readers, I have to state that I can make no claim to any truly scholarly competence in this field. I am fascinated by but not learned in classical languages and consequently crave the indulgence of the real scholars who, I hope, will find *The Life and Times of Samuel Prideaux Tregelles* to be of interest albeit written by an historian who is little more than a linguistic *dilettante*!

The number of debts incurred during sixty years is far too great for me to enumerate. I trust that the expression here of my sincere gratitude to all who have assisted and often patiently suffered in the gestation of this project will be sufficient. I am sure that none of them will resent my singling out my wife Nancy as the person who, *grace à Dieu*, ensured that I would live to complete this protracted work.

Naples, Florida   Timothy C. F. Stunt
Summer 2019

CONTENTS

ABOUT THE AUTHOR

Timothy C. F. Stunt was born in Chelmsford and was educated at St Lawrence College, Ramsgate and Sidney Sussex College, Cambridge. For almost fifty years, he taught ancient and modern history to secondary school students in Britain, Switzerland and the United States. His published work includes *From Awakening to Secession: Radical Evangelicals in Switzerland and Britain 1815–35* (Edinburgh, 2000) for which his *alma mater* awarded him a Ph.D. He is the author of some forty contributions to the *Oxford Dictionary of National Biography*. His most recent publications have been concerned with the nineteenth-century Italian *Risveglio* and the early career of John Nelson Darby.

He has two children and lives in south-west Florida.

Abbreviations

AHTL	Andover-Harvard Theological Library
Al. Cantab.	*Alumni Cantabrigienses...* see Venn, J.A.
Al. Oxon.	*Alumni Oxonienses...* See Foster, Joseph
AV	*Authorized Version* (a.k.a. *King James Version*)
BFBS	British and Foreign Bible Society
Bibl. Corn.	*Bibliotheca Cornubiensis...* see Boase, G.C.
BL	British Library
BML	Biblioteca Medicea Laurenziana
BNC	Biblioteca Nazionale Centrale, Florence
Bod	Bodleian Library
CBA	Christian Brethren Archive, John Rylands University Library of Manchester
CRO	County Record Office, Truro, Cornwall
CUL	Cambridge University Library
CW	*Christian Witness*
DBI	*Dizionario Biografico degli Italiani*
DQB	Dictionary of Quaker Biography (typescript)
DWB	*Dictionary of Welsh Biography*
ECM	*Editio Critica Maior* of the Greek NT
EQ	*Evangelical Quarterly*
FQE	*Friends Quarterly Examiner*
JRUL	John Rylands University Library, Manchester
JSL	*Journal of Sacred Literature*
JURCHS	*Journal of the United Reformed Church History Society*
LPL	Lambeth Palace Library
LSF	Library of the Society of Friends

LXX	Septuagint version of the OT
MA	Massachusetts
MS[S]	Manuscript[s]
NLW	National Library of Wales, Aberystwyth
NT	New Testament
ODNB	*Oxford Dictionary of National Biography*
OR	Oregon
OT	Old Testament
s.n.	*Sub nomine* [under the name of the subject]
UGL	University of Glasgow Library

CHAPTER 1

A Falmouth Childhood

1.1 FALMOUTH

When the news of the battle of Trafalgar and the death of Lord Nelson reached England in November 1805, it was the people of Falmouth, in Cornwall, who were the first to learn the news. It may well be asked why a little town like Falmouth was distinguished in this way, rather than one of the great ports like Bristol or Plymouth. The simple answer is that not only is Falmouth the third deepest natural harbour in the world, but it was also the first port of safety available to a British ship entering the English channel in an Easterly direction, especially if it was being chased by a larger French ship—a familiar situation in the eighteenth century and early nineteenth century as the French and the English were at war for much of that period. In fact, on that day in 1805, a larger French vessel was pursuing Captain Lapenotiere, who was carrying the Trafalgar dispatches in a very small schooner, the HMS Pickle, and for him, Falmouth was indeed a place of safety.

But Falmouth was more than just a haven in wartime. During the previous two centuries, it had grown sufficiently in importance to have become the first port of call for the packet service, carrying mail from the United States and other countries. In fact, Falmouth's distinction as a port had resulted in a significant growth in the town's trading wealth and prosperity and one family that participated in this process with great success is of particular interest for our purposes.

© The Author(s) 2020
T. C. F. Stunt, *The Life and Times of Samuel Prideaux Tregelles*,
Christianities in the Trans-Atlantic World,
https://doi.org/10.1007/978-3-030-32266-3_1

From the mid-seventeenth century, the Fox family increasingly dominated the commercial and industrial life of Falmouth.[1]

1.2   Quakers in Falmouth

Although they were not related to George Fox, the founder of the Quaker
movement, the family of that name in Falmouth was deeply committed to
the principles of the Society of Friends and to their pacifist ideals, which
forbad their producing materials that would be used in warfare. Their reputation for probity meant that they were respected as a pre-eminently reliable
family with whom to have good commercial dealings, and George Croker
Fox's[2] shipping business was so successful that members of his family acted
continuously, from 1792 to 1905, as consuls in Falmouth for the United
States as well as a number of other countries.

In examining life in Falmouth during the late eighteenth century and the
part played in it by the Quaker element in its population, we are considering
the world into which the subject of this book was born in 1813. There
is a dearth of contemporary material relating to the early life of Samuel
Prideaux Tregelles and his family, but by investigating the society in which
he grew up, we can usefully discover something about the circumstances
that influenced his early development.

On a smaller scale than the Fox dynasty but nevertheless with some success, the old Cornish family of Tregelles was one of several other Quaker
families that throve in Falmouth. In the South West of England, one of
the earliest followers of the founder-Quaker, George Fox, had been a tai-
lor John Tregelles (?1627–1706), who in 1676 had married Honoria the
daughter of a Spanish immigrant, Nicholas José.[3] Imprisoned on more
than one occasion in Pendennis Castle and Launceston gaol, for his Quaker

---

[1] For Falmouth in its Cornish context, see James Whetter, *The History of Falmouth*
(Redruth: Truran, 1981). For the Fox family in Falmouth, see T.H. Bradley, 'The Fox Fam-
ily of Falmouth: Their contribution to Cornish Industrial History, 1640–1860,' *Cornwall
Association of Local Historians' News Magazine* 14 (October 1987): 9–17.

[2] George Croker Fox I (1727–1782). His eldest son and grandson were identically named.

[3] Copy of marriage certificate, Truro/CRO, Stephens of Ashfield Papers, ST/874.

convictions,[4] Tregelles and his family faithfully maintained the Quaker tradition and the 'Tregelles meeting house' is mentioned in the Falmouth records of the late seventeenth century.[5]

One of John's great-grandsons was Samuel Tregelles,[6] our subject's grandfather, who established a rope factory in Ashfield, Budock, on the outskirts of Falmouth, and whose links with the Fox family are well illustrated by the marriage of two of his younger sisters, Elizabeth (1768–1848) and Mary (1770–1835), to Robert Were Fox (1754–1818) and Thomas Were Fox (1766–1844), brothers of George Croker Fox II, whose father's shipping business we mentioned earlier. It is apparent from the minutes of the Quaker regional monthly meetings that when Samuel Tregelles (the owner of the rope factory) was about thirty-five years old, he was in trouble with the Quaker authorities. In October 1801, he 'came forward and declared that he had departed from the standard of truth and rectitude'. On consideration of the circumstances, details of which were not recorded, the Quakers disowned him in December for 'grossly immoral conduct'. When more than two years later, in March 1804 he asked for readmission to the Society, the application remained a matter for discussion for a further six months.[7]

Of his many children, the eldest son Samuel (1789–1828), the father of our subject, is an elusive figure about whom there is little recorded information. However, his standing among the Falmouth Friends doesn't seem to have been affected by his father's misconduct and, a few years later, when he announced (21 November 1810) his intention of marrying Dorothy Prideaux (1790–1873), the Friends monthly meeting (19 December 1810) raised no objection and gave their approval.[8]

---

[4] *The Friend* 6 (1848) 98; 80 (1907) 367; cited in 'Dictionary of Quaker Biography' [DQB] (typescript in London/LSF); see Mary Coate, *Cornwall in the Great Civil War and Interregnum, 1642–1660: A Social and Political Study* (Oxford: Clarendon, 1933), 348.

[5] Susan Gay, *Old Falmouth: The Story of the Town* … (London: Headley Brothers, 1903), 40.

[6] 10 June 1766–1763 June 1831. In 1787 he married Rebecca Smith who died 6 August 1811, aged 45.

[7] Minutes of the West Cornwall Monthly Meeting, November 1801–October 1804 (Truro/CRO, Society of Friends Archive, SF/105). Confusingly, SPT's grandfather is here referred to as 'Samuel Tregelles, junior' because his uncle Samuel Tregelles (1725–1805) was still living.

[8] Minutes October 1808–March 1813 (Truro/CRO, SF/108), in which the designation 'Samuel Tregelles, junior' is now assigned to SPT's father.

Dorothy Prideaux, whose father George (1744–1815) was a solicitor,[9] came from an old Cornish family living in Kingsbridge, Devon. Like the Tregelles family, her ancestors were also Quakers and it was in their meeting house at Kingsbridge that the Quakers regularly held one of their quarterly divisional meetings.[10] It is clear therefore that although we have scant information about the childhood of Samuel Prideaux Tregelles, who was born at Wodehouse Place, Falmouth on 30 January 1813, he was from the very outset of his life part of an extended family with long-established Quaker roots, and indeed, the town in which he grew up was significantly characterized by Quaker culture and practice.

A few years before SPT's birth, his father, together with Lord Wodehouse, planned to build an Almshouse on some land provided by the baron, at the foot of Mount-Sion in Porhan Lane, Falmouth. It was a typically Quaker work of philanthropy, and in 1810, the building was erected, consisting of a row of small tenements, which provided accommodation for ten widows 'of good character, who have not received parochial relief'.[11]

Whether this act of conspicuous charity on the part of SPT's father was an attempt to redeem the family's reputation is far from clear, especially as we are ignorant of the nature of the older Samuel's indiscretions, but at this stage, the newly married Samuel Tregelles (SPT's father) was living up to the expectations to which other worthy Quakers in Falmouth had given rise. The shadow of a future bankruptcy was not yet hanging over the family.

1.3   Years of Uncertainty

On the wider canvas of national and international events, Samuel Prideaux Tregelles was born into a world of anxiety. England had been at war with France for the best part of twenty years, and people who lived on the South

---

[9] Joseph Jackson Howard, Frederick Arthur Crisp [eds.], *Visitation of England and Wales*, xv (priv. printed, 1908) [Howard, Crisp, *Visitation*] 140. Cf. R.M. Prideaux, *Prideaux, A West Country Clan* (Chichester, Phillimore 1989).

[10] Anonymous, *Kingsbridge and Salcombe, with the Intermediate Estuary, Historically and Topographically Depicted. Embellished with Four Views* (Kingsbridge: R Southwood, 1819), 38.

[11] R. Thomas, *History and Description of the Town and Harbour of Falmouth* (Falmouth: J. Trathan, 1827), 90n. Cf. Anonymous, *Panorama of Falmouth Containing: A History of the Origin, Progress, and present state of the Port; particulars of the Packet and other Establishments; directions to the Public Offices, Taverns, Lodging Houses, etc.* (Falmouth: Philp [*sic*] 1827), 54.

Coast could not but be aware of the hostilities. In addition to the possibility that the press gang could arrive at any moment and seize able-bodied men for the naval forces, the war itself was on their doorstep. Quite apart from ships putting into Falmouth, seeking refuge from French men-of-war, there had been the liability of French invasion. The mother of Benjamin Newton, later to be SPT's close friend and confidante, recalled how when she was living in Falmouth in 1803, many had fled the town, fearing a French raid. Newton himself was five years older than Tregelles, but he too had grown up in a Quaker family on the South Coast of Devon and Cornwall and vividly recalled returning from school, in February 1815, to find his mother, having learnt of Napoleon's escape from Elba, wringing her hands in despair and exclaiming, 'Now torrents of blood will be shed'.[12]

Although Napoleon was finally defeated in 1815 when SPT was only two years old, the post-war years were similarly difficult times. For years, the economy had been on a war-footing and the end of the war brought serious unemployment and financial problems. Samuel Tregelles (SPT's father) is usually described as a merchant, but we have little evidence as to the commodities in which he dealt.

There are some indications that he may have worked with his father in the rope manufacturing business, but it seems that he took some risks that landed him in bankruptcy. Some random papers have survived, but they give no indication of the nature of Samuel Tregelles's folly.[13]

In addition to his son, who was always known by his second name, Prideaux—his mother's maiden name—Samuel Tregelles had two daughters: Anna Rebecca (1811–1885) was fifteen months older than her brother, and a third child Dorothea was born five years after her brother, but she only lived for a couple of weeks. In his early years, Prideaux attended a school at Ashfield on the outskirts of Falmouth, managed by his aunts Lydia (1800–1891) and Rachael Tregelles (1805–1874). Lydia who outlived our subject recalled his eagerness to learn and his remarkable memory.[14]

---

[12] T.C.F. Stunt, *The Elusive Quest of the Spiritual Malcontent: Some Early Nineteenth Century Ecclesiastical Mavericks* (Eugene OR: Wipf and Stock, 2015), 26 n.88.

[13] Truro/CRO, ST/882 debts of Samuel T., 1820. The only direct account is in B.W. Newton's recollections: 'His [SPT's] father had £30,000 which he lost in speculation and died leaving a boy and a girl unprovided for'. Wyatt MSS 4 (Manchester/JRUL/CBA 7059), 121.

[14] Cambridge MA/AHTL, Special Collections, Papers of Caspar René Gregory (bMS

One other scrap of anecdotal information confirms this picture of Prideaux Tregelles's early development and precocity. Their very distant cousins in the Fox family, Ellen, Jane and Tabitha Fox,[15] who lived at Perranarworthal a few miles North of Falmouth, were rather older than Prideaux and his sister Anna, but nevertheless were their 'frequent playmates'. Ellen had a particular memory of the 'grave' young Prideaux delighting to use antique language as when he observed one afternoon: 'This bread-and-butter cumbers me'.[16] Clearly 'Little Prid', as they used to call him,[17] was a serious boy—a scholar in the making.

1.4   A New School

In 1825, at the age of twelve, Prideaux Tregelles was one of the first pupils to be enrolled in the Classical and Mathematical School in Falmouth. Some idea of this newly founded school is given in a contemporary account. There were seventy-five shareholders or Proprietors each contributing £15. Located in the New Road above Killigrew Street, the school was

> admirably situated and presents a handsome classical elevation; the interior consists of a noble lofty School-Room, a vestibule, and two apartments, one for the Governors and Committee, and the other for the person in care of the premises, with suitable attached offices, and at the back a good Play-ground; in front is a Garden within iron rails and a carriage-drive to the flight of steps at the door.

The local benefactor, Lord Wodehouse (who, as we noted earlier, had cooperated with Samuel Tregelles in the Almshouse project), was responsible for the gift of the land for the site of the property.

> The School-room is 60 feet long, 26 wide, and 21 high, and the number of Boys which are admitted is 100. The Noble Patron and the Proprietors,

---

560/125 [7]) Augusta Prideaux, 'Life of Dr Samuel Prideaux Tregelles' [hereafter Prideaux, MS Life] [p. 2].

[15] Ellen (1807–1890) and Jane (1808–1863) both later married into the Crewdson family, while Tabitha married into the Lloyd family of banking fame. The sisters were great-great granddaughters of George Croker Fox II's grandfather, George Fox by his first marriage.

[16] Ellen Crewdson, *Our Childhood at Perran* and *Postscript to Mother's Diary*, by F. Mary Broadrick (Liverpool, 1926), 34.

[17] See below Chapter 11, Footnote 31.

according to their shares, have nominations of one boy each, the parents paying the moderate sum of 7 guineas per annum. The Masters have three nominations each, at nine guineas per annum; and gentlemen not being proprietors may propose scholars by paying first a fixed sum for each one admitted, and seven guineas per annum, so far as will complete the above number. …

There are five Masters including the French Teacher, at graduated Salaries; the two first must be graduates of one of the Universities. The Head-Master has the whole management of the School, so that it be conformable to the Laws and Rules made for its guidance. A public examination of the Scholars is held once a year on four following days previous to the Midsummer holidays, and PRIZES are adjudged to the most deserving youths.[18]

This then was the school in which Samuel Prideaux Tregelles at the age of twelve began his secondary studies. As one of the first students to be enrolled, Prideaux Tregelles would almost certainly have attended the opening ceremonies also described in the contemporary account:

The Mayor, Aldermen, and Corporation met the President, Officers and Committee of Management at the Town-hall, and proceeding towards the School House were met by the Proprietors, and the Masters in their Academic gowns at the head of their Scholars, the procession then passed into the spacious School-Room, where a number of Ladies and Gentlemen were assembled as spectators. The Head-Master read a portion of the Church service with a selection of psalms and offered up two appropriate prayers for the occasion, after which he delivered an excellent address, — on the advantages of an education which would combine sound learning with religious instruction, which without doubt would be the means of bestowing on, many hundreds incalculable benefits; concluding with an exhortation for ALL to perform their duty, with a firm trust in Providence for a furtherance in their laudable endeavours.

It was here for the next three years that Prideaux pursued his studies but perhaps a word about his headmaster would be appropriate at this point.

---

[18] Anonymous, *Panorama of Falmouth*, 55–57.

1.5   A Scholar in the Making

Thomas Sheepshanks had previously been a student at Shrewsbury School (1812–1816) where, after securing his degree at Trinity College, Cambridge in 1820, he had been a teacher for five years. Ordained in 1825, he became the curate of Penwerris in Falmouth, a position that he held in conjunction with his headmastership. There may have been an element of nepotism in his appointment as his uncle John Sheepshanks (1765–1844) was the vicar of St Budock (1824–1844) and Archdeacon of Cornwall (1826–1844). Thomas Sheepshanks was later briefly Rector of Edinburgh Academy (1828–1829) before his appointment as Headmaster of Coventry Grammar School (1834–1860) where he numbered among his pupils the future novelist George Eliot to whom he gave Latin and Greek lessons.[19]

We may reasonably assume that SPT's enthusiasm for ancient languages must have benefited from this scholar's teaching at Falmouth, and according to one account, he made such good progress that Sheepshanks did his best to persuade the lad's family to send him to Oxford or Cambridge[20] but, as entrance to the universities was only open to Anglicans at that time, this would have required Prideaux to be baptized in the Church of England—a suggestion that would have been unacceptable to the Quakers into whose circle he had been born. In any case, with the crisis in his father's business affairs, the proposal was not remotely feasible from a financial point of view, and as if to finalize the matter, in March 1828 at the age of 39, Prideaux's father died. The boy's academic career now came to an abrupt halt when his widowed mother appears to have reckoned that a more practical training was called for.[21]

---

[19] Fisher, G.W., Hill, J.S., [eds.] *Annals of Shrewsbury School* (London: Methuen and Co., 1899) 286; *Alumni Cantab.* iv. 486. His son John became a Bishop of Norwich.

[20] Cambridge MA/AHTL, Prideaux, MS Life [p. 2]. The suggestion that he might go to Oxford or Cambridge is mentioned in Newton's recollection where he unaccountably refers to Sheepshanks as 'Archdeacon Elliot, Archdeacon of Cornwall'—a cleric of whose existence there appears to be no record (Wyatt MSS 4 [Manchester/JRUL/CBA 7059] 121).

[21] From an anonymous newspaper cutting preserved in the Cornwall County Record Office (Truro/CRO, ST/905), we learn that Sheepshanks resigned in July 1828, as the school was a financial failure. Prideaux Tregelles's departure, therefore, coincided with the closure of the school. The school appears to have been revived at a later date. Another textual scholar Prebendary Scrivener (born in the same year as SPT) was proud to recall that 'twenty years later', he had been the school's headmaster; Frederick Henry Ambrose Scrivener, *A Plain Introduction to the Criticism of the New Testament for the Use of Biblical Students*, 4th ed., Rev. Edward Miller [ed.] (London: Geo. Bell, 1894), 2: 241.

One of her late husband's aunts, Anna Tregelles (1759–1846), had married, Peter Price (1739–1821) the manager of a successful iron works in Glamorganshire, South Wales, and the possibility of an apprenticeship in Price's establishment seemed to offer, for young Prideaux, a more realistic future than the world of *academe*. In a matter of months, the family had moved to Neath Abbey in South Wales.

CHAPTER 2

A Welsh Interlude

2.1   Neath Abbey, Glamorgan

The Iron Foundry at Neath Abbey, where Prideaux Tregelles began his apprenticeship in 1828, had come under new management in 1790 when it was leased to a consortium of members of the Fox Family and their brother-in-law, Samuel Tregelles (SPT's grandfather). The arrangement was unmistakably typical of the Fox family whose investments were not confined to a particular field of enterprise. In the words of a recent family historian:

> In mining, their [the Fox Family's] assets were widely spread whenever possible as minority interests, so as to reduce the risk in that unpredictable industry. They were among the first to look beyond the primary aim of digging holes in the ground and to realise that by creating ports, providing mining supplies, selling coal and exporting ore, they could automatically reap great benefits from a whole mining area and divorce themselves from the worst consequences of a single mine failure.[1]

The Neath Abbey ironworks were ideal for such a global approach to industry. The River Neath provided transport to Swansea, and this in turn gave

---

[1] T.H. Bradley, 'The Fox Family of Falmouth: Their Contribution to Cornish Industrial History, 1640–1860,' *Cornwall Association of Local Historians News Magazine* 14 (October 1987): 12.

© The Author(s) 2020
T. C. F. Stunt, *The Life and Times of Samuel Prideaux Tregelles*,
Christianities in the Trans-Atlantic World,
https://doi.org/10.1007/978-3-030-32266-3_2

access to the harbour at Portreath, on the North Cornish coast, where the Fox family had cooperated with the Bassett family in the construction of a tram road company. The works at Neath were thus supplied with Cornish iron ore from Perran, which was another centre of Fox activity. The quality of production in the Neath Abbey ironworks during the nineteenth century became almost legendary and 'for a long period of years the firm had the reputation of pre-eminence for the manufacture of all kinds of machinery, pumps, boilers, marine and stationary engines, etc.'[2]

Perhaps of greatest importance for this notable enterprise of the Fox and Tregelles family was the fact that for the first twenty years of the nineteenth century, the foundry in Neath was managed by a man whose professional credentials and religious experience were exactly suited to the family's Quaker ideals. Peter Price (1739–1821) had worked with the Quaker ironmaster Abraham Darby, the younger, whose father of the same name had been a pioneer of the iron industry in Coalbrookdale. Price had also been the manager of the machine shop of the largest iron foundry in Scotland, and, being held in high regard by James Watt himself, he was singularly well qualified to become the manager of the Fox mine at Perran in Cornwall and then a few years later to move to Neath Abbey itself where he took up a similar position.[3] Of significance too, was the fact that he was a first generation Quaker. Born a Roman Catholic who was said to have been fondled as a baby by Bonnie Prince Charlie, he had experienced an unusual conversion, during a month-long illness as a teenager in France in 1754 when he was said to have had visions of both heaven and hell. The absence of any awareness of purgatory in his visions was said to have contributed to his decision to renounce Roman Catholicism. As a young man in America on the outbreak of war, he was reluctant to take up arms, and on his return to England, he became a Quaker.[4] In 1781, he married Anna Tregelles (1759–1846), a sister of SPT's grandfather, Samuel, thus

---

[2] W.W. Price, 'Joseph Tregelles Price (1784–1854), Quaker and Ironmaster,' in J.E. Lloyd, R.T. Jenkins [eds.], *Dictionary of Welsh Biography Down to 1940* [*DWB*] (London: Society of Cymmrodorion, 1959).

[3] D. Rhys Phillips, *The History of the Vale of Neath* (Swansea: Beili Glas, 1925), 290.

[4] See Hannah Southall, 'The Price Family of Neath,' in *FQE*, 28 (1894) 189–90, reproduced in *Friends' Intelligencer and Journal* 51 (Philadelphia, 22, 29 September 1894): 601–602, 619–20 and cited in article 'Peter Price' in DQB (typescript in London/LSF). Cf. Rev. T. Mardy Rees, *A History of the Quakers in Wales and Their Emigration to North America* (Carmarthen: Spurrell and Son, 1925), 95–96. 'Unlike other ironmasters in South Wales, they did not get together a fortune by casting or boring cannon for scenes of warfare', J. Lloyd,

cementing the Quaker link with Falmouth. In his later years, he was ably assisted by his son Joseph Tregelles Price (1784–1854) who took over the management of the Neath Abbey ironworks in 1818.[5]

2.2 A QUAKER APPRENTICESHIP

It was to this thriving Quaker establishment that Prideaux Tregelles came from Falmouth, with his widowed mother and sister Anna Rebecca, to take up an apprenticeship at the age of 15.[6]

Bringing with them, Quaker letters of commendation from Falmouth,[7] the family now became part of the Neath Quaker meeting, and the few of his letters that have survived from these years have all the hallmarks of the boy's Quaker upbringing. As was the custom with all good Quakers, he avoids the pagan names of the months, referring to July as the '7th mo.', and likewise, he addresses his correspondents with the pronoun *thou* or *thee*. Quaker morality was something SPT held in high regard, especially as exemplified by the noble conduct of his father's cousin Joseph Tregelles Price who was now SPT's employer.

During the social unrest of 1831 at the time of the Merthyr Riots, it was well known that Joseph Price had travelled to London to intercede at the highest level for a prisoner whom he considered to have been unjustly accused. As an eighteen-year-old, SPT had immense respect for his employer and wrote at length to his aunt Lydia in Falmouth with an

The Early History of the Old South Wales Ironworks (1760 to 1840) (London: Bedford Press, 1906), 102.

[5] For Joseph Tregelles Price, see *DWB. s.n*; G. Eaton, *Joseph Tregelles Price, 1784–1854: Quaker Industrialist and Moral Crusader: A Portrait of His Life and Work* (Neath: Glamorgan Press, 1987). Cf. Laurence Ince, *Neath Abbey and the Industrial Revolution* (Stroud: Tempus, 2001), 82.

[6] If his uncle Edwin's experience, eight years earlier, was anything to go by, they would have taken a boat from Portreath (on the northern Cornish coast) to Ilfracombe, and from there the packet boat to Swansea whence on a pony to Neath Abbey; Sarah E. Fox [ed.], *Edwin Octavius Tregelles: Civil Engineer and Minister of the Gospel* (London: Hodder and Stoughton, 1892), 3–4.

[7] Minutes of West Divisional Monthly Meeting of Cornwall 1824–29 (Truro/CRO, SF/113), and ibid., 1829–1834 (SF/114).

account of Price's efforts on behalf of the innocent victim.[8] Clearly, at this stage, young Prideaux had no problems with his Quaker identity. The issues that challenged him were of a more mundane character and lay in the nature of his employment as an apprentice in the ironworks—a problematical situation for a teenager whose real enthusiasms were in the more academic fields of language, literature and history.

As an apprentice, he was expected, with other lads, to light the fires at five o'clock in the morning, so that they would be ready for the craftsmen at six. Evidently, Prideaux had difficulty with this task, and sometimes the fires were not kindled by the time appointed. When, on such occasions, the moulders gave the apprentice a hard time, Prideaux is said to have responded—we may assume somewhat sarcastically—with an apt quotation from the classics or better still 'a disquisition on the scientific properties of damp wood and poor coal'.[9] In due course, he appears to have been given some administrative responsibilities in which his clerical abilities could be exercised,[10] but in his spare time, he was building on the foundations laid under Sheepshank's earlier tutelage and extending his classical learning.

According to his sister-in-law, it was at a time when sickness prevented his going to work that SPT began teaching himself Hebrew with the help of only printed materials.[11] Clearly, this was related to his voracious appetite for history and his fascination with the Hebrew Bible—one of the principle sources for any student of ancient history. This was no passing fad, and, as we shall see, he acquired in these years an astonishing familiarity with the Old Testament scriptures. However, in addition to these studies, Tregelles was also devouring anything he could find concerning Welsh history, for which purpose he undertook the business of learning to speak and read Welsh. From an account written by his cousin, George Fox Tregelles, some

[8] The contents of SPT's letter (which apparently has not survived) were known to Hannah Southall when writing her account of 'The Price Family of Neath,' *Friends Intelligencer and Journal* (1894): 620.

[9] Phillips, *Vale of Neath*, 439.

[10] According to SPT's cousin, George Fox Tregelles, 'He did not go through all the processes and departments, like other youths, but had some superintendence over the forge...' 'The Life of a Scholar,' in *FQE* (October 1897): 449. In confirmation of this, Rev. J. Vernon Lewis writing in 1933 claimed that E.R. Phillips, of Neath Abbey, had seen a bill in the works signed by Tregelles in his own hand, and he gathered from that that he was a clerk in the office of the ironworks. J. Vernon Lewis, 'S.P. Tregelles ac Eben Fardd,' *Y Dysgedydd* (March 1933): 69.

[11] Prideaux, MS Life [p. 4].

twenty years after his death, we learn that Prideaux Tregelles's initial study of Welsh was made possible by an unusual friendship: 'The Welsh he learned from David Jones, of the "Star" public house, and he taught this remarkable publican some classics in exchange'.[12]

The Quakers among whom he had been brought up were far from cultural Philistines, and although they had drawn the line at the suggestion of SPT going to Oxford or Cambridge, they were not opposed to learning and education as such, and it must rapidly have become apparent that this youth in his late teens was very much an intellectual with a veritable thirst for learning particularly in the study of history and languages. The impression that Prideaux Tregelles made, at this time, on a younger boy whose father had been the headman at the Neath Abbey forge gives us some idea of how the Cornish apprentice was perceived by those around him. In later years, the man recalled that as a boy, carrying food to his father at his place of work, he [the boy] had been 'quite afraid to pass S.P.T. who stood in the middle of the road absorbed in thought; [though] at other times he [S.P.T.] would be quite communicative'.[13] Prideaux Tregelles seems to have been the sort of youth whose thoughts were usually elsewhere, and it is not surprising to discover that the few of his letters that have survived from these years are preoccupied with questions about the Welsh Chronicles and Welsh poetry.

2.3   THE FASCINATION OF WELSH CULTURE

To understand the significance of this additional enthusiasm, we must briefly consider developments in Wales in the early nineteenth century. Prideaux Tregelles had arrived in South Wales at the end of the 1820s, a decade during which a remarkable Welsh cultural reawakening had begun fully to flower. These were the years that saw the revival of the Gathering (*gorsedd*) of the Bards with the establishment of local festivals (*eisteddfodau*) to celebrate Welsh literature and music,[14] and SPT seems to have immersed himself in this growing enthusiasm for Welsh culture. Given that

---

[12] Tregelles, 'Life of a Scholar,' 450. George Fox Tregelles (1853–1943) was a son of SPT's uncle Edwin Octavius Tregelles, the youngest son of Samuel Tregelles, snr (1766–1831).

[13] Tregelles, 'Life of a Scholar,' 450.

[14] For this Welsh cultural awakening, see Shawna Lichtenwalner, *Claiming Cambria: Invoking the Welsh in the Romantic Era* (Newark, DE: University of Delaware Press, 2008); cf. C. Charnell-White, *Bardic Circles: National, Regional and Personal Identity in the Bardic Vision*

he was clearly not cut out for employment in the ironworks, we have no reason to suppose that his mother and her relatives discouraged his literary enthusiasm. In fact, the progress that Tregelles made in reading and writing Welsh in the few years when he was living in Neath is little short of astonishing when we remember that he was also teaching himself Hebrew. When he was only twenty years old, we find him writing in July 1833 to Aneurin Owen[15] (1792–1851) a Welsh scholar, whose father had been the principal editor of *The Myvyrian Archaiology of Wales*, one of the first collections of mediaeval Welsh literature. In his letter, the young SPT has a host of questions which have arisen in his mind from reading the Welsh 'Chronicle of the English' (*Brut y Saeson*), the 'Chronicle of the Princes' (*Brut y Tywysogion*) and the Welsh version of Geoffrey of Monmouth's 'Historia regum Britanniae' (*Brut y Brenhinedd*). What part, he asks, did the Welsh monk Caradoc of Llancarfan play in the production of these works and what MSS of these works have survived and where can they be found?

Aneurin Owen, who was probably already at work on his edition of the *Brut y Tywysogion*, was the right person with whom to raise questions of this sort, and, recognizing the careful enthusiasm of his young correspondent, he replied promptly and in turn asked Tregelles about which MSS might be in the possession of William Williams whose country house, Aberpergwm, was not far from Neath. At this point, Prideaux had to admit that his understanding of these matters was only limited:

> I am myself but a novice in Welsh matters, having only come in this country between four & five years ago. I have however acquired a pretty decent knowledge of the language, & am doing what lies in my power to gain some acquaintance with the historical antiquities of Wales.[16]

---

of Iolo Morganwg (Cardiff: University of Wales Press, 2007), especially Chapter 3, 'Wales: A Civilized Nation,' 44–81.

[15] For Aneurin Owen (1792–1851), see W.L. Davies, art s.n., *DWB*. His edition of the *Brut y Tywysogion* was only properly published more than ten years after his death. He was a son of William Owen (-Pughe) the lexicographer whose mistaken theories dominated the study of the Welsh language in the first half of the nineteenth century (see G.J. Williams, art. s.n., *DWB*).

[16] S.P. Tregelles (12 September 1833) to Aneurin Owen (Aberystwyth/NLW, Pughe papers, MS 13232E #33).

However, he went on to explain that after making enquiries at Aberpergwm, he had found that the Caradoc Chronicle was missing from the library, as were other manuscripts, which had been there until recently. Displaying all the enthusiasm of a young man with a passion for history, Tregelles then launches into the errors in Caradoc's chronicle, which have given him reasons for doubting the reliability of the *Brut y Tywysogion*.

2.4   QUESTIONS OF SCHOLARSHIP

From another part of his letter, it is apparent that SPT had cultivated the acquaintance of John Montgomery Traherne (1788–1860) of Coedriglan, near Cardiff, 'one of the chief authorities of his time on the genealogies, history and archaeology of Glamorgan'.[17] He was also receiving help and encouragement from 'my friend Henry H[ey] Knight, the Rector of Neath, a zealous, well informed, & *cautious* antiquary' who evidently provided Prideaux with a variety of scholarly works from his own library.[18]

To discover a young man, barely twenty years old, who, completely from self-motivation, has taken up the study of ancient Hebrew, is remarkable in itself but then to find that this same youth has also immersed himself in what is for him a living cultural world, stumbled upon by the chance of family circumstances—this should give us pause for thought! It helps to explain Tregelles's interest in finding the Rev. Evan Griffiths of Swansea busily engaged in translating Matthew Henry's commentary into Welsh,[19] and his respect for the single-mindedness of Griffiths, who, finding that his printer had gone bankrupt, purchased the business to ensure that his work

---

[17] For Traherne, see D.L. Thomas, rev. B.F. Roberts, art. *s.n.* in *ODNB*. Cf. 'the most distinguished Glamorgan antiquary of his time,' H.J. Randall, art. *s.n.* in *DWB*.

[18] For Henry Hey Knight (1795–1857), see R.T. Jenkins, art. *s.n.* in *DWB*. Among the books mentioned in his letter, Tregelles had evidently consulted (probably in Knight's library) *The Myvyrian Archaiology of Wales Being a Collection of Historical Documents from Ancient Manuscripts*. Volume II: Poetry (London: Rousseau, 1801); Thomas Gale, *Historiae Anglicanae Scriptores veteres* (Oxford 1687); and Gerardus Ioannis Vossius, *De Historicis Latinis, Libri Tres* (Leyden: Maire, 1627).

[19] Seventeen years later when arguing that Papias's written testimony concerning the early Christians was a more reliable source of evidence than conjectures based on 'probability', Tregelles suggested, by way of analogy, that although it might seem logically 'probable' that Matthew Henry would have written his commentary in Welsh, the evidence of Tregelles's testimony, as an eyewitness of Evan Griffith's work of translation, was superior to such conjecture; S.P. Tregelles, 'On the Original Language of St Matthew's Gospel,' *JSL* 5 (January 1850): 167–68.

would see the light of published day.[20] This was the sort of scholarship for which young Prideaux had nothing but admiration, particularly as it tallied with his own fascination with Welsh and Cornish literature—an enthusiasm, which, it should be stressed, remained with him for the rest of his life. In letters, written to Welsh friends in the 1840s, and some thirty years later in a little book describing a Tour of Brittany, he refers repeatedly, as we shall see, to his continuing interest in these subjects.[21]

There is however a curious irony in the story of Prideaux's passionate enthusiasm for Welsh culture. One of his heroes in this new field of enquiry was Edward Williams, known to the Welsh as Iolo Morganwg (1747–1826), 'the Bard of Glamorgan' for whom he had great admiration. In 1831, SPT went, with Isaac Redwood, to Flemingston [Trefflemin] to visit Iolo's tomb on which, he was proud to recall in later years, he had planted evergreens.[22] In addition to his encouragement of the *eisteddfod* movement, the Bard of Glamorgan was renowned for his exposition of the *Coelbrenn y Beirdd* (a runic alphabet), which he claimed had been used by the ancient Druids. The case for the authenticity of his claims was powerfully argued by his son Taliesin [ab Iolo] Williams (1787–1847),[23] but in the late nineteenth century, many of Iolo Morganwg's supposed ancient MSS were discredited as forgeries and the *Coelbrenn y Beirdd* was exposed as his own invention.

This was a development with which Tregelles could never come to terms. Indeed when Taliesin Williams's defence of his father's integrity was called in question, Tregelles ventured unequivocally to defend it as 'by far the

---

[20] For Evan Griffiths (1795–1873), Independent minister in Swansea from 1828, see R.M.J. Jones, Mari A. Williams, art. s.n., *ODNB*.

[21] *Y Brython* [*The Briton*] 5:41 (Summer 1862–1863): 344; *Y Traethodydd* [*The Essayist*] 29 (July 1884): 292–93 (letter from Granada, in Spain, [June 30th 1860] to Eben Fardd); S.P. Tregelles, *Notes of a Tour in Brittany* (Edinburgh: Johnstone and Hunter [1881]), 17–18, 27, 51–54, 58–62. For help (very many years ago) with the translation of several lengthy pieces of Welsh writing (see Chapters 4 and 5), I am hugely indebted to Mrs. Olwen Wonnacott (*née* Williams) of Bristol, a musician who taught my younger sister some fifty years ago.

[22] Writing from Paris in 1849 SPT mentions his visit 'eighteen years ago [sc 1831] … when we found he [the Bard] was buried in a dismal corner of the church. I have been [in Italy] at the grave of Tasso [1544–95] … and that of Alfieri [1749–1803], … but these, and many others, have not made me the less remember the *Bard of Glamorgan*'. Elijah Waring, *Recollections and Anecdotes of Edward Williams, the Bard of Glamorgan, or Iolo Morganwg, B.B.D.* (London: Charles Gilpin 1850) 198–99.

[23] Williams, Taliesin. (ab Iolo), *Coelbren Y Beirdd; A Welsh Essay on the Bardic Alphabet* (Llandovery: W. Rees, 1840).

best thing that Taliesin ever wrote'.[24] It is perhaps, specially ironic, that one very early (undated) letter written by Tregelles to Taliesin Williams has survived, in which the young enthusiast for Welsh culture appears to be somewhat sceptical about Iolo Morganwg's claims for his runic alphabet: 'Have not the Bards some account of a more ancient alphabet than the *Coelbren y Beirdd* invented by Einigan Gawr and did not they correspond in? power with [the letters] A E I O C Ll P R S T'.[25]

But the discovery of the truth about Iolo Morganwg lay many years away in the future, and in the early 1830s, SPT was an avid enthusiast for Welsh culture. When an auxiliary of the Cymmrodorion—a society seeking to promote the practice and development of the Language, Literature, Arts and Sciences of Wales—was founded in Neath Abbey in 1833, it was the young Prideaux Tregelles who was chosen to be its secretary.[26] Some ten years later this scholar would try his hand at preaching in Welsh but that too was still very much in the future, because preaching the Christian gospel was not yet a part of his agenda. It was only in 1835, when he turned his back on the Neath Abbey ironworks and returned to his native Falmouth with the intention of taking pupils for tutoring, that he found himself facing a rather different set of questions that would radically affect the direction of his studies.

[24] Waring, *Recollections of Iolo Morganwg*, 198. For some essays on a variety of aspects of the Bard of Glamorgan's life, see G.H. Jenkins [ed.], *A Rattleskull Genius: The Many Faces of Iolo Morganwg* (Cardiff: University of Wales Press, 2005). See also Prys Morgan, art. 'Williams, Edward' in *ODNB*. We do not know how SPT may have reacted to the growing awareness, later in the century, that Iolo Morganwg was an accomplished forger of Welsh manuscripts (and an alphabet to go with them!), which he used to perpetuate his romantic nationalist myths and inventions. Perhaps SPT's focus on biblical studies enabled him to ignore it.

[25] Samuel Prideaux Tregelles to Taliesin ab Iolo, undated letter (Aberystwyth/NLW, Iolo Morganwg Papers, MS 21277E #770).

[26] Phillips, *Vale of Neath*, 439, n.1.

CHAPTER 3

A Significant Change

3.1 Disagreement Among Quakers

When Prideaux Tregelles returned from Wales to Falmouth in 1835, the life of the Society of Friends, among whom he had been brought up, was in crisis. Two distinct parties had emerged, and the nature of the division in the movement requires some explanation. From the start in the seventeenth century, the faith of the Society was one in which the Holy Spirit was a central reality. Quakers had acquired their nickname because it was said that they trembled in the presence of the Spirit of God. Their meetings were often entirely silent, except when a minister felt 'led' to share a thought with the congregation, and there was little by way of systematic biblical exposition. This was because they believed in the 'Inner Light' of John i.9— 'the true light which lighteth every man that cometh into the world'. If, as they believed, there was an 'Inner Light' illuminating their thought and understanding, then the scriptures and their teaching would inevitably take an inferior place in the process of revelation and spiritual understanding.

By a similar process of reasoning, the early Quakers had paid little attention to the sacraments, claiming that just as we do not reenact the Lord's humility in the washing of each other's feet, so baptism should be a spiritual rather than physical experience. By the same token, any meal shared by Quakers could be 'the Lord's Supper', because biblical instructions relating to such matters were not treated, in the Society of Friends, as authoritative

© The Author(s) 2020
T. C. F. Stunt, *The Life and Times of Samuel Prideaux Tregelles*,
Christianities in the Trans-Atlantic World,
https://doi.org/10.1007/978-3-030-32266-3_3

sacramental teaching for all time. Feeding spiritually on Christ, the Bread of Life was more important than a liturgical commemoration.

Working from this principle, some of those who regarded the 'Inner Light' as the true source of spiritual understanding took the question of scriptural inspiration a step further and ventured to criticize the Quaker yearly meeting's use of scripture, complaining that in so doing, they were interfering with the role of the Holy Spirit. Indeed, some of them took the argument still further and claimed that there were rational grounds for regarding the Bible as unreliable. An Irish Quaker, for example, Abraham Shackleton (1752–1818) complained about the scriptures being referred to as 'sacred' writings and questioned the morality (and therefore the inspiration) of a book in which 'the extirpation of the Canaanites … was undertaken by the express command of God'.[1]

In contrast to such attitudes, there had grown up in the eighteenth century an evangelical wing to the movement. Influenced by such men as John Wesley and George Whitefield, they had 'discovered' biblical doctrines like 'justification by faith' and the importance of conversion in Christian experience. The study of the Bible became an important element in the devotions of this brand of Quaker piety, and in contrast to the traditional Quaker attitude, the evangelical Quakers' study of scripture led them to take the idea of baptism and the Lord's Supper more seriously.

The movement was thus radically dividing between the old fashioned piety of the early movement and an increasingly vocal evangelical wing which was less isolated from non-Quaker piety and was calling for Quakerdom to adopt a more evangelical and biblical emphasis.[2] Although generalizations are liable to over-simplify matters and therefore may be misleading, one may observe that there were fewer evangelical Friends in Cornwall, Devon and Wales, and the Foxes of Falmouth were generally characterized by the more traditional sort of Quaker piety. Whether they can be said to have been sceptical with regard to the authority of scripture is more of an open question. Influenced by the rationalism of the enlightenment, some of them were inclined to question whether the miracles recorded in the Bible were truly miraculous. 'I remember well', wrote Prideaux Tregelles

---

[1] [W. Rathbone], *A Narrative of Events, That Have Lately Taken Place in Ireland Among the Society Called Quakers, with Corresponding Documents and Occasional Observations* (London: Johnson, 1804), 50–52. For fuller details, see Stunt, *Elusive Quest*, 16–18.

[2] For a fuller analysis of these different wings of the Quaker movement, see Stunt, *Elusive Quest*, 8–16.

in 1850, 'how twenty years ago or more [sc. circa 1830, when he was associated with Quakers in South Wales] it was rather customary to explain away Elijah having been fed by *ravens:* [the Hebrew word could be translated as] ... *Arabians* or the people of *Orbo,* or anything rather than admit a miracle'.[3] There are, indeed, indications, as we shall observe that Tregelles himself was inclined to think in that way and had serious doubts about the reliability of scripture.

3.2   A LEARNED CRITIC

In the West Country, however, there was one former Quaker, a native of Plymouth, who was highly vocal in his criticism of traditional Quaker attitudes, which he found to be at total variance with the evangelical faith that he had adopted as an undergraduate at Oxford. This was Benjamin Wills Newton (1807–1899), a Fellow of Exeter College. Brought up among Quakers, Newton became increasingly troubled, after his evangelical conversion in 1826, that his family were still attending Quaker services.[4] From 1830 onwards, he took the lead in the establishment of an independent evangelical congregation whose members came to be known as 'Plymouth Brethren',[5] but his concern about what he considered to be the errors of the Society of Friends continued unabated.

The disagreements within the Quaker community came to a head in 1835 with the publication of *A Beacon to the Society of Friends,* an outspokenly evangelical booklet by Isaac Crewdson, a Quaker from Manchester.[6] In the same year, Newton, riding on the momentum of Crewdson's work, published *A Remonstrance to the Society of Friends.* It was almost certainly in that year too that Prideaux Tregelles, back in Falmouth after his time in

---

[3] S.P. T[regelles], 'Definitions of Miracles,' *JSL* 5 (April 1850): 512.

[4] For Newton, see my article in *ODNB.* For fuller details of his evangelical conversion and his subsequent relations with his Quaker family, see Stunt, *From Awakening,* 195–96, and *Elusive Quest,* 27–30.

[5] For the beginnings of this congregation, see Stunt, *From Awakening,* 291–99; T. Grass, *Gathering to His Name: The Story of Open Brethren in Britain and Ireland* (Milton Keynes: Paternoster, 2006), 32–37, and *infra* Chapter 4.

[6] For the 'Beaconite' controversy and some of the consequences of Crewdson's publication, see Stunt, *Elusive Quest,* 33–34.

Wales, called on Benjamin Newton, whose wife, Hannah, was one of SPT's many distant cousins.[7]

Newton's first impressions of this intellectual young Quaker, whom he later described as having been 'of a sarcastic turn', were not favourable. As Newton recalled many years later, his wife's cousin 'was on the very borders of scepticism and almost had decided for infidelity'.[8] For some time, SPT's interest in biblical history had led him to study the Hebrew scriptures, but where many believers, following the Christian apologist, Alexander Keith,[9] found the apparent fulfilment of prophecy to be a proof of scriptural inspiration, SPT found the evidence did just the opposite. In fact, he had reached the conclusion that some of the biblical prophecies were manifestly unreliable.

3.3   THE CHALLENGE OF BIBLICAL PROPHECY

About twenty years previously in 1812, the Swiss traveller Jean Louis Burckhardt (1784–1817) had discovered the ancient Nabataean city of Petra, supposedly the Edomite capital mentioned in the prophetic scriptures,[10] and in 1823, the published account by two British naval officers James Mangles and Charles Irby, who had visited the city in 1818,[11] caused a sensation—particularly among 'historicist' interpreters of prophecy who reckoned that the desolate state of Petra today indicated that the prophecies in Isaiah (Chapter 34) concerning the judgement of Edom had been fulfilled. For Tregelles, however, the passage in Isaiah posed more problems than it solved:

---

[7] The mother of Newton's wife, Hannah (*née* Abbott, 1799–1846), was Sarah Abbott (*née* Tregelles, 1772–1802), a younger sister of SPT's grandfather.

[8] Wyatt MSS 4 (Manchester/JRUL/CBA 7059) 121.

[9] A. Keith, *Evidence of the Truth of the Christian Religion Derived from the Literal Fulfilment of Prophecy; Particularly as Illustrated by the History of the Jews, and by the Discoveries of Recent Travellers* (Edinburgh: Waugh & Innes, 1826). The ongoing popularity of this work, which has been repeatedly republished for the last two hundred years, is extraordinary.

[10] John Lewis Burckhardt, *Travels in Syria and the Holy Land*, ed. William Martin Leake (London: John Murray, 1822); cf. G.W. Bowersock, *Roman Arabia* (Cambridge, MA: Harvard, 1983); J. Taylor, *Petra and the Lost Kingdom of the Nabataeans* (Cambridge, MA: Harvard UP, 2002); and Richard Cavendish, 'The Discovery of Petra,' *History Today* 62 (8 August 2012).

[11] C.L. Irby, J. Mangles, *Travels in Egypt and Nubia, Syria and Asia Minor During the Years 1817 and 1818* (London: T. White and Co, 1823), 415.

The streams thereof shall be turned into pitch, and the dust thereof into brimstone, and the land thereof shall become burning pitch. It shall not be quenched, night nor day …

In his opinion, these verses (Isaiah xxxiv.9–10) had clearly *not* been fulfilled. Could it really be claimed, on the basis of this passage, that the biblical record was reliable? Tregelles, who was passionately involved in historical study, was inclined to present his opinions emphatically and could be quite scornful and dismissive of those who disagreed with him.

Newton was at something of a loss for a topic of conversation when visited by his intellectual young relative, but noticing his interest in historical studies, he evidently mentioned some of the scriptures which referred to Babylon and Edom and this led to a lively discussion during which Tregelles apparently made light of the biblical references to the cities and forcefully expressed his opinion that the prophecies were a reason for doubting the scriptures.

However, to the surprise of the scoffing young sceptic, the former Quaker with whom he was speaking saw the subject differently and had an explanation that had not occurred to Tregelles. In his scheme of prophetic interpretation, Newton was not a historicist but a futurist, and according to this framework, the prophecies, which were such a stumbling block to Tregelles, were only due for fulfilment at a later date, which meant that the final judgement of Edom was incomplete.

Tregelles became 'exceedingly interested' and a few weeks later he told Newton how this different interpretation had impressed him: 'I freely say to you that I was on the verge of infidelity. I couldn't believe those prophecies, because tourists find no pitch, burning in Edom'. According to Newton's recollections, it was 'about a fortnight afterwards, he [Tregelles] heard me [Newton] preaching the gospel and believed and was converted'.[12] It is true that our only source for this encounter and discussion concerning Babylon and Edom is in Newton's recollections recorded more than sixty years later, but we have independent evidence that verifies the importance of the prophetic dimension in the development of Tregelles's thinking at this time.

---

[12] These recollections of Newton were recorded in September 1896 by Frederick Wyatt Wyatt MSS 8 (Manchester/JRUL/CBA 7062) 94 and later copied into the Fry MS (CBA 7049) 81.

About a year later, in 1836 the *Christian Witness* carried a series of articles written by Tregelles, identifying quotations from the Old Testament in the Book of Revelation. In the first of these, we find him writing to a friend as early as December 1835: 'I believe that those prophecies [against Babylon and Edom] (however fulfilled in some important particulars) are not *exhausted* and that the events of the latter day alone will entirely show their accomplishment'.[13] Six months later, in a paper on 'Babylon' he gives some details as to how his opinions changed on the subject:

> When I first thought, from reading the prophetic word, that these things were yet unfulfilled, the idea seemed so strange, so entirely contrary to my own pre-conceived opinions, that I was disposed to look on it as an untenable hypothesis: but the more I have searched into the evidence of Scripture and compared it with incontrovertible facts, the more have I been confirmed in regarding the true and literal Babylon to be the city on which God's judgments are yet to be poured out.[14]

In a later paper on Edom, when he sets out again to refute the idea, popularized by Alexander Keith, that the prophecies of judgement on Edom have already been fulfilled, it seems more than likely that he is thinking of his own earlier scepticism when he exclaims:

> Well might an infidel argue [on the basis of Keith's exposition]:
> "If the Truth of Christianity be based on nothing but supposed literal fulfillments such as these, then that religion must be false."[15]

---

[13] S.P. T[regelles], 'Passages in the Book of Revelation connected with the Old Testament,' No 1, *CW* 3 (January 1836): 85.

[14] S.P. T[regelles], 'Babylon,' *CW* 3 (July 1836): 285–86. A similar example of an ancient city whose destruction appeared to be less than one might have expected from the prophetic account was Tyre. In the same article in the *Christian Witness* (p. 286n), SPT recalled reading 'a year or two ago' the account of John Carne, *Letters from the East* (London: H. Colburn, 1826) where Carne described Tyre as 'by no means so desolate as it has sometimes been represented' (p. 233).

[15] S.P. T[regelles], 'Edom,' *CW* 4 (April 1837) 112.

3.4   A NEW PERSPECTIVE

Clearly, this had been something of a Damascus road moment for Prideaux Tregelles, and it changed his whole way of thinking. Benjamin Newton was a man of learning and profound religious conviction—qualities that immediately commended themselves to the slightly younger Tregelles, for whom this was a crucial juncture in his life. He now followed Newton's example and, as an evangelical, totally abandoned his Quaker identity and soon began to meet with the independent congregation of Brethren in Plymouth of which Newton was a respected elder. According to Newton's recollections, when the Tregelles family learnt that one of their number had joined the Plymouth Brethren 'they cut him completely and would do nothing for him. He was penniless and he lived three months with Newton'.[16]

Newton, himself, had been converted to evangelical Christianity nearly ten years before, when he was a Fellow of Exeter College and he had had time to immerse himself in the writings of the early fathers and the theology of the Reformation. It is evident that Tregelles, who, having left school at fifteen, was more of an autodidact, stood somewhat in awe of Newton's scholarship, so that Newton seems to have become in effect a role model for him. Following Newton's guidance, Prideaux Tregelles grounded himself not just in the ancient Christian writings of the fathers but also in the Protestant texts of the sixteenth and seventeenth centuries, which Newton esteemed so highly. Writing some thirty years later in September 1863, Tregelles recalled:

> When I was first led by the mercy of God to value the Gospel of Christ, and to seek instruction in revealed truth, as that in which I had an interest, it was my lot in the good providence of God, to be placed in close association with a teacher who, beside the Scriptures, pretty much confined my attention to three books, — 'Calvin's Institutes', 'Pearson on the Creed' and 'Marshall's Gospel Mystery of Sanctification'.[17]

---

[16] Wyatt MSS 4 (Manchester/JRUL/CBA 7059) 121; exceptionally, this was not taken down from Newton's words *verbatim* but is Wyatt's account of what he recalled that Newton said.

[17] 'Letter V: The Dangers of Loose Theology,' in S.P. Tregelles, *Christ the End of the Law for Righteousness: Five Letters to the Editor of 'The Record', on Recent Denials of Our Lord's Vicarious Life*, 2nd ed. 1864 ([reprinted] London: Hunt, Barnard & Co, 1910) [Tregelles, *Five Letters*], 32.

This of course was but the starting point in the voluminous reading that would characterize the scholarship of our subject, but, thanks to Newton, SPT's thinking had a fundamentally Reformed orientation. In the process, however, his faith in the inspired reliability of scripture was strengthened and this now became an issue of cardinal importance in his thinking.

3.5   BIBLICAL STUDIES

Effectively from now on, SPT's career was dictated by his total conviction that the text of the Bible had been given to the original writers by the Spirit of God and was therefore the revealed 'Word of God'. This did not preclude discussion of textual questions about, for example, the language in which Matthew's gospel had originally been written,[18] but one consequence was that the principal quest for the remainder of his life would be to establish a text for the Greek New Testament that was as near as possible to that of the MSS as they were originally written. However, we should also recognize that SPT's biblical studies did not begin with his evangelical conversion. Bearing in mind the importance of the Bible as a primary source for ancient historians, it is evident that when, as a teenager in Wales some years before his conversion, he had opted to teach himself Hebrew, it was with a view to studying the Old Testament Scriptures. This explains not only his familiarity with the prophecies concerning Babylon and Edom, but also his ability, barely a year after his conversion, to produce a comprehensive analysis of the Book of Revelation identifying in it, all the quotations from and allusions to passages and phrases in the Old Testament.[19]

One of the members of the congregation of 'Plymouth Brethren', in the founding of which Benjamin Newton had played an important part, was an unusual young man with whom Prideaux Tregelles now became acquainted. George Vicesimus Wigram (1805–1879) was the twentieth

---

[18] This was the subject of a well-argued paper by SPT, 'On the Original Language of St Matthew's Gospel, with particular reference to Dr. Davidson's Introduction to the New Testament,' *JSL* 5 (January 1850): 151–86, independently produced later in the year as a thirty-seven page booklet, by the London publishers, Samuel Bagster and Sons.

[19] The analysis appeared in the form of letters to 'My Dear Brother', signed 'S.P.T.' as 'Passages in the Book of Revelation connected with the Old Testament', in three instalments in the *CW* 3 (January, April and October 1836): 55–86, 182–214, 317–59.

child of an exceedingly successful trader, Sir Robert Wigram, whose business in the Far East had made him very wealthy.[20] For a time, George Wigram had been in the Guards but after his conversion in 1824, he matriculated from the Queen's College at Oxford where he was part of the evangelical circle frequented by Newton in the late 1820s.[21] He soon joined Newton in Plymouth where his ample means enabled him to buy the Raleigh Street chapel in which the Brethren congregation began to meet in 1831. There was a curiously ascetic streak to Wigram so that although he had ready access to money when he needed it, his lifestyle was severe and self-denying.[22]

A few years before Tregelles's evangelical conversion, Wigram had met a brilliant scholar of Hebrew, William Burgh, with whom he had conceived the idea of producing two biblical concordances—one of which would include all the Greek words in the original text of the New Testament and in the other would be found all the Hebrew words in the Old Testament.[23] It was an ambitious project and was not completed for another fifteen years, but when they finally appeared, the volumes were published as *The Englishman's Greek concordance of the New Testament* and *The Englishman's Hebrew and Chaldee concordance of the Old Testament* both of which have remained in print to this day.[24]

---

[20] For the remarkable career of Sir Robert Wigram, see A.P. Baker, art *s.n.*, *ODNB*. For the various successes of George Wigram's twenty siblings see S. Wills, *The Wreck of the S.S. London* (Stroud: Amberley, 2016) Chapter 2.

[21] For G.V. Wigram's early life and conversion, see Stunt, *From Awakening*, 198–200, 209. For Newton and his evangelical circle at Oxford, see Stunt, 'J.H. Newman and Proto-Plymouth Brethren at Oxford,' in *Elusive Quest*, 91–101.

[22] 'He used to rub a new coat against the wall to make it shabby, lest it should minister to pride' (cited in Stunt, *From Awakening*, 209, from Newton's recollections, Wyatt MSS 4 [Manchester/JRUL/CBA 7059] 117).

[23] For William Burgh (later de Burgh) to whose original idea the project owed its inception and for details of Wigram's encounter with him in 1830, see T.C.F. Stunt, 'Trinity College, John Darby and the Powerscourt *milieu*,' in J. Searle, K. Newport [eds.], *Beyond the End: The Future of Millennial Studies* (Sheffield: Sheffield Phoenix Press, 2012), 62–63.

[24] [G.V. Wigram, ed.], *The Englishman's Greek Concordance of the New Testament; Being an Attempt at a Verbal Connexion Between the Greek and the English Texts* (London: Central Tract Depot, 1839) and [G.V. Wigram, ed.], *The Englishman's Hebrew and Chaldee Concordance of the Old Testament, Being an Attempt at a Verbal Connexion Between the Original and the English Translation* (London: Longmans and Co, 1843). More widely circulated editions were later produced by Bagster and Sons. For SPT's rebuttal of some apparently groundless

As the titles suggest, the words of the Bible were to be listed according to the words in the original language. Thus, for example, the English word *crown* occurs many times in the New Testament, where occasionally (in the Book of Revelation) this is a translation of the Greek word *diadema* (διάδημα), but far more frequently, it is a translation of the Greek word *stephanos* (στέφανος). In Wigram's New Testament Concordance, there were separate listings under *diadema* and *stephanos*. Such a work would be immensely useful for the scholarly student of the Bible, of whom there were not a few in the circle of Christians with whom Wigram was connected at Plymouth, but the project had languished probably because it was too ambitious for Wigram to achieve on his own. The realization that there had arrived in Plymouth an enthusiastic student of the ancient biblical languages changed the situation significantly. At Newton's suggestion, Tregelles became a key figure in Wigram's project during the years that followed, and in due course (April 1836), he moved to London[25] where he played a crucial part in the production of the concordances. His eye for detail and his formidable memory turned the project into a reality.[26] Although Tregelles was probably unaware of it at the time, his evangelical conversion and his consequent involvement in Wigram's project were a key development in his career. For more than seven years, he now worked tirelessly on Wigram's Concordances.[27]

Earlier we mentioned Wigram's ascetic tendencies, and there is reason to believe that Tregelles was probably under-remunerated for his services to the project. This may explain a secondary task that he undertook sometime in the late 1830s. When Bagsters decided to produce a magnificent edition of Scholz's Greek New Testament with a six columned English

---

accusations, made in 1844, that Wigram had been dishonest in his dealings with Burgh, see below, Chapter 4, p. 10, Footnote 19.

[25] In SPT's 'Account of Mr. Newton's paper on the doctrines of the church in Newman Street' made in November 1847 and included as an appendix to B.W. Newton, *Statement and acknowledgment respecting certain doctrinal errors* (Plymouth 1847) 9 he gives April 1836 as 'the month I quitted Plymouth'.

[26] An interesting anecdote illustrating Tregelles's memory was told by the sister of Newton's second wife. 'They travelled by train with him [Tregelles] and some mention was made of some advertisement in Bradshaw [the railway time-table]. He had been cursorily looking it through, and could repeat every advertisement in proper order, and did so without mistake'. Newton's recollections, Fry MS book (Manchester/JRUL/CBA 7049), 32–33.

[27] In a letter dated 2 September 1843 apparently addressed to someone in the Longman publishing house, SPT refers to being now able to 'complete our many years work on the Concordance' (Original MS letter deposited by the author in the CBA [Manchester/JRUL] in January 2015, and now catalogued as Box 585, file 2.

text using the translations of Wycliff, Tyndale and Cranmer together with the Genevan, Anglo-Rhemish and Authorized versions, they commissioned Tregelles to write a lengthy introduction.[28] This was 'An Historical Account of the English Versions of the scriptures, in connection with the Progress of the Reformation: with Biographical Notices of Various Translators'. Newton recalled 'that Tregelles' memory was so exact that he wrote the 166 [sc. 160] large pages (quarto) with very little assistance (if any) but his memory, as to dates and facts … [and] that Bagsters gave him £100 for it'.[29] In fact, SPT's footnotes make clear that he was familiar with the latest scholarship on the subject and consulted with other scholars like the antiquarian book collector George Offor and Myles Coverdale's biographer, the barrister John James Lowndes.

This secondary employment however was probably light relief for an enthusiastic historian with a prodigious memory. Far more impressive, in many ways, was his single-minded perseverance with the work on the Concordance, in the course of which he became increasingly troubled by the variations in the surviving MSS of the text of the Greek New Testament and the need for the production of a better and more accurate text than that of Scholz, used by Bagster in the Hexapla.

It is clear from his early writings in the *Christian Witness* in 1836, where on several occasions he refers to variant readings in Griesbach's edition of the Greek text, that SPT had been well aware for some time of the textual difficulties faced by the serious student of scripture. His interest in the prophetic scriptures—another aspect of biblical study that Newton had encouraged him to pursue—had immersed him in the reading of the *Book of Revelation*, the text of which he found to be very variable in the MSS, which he consulted. So, during the first years of his life as an evangelical believer he had increasingly come to see that scholarly biblical study would be effectively crippled until a reliable text for the scriptures could be established. He shared his anxieties in the matter with several scholars whom he reckoned were better equipped than himself to produce and publish the

---

[28] *The English Hexapla: Exhibiting the Six Important English Translations of the New Testament Scriptures … the Original Greek Text After Scholz, with the Various Readings of the Textus Receptus and the Principal Constantinopolitan and Alexandrine Manuscripts, and a Complete Collation of Scholz's Text with Griesbach's Edition of MDCCCV …* (London: Bagster, 1841). Later editions abbreviated or even omitted SPT's introduction.

[29] Wyatt MSS 4 (Manchester/JRUL/CBA 7059), 124. Exceptionally, this is not taken down from Newton's words *verbatim* but is Wyatt's account of what he recalled that Newton said.

text of the Greek New Testament based on the most ancient MSS, but none of them was ready to take up the task.[30] At some point, in the late 1830s when he was not yet thirty years old, Prideaux Tregelles recognized the need for the establishment of a definitive biblical text as an undeniable challenge to which his personal gifts were perhaps uniquely fitted to respond, but in undertaking such a work, he was now confronted with the *magnum opus* that would become his life's work.

3.6   MARRIAGE AND LIFE IN LONDON

Although Newton recalled, as we noted earlier, that Prideaux Tregelles's evangelical conversion led to his being cut off from his family, this would appear to have only been on his father's side. His relations with his mother and her relatives in the Prideaux family were evidently good and remained so.[31] On 12 March 1839, he married his cousin, Sarah Anna (1807–1884), the second child of Walter and Elizabeth Prideaux, and the young couple settled in Theberton Street in Islington, London, where Samuel had moved three years earlier.

This was a particular source of pleasure for Sarah Anna as it brought them into frequent contact with her younger brother Frederick Prideaux (1817–91) to whom she was particularly attached. Frederick was slightly younger than Tregelles and they became firm friends.[32]

Years later Frederick's widow, Fanny, recalled those days in London. Her husband had begun his legal studies and had chambers in Chancery Lane, at just the time when SPT 'was struggling into recognition as a literary man'. Like Tregelles, Frederick Prideaux had great respect for Benjamin Newton by whom he had previously been tutored for a time. In Fanny Prideaux's words, Newton had always done 'his utmost to draw out and

---

[30] S. Prideaux Tregelles, *A Prospectus of a Critical Edition of the Greek New Testament, Now in Preparation, with an Historical Sketch of the Printed Text* (Plymouth: Jenkin Thomas, printer, 1848), 16. Cf. Samuel Prideaux Tregelles, *An Account of the Printed Text of the Greek New Testament, with Remarks on Its Revision Upon Critical Principles…* (London: Bagster, 1854), [Tregelles, *Account*], 154.

[31] It was ironic that in the end, Tregelles himself was already incapacitated by paralysis when his greatly loved, eighty-four-year-old, mother died on 28 July 1873 and was buried in the Friends' cemetery in Kingsbridge.

[32] For Frederick Prideaux, see J.M. Rigg, art s.n.in *ODNB*. He is immortalized in the memory of lawyers as the author of *The Handbook of Precedents in Conveyancing* (1st ed., 1852) [a.k.a. *Prideaux's Precedents*] 25th ed. (1959).

inform the minds of the few young men who read with him ... [and Frederick Prideaux] always recalled his work under him [Newton] with gratitude and pleasure especially the readings in Thucydides ... '[33] Their shared appreciation and admiration of Benjamin Newton was clearly an important contributing factor in SPT's close friendship with his brother-in-law.

Frederick's widow later remembered a particularly striking incident that occurred at this time. In June 1840, Frederick's younger brother Joseph Hingston Prideaux (born 1823) was tragically drowned when swimming off Plymouth Hoe. It was the twenty-seven-year-old Tregelles 'who undertook to be the bearer of the deplorable news' to the older brother and went to Frederick's chambers for that purpose. 'F.P. saw his face and immediately cried out "I know what it is. Hingston is drowned"'.[34] Such painful moments may exemplify the varied responsibilities of friendship, but they were hardly typical of the day-to-day life of SPT for whom the ceaseless concentration on textual details would soon take its toll on his eyesight. He was already wearing spectacles in 1844.[35]

The preparation of a reliable text of the Greek New Testament based on his reading of ancient MSS rather than the traditional *textus receptus* was to become his life work—a task which would take him to countless libraries on the European continent starting in 1845 with his well-known attempt to collate the precious fourth century uncial codex in the Vatican Library, but before we consider this development in his life, we must look more closely at the assembly of Christians in Plymouth with whom he was closely associated for more than twenty years.

---

[33] F[rances] A[sh] P[rideaux], *In Memoriam F[rederick] P[rideaux]* (1891), 29–30.

[34] Prideaux, *In Memoriam*, 44.

[35] See the description of him below in Chapter 4, p. 15, Footnote 30.

Brethren in Plymouth and Wales

4.1   Plymouth Brethren

4.1.1   A New Congregation with Some New Ideas

When Prideaux Tregelles followed Newton's example and totally abandoned his Quaker identity, he began to associate, in early 1835, with the
Plymouth Brethren.[1] In doing this, he was joining a recently founded
(1831) independent congregation with a somewhat heterogeneous membership.[2] The larger and more vocal part of this community came from
an Anglican background. Numbered among these was George Vicesimus
Wigram, with whom, as we noted earlier, Tregelles worked on the *Englishman's Hebrew and Greek Concordances*. Others in the congregation, like
Newton and Tregelles himself, were of Quaker origins,[3] including some of
Tregelles's relatives on his mother's side.

---

[1] S.P. Tregelles, *Three Letters to the Author of 'A Retrospect of Events That Have Taken Place
Among the Brethren'*. [1849] 2nd ed. (London: Houlston and Sons, 1894) [Tregelles, *Three
Letters*], 4.

[2] For an account of early developments in Plymouth, in the most recent and comprehensive
history of the (Plymouth) Brethren, see Grass, *Gathering*, 32–39. Cf. Stunt, *From Awakening*,
291–96.

[3] For the Quaker element in the Plymouth congregation, see Stunt, *Elusive Quest*, 36–37.

© The Author(s) 2020   35
T. C. F. Stunt, *The Life and Times of Samuel Prideaux Tregelles*,
Christianities in the Trans-Atlantic World,
https://doi.org/10.1007/978-3-030-32266-3_4

The Prideaux family had West Country banking connections.[4] Walter Prideaux (1779–1832) was an older brother of Tregelles's mother, Dorothy, and when he moved from Kingsbridge to Plymouth in 1812, he established the Hingston and Prideaux Bank, which on his death in 1832 became the Plymouth and Devonport Banking Company. The Prideaux bank had business dealings with another Plymouth company, Symons, Soltau and Co, and the widows of both Walter Prideaux and George Soltau were evidently friends of Benjamin Newton, to whom they turned for the tutoring of their sons. Not unexpectedly, therefore, we find members of these families becoming part of the Plymouth Brethren congregation, in the establishment of which Newton had played a significant part.[5] We cannot be sure but it may have been through his Prideaux relatives that SPT himself, on his return to Falmouth, was introduced to Newton. One is hardly surprised to find that a few years later, in 1839, he married one of Walter's daughters, his cousin Sarah Anna Prideaux.

In the early years of the movement, the Brethren made much of their readiness to receive at the 'Lord's Table' any committed Christian, no matter the nomenclature of his or her denomination,[6] and although in later years Prideaux Tregelles was anxious to dissociate himself from the Plymouth Brethren, there is no doubt that as a young man, in his twenties and thirties, he was in full sympathy with this 'œcumenical' ideal and with the Brethren's aspirations to be non-denominational. A few years after his

---

[4] Howard, Crisp, *Visitation*, 140–44; *Kingsbridge and Salcombe*, 42–43.

[5] Prideaux, *In Memoriam*, 14–15, where the author (Frederick Prideaux's widow) recalled Sarah Hingston, the maternal grandmother of SPT's wife [i.e. Walter Prideaux's mother-in-law], 'a vigorous and decided old lady of the Quaker type, though she had left the Society of Friends some years before and like many members of your Uncle's family and of mine was associated with the Plymouth Brethren'. Frederick, who was tutored by Newton (see above Chapter 3) was Walter's fourth son, and therefore SPT's cousin as well as his brother-in-law. For the Soltau family's connection with Newton, see Stunt, 'The Soltau Family of London and Plymouth' in *Elusive Quest*, 170.

[6] See Harold H. Rowdon, *The Origins of the Brethren, 1825–1850* (London: Pickering and Inglis, 1967), 288–89; F. Roy Coad, *A History of the Brethren Movement: Its Origins, Its Worldwide Development and Its Significance for the Present Day* (Exeter: Paternoster, 1968), 100–101. To demonstrate the practical outworking of this œcumenical ideal, one of the leading early Brethren could insist: 'Though the fullest devotedness and separation from the world are enjoined as a privilege and duty, yet gladly would we have admitted [to the Lord's Table] the late emperor of Russia before he died, as we would the archbishop Fenelon, without obliging or calling upon either to give up their thrones'. P.F. Hall, *To the Christians who Heard … Mr Venn's Sermon, Preached at Hereford, December 9th, 1838* (Leominster: Chilcott, 1839), 21. I am indebted to Herr Michael Schneider for this reference.

conversion, in 1840, he gave expression to the idea in a pamphlet *The Blood of the Lamb and the Union of Saints*, in which he argued that if the work of Christ was sufficient to unite believers in heaven, then their shared faith in Christ should also be a sufficient basis for fellowship here on earth.[7]

The other side to this œcumenical coin was the distinction that Brethren made between believing Christians and nominal ones. One of the reasons for their dissatisfaction with the Established Church was that it made no such differentiation and was usually ready to provide Christian baptism, marriage or funeral rites and Holy Communion to anyone regardless of their personal faith and behaviour—aspects of life, which the Brethren took very seriously.[8] In other doctrinal and sacramental matters, there was a remarkable elasticity in the early Brethren's practice. In his association with them, Tregelles had thus become part of a unique congregation of Christians where Zwinglian, Lutheran and Calvinist teachings were equally likely to be heard in the exposition of the Lord's Supper, and where both paedobaptism and adult baptism were practised. What had begun as a series of evening lectures organized by a group of discontented Anglican intellectuals, with evangelical sympathies, had rapidly developed into an independent church where a considerable variety of doctrinal opinion could be heard. It should perhaps be noted that one of its leaders, Benjamin Newton, had serious misgivings about this imprecise approach to matters of doctrine—a phenomenon which some years later would lead him to separate from and disown the movement.

Equally important in the ecclesiastical position of the Brethren was their growing rejection of any formal liturgical order or ceremony in congregational worship, and, with this, their repudiation of the idea of a clerical system, to which they often referred disparagingly as a 'one man ministry'. The gifts of God, they argued, were not bestowed on Christians by an ecclesiastical process of education and ordination. Rather they should be recognized wherever they could be found, and they might be exercised by believers, who had received no ordination or even by an uneducated believer if he had nevertheless been given spiritual discernment and understanding. In a gathering where ministry and teaching were in the hands

[7] SPT's 'The Blood of the Lamb and the Union of Saints' was originally published in *The Inquirer* (London: Central Tract Depôt), 3 (January 1840), 1–10.

[8] The evils of what they called 'indiscriminate communion' and the 'promiscuous use of the burial service' were rehearsed at length in pamphlets by several of the early Brethren, for example, Henry Borlase, Charles Brenton, John Darby, and Benjamin Newton.

of several gifted brethren, who were not necessarily unanimous in their doctrine and practice, there was a considerable potential for disagreement and conflict, but such developments were kept at bay for a while. It was somewhat ironic that when divisions did emerge they were more especially concerned with eschatological questions on which historically many Christians have often been prepared to agree to differ.

4.1.2   Previous Developments: B. W. Newton and J. N. Darby

The beginnings of the Plymouth Assembly take us back to late 1830, some years before Tregelles's conversion, when Benjamin Newton, a native of Plymouth, invited an Irish cleric, John Nelson Darby, to engage in Christian work with him in Plymouth. With an Oxford Fellowship, which he only vacated (by marriage) in March 1832, Newton was still officially a member of the Church of England, of which Darby was an ordained minister. Both of them were in the process of separating themselves (somewhat reluctantly) from the Establishment, and as their ecclesiastical positions became clearer, the little congregation in Plymouth became increasingly the focus of their attention. Darby's ministry, between 1832 and 1835, was chiefly in Ireland, but his involvement in and deep attachment to the emerging assembly of Brethren in Plymouth was a key element in his own development. In a letter of April 1832, he could write:

> Plymouth, I assure you, has altered the face of Christianity to me, from finding brethren, and they acting together ... [This was in contrast to the Brethren in Ireland where] There are, as you know, individuals here, but scattered as missionaries over the country.[9]

In thinking of these developments we need to bear in mind that the years just before Tregelles's conversion and his involvement with the Brethren at Plymouth were ones that had been characterized in Britain by significant social change and upheaval. Catholic emancipation in 1829 seemed to have opened the door to major political developments in the Reform Act of 1832 and the Whig legislation that followed it. The accompanying political and social uncertainty, together with the echoes of revolutionary change in Europe, not to mention the grim spectre of the spread of cholera—all this

---

[9] J.N. D[arby], *Letters*, 3 vols. (Kingston on Thames: Stowe Hill Bible and Tract Depot, n.d.), 3: 230 (13 April 1832).

encouraged many religious people at every level to wonder whether the end of the world was at hand. Ever since the French Revolution, forty years earlier, eschatology and the study of prophecy had been matters of anxious concern for many, and with such inquiries now becoming still more intense, both Newton and Darby were important participants in the 'millenarian' debates of diligent students of scripture who paid special attention to the order of events connected with the expected return of Christ. It was a significant line of biblical enquiry that Prideaux Tregelles would share with them.

Both Newton and Darby rejected the idea that with the spread of the gospel, the 'earth would be filled with the knowledge of the glory of the Lord',[10] nor could they accept the possibility that Christ would return *after* the millennium. Such a 'post millennial' view of the Second Coming had been widespread in the eighteenth century but the shadows of revolutionary change and uncertainty called in question some of the optimistic attitudes of the enlightenment. It was clear to men like Newton and Darby that Christ's return would be a moment of deliverance from the rising tide of evil and impiety, but even they were not agreed as to the detailed order of events. Newton seems to have been very cautious in the development of his ideas while Darby could easily be taken for a time with a new idea, which at a later stage he would abandon. Later (in 1857) Tregelles recalled that when he first knew him, in 1835, Darby was full of enthusiasm for the prophetic expositions of Père Bernard Lambert (1738–1813), a French Dominican priest, and of the Jansenist scholar Pierre Agier (1748–1824).[11] Darby himself was a dynamic character and it seems likely that initially Tregelles was impressed by him. They were both fascinated by history and language, but soon after they became acquainted, Darby left, in 1837, for the continent where he worked in Switzerland for several years with only occasional brief visits back in the UK.

[10] Cf. Habakkuk ii.14.

[11] Cf. Stunt, *Elusive Quest*, 138–40. 'Lambert and Agier were the writers Mr. J.N. Darby studied earnestly before he left the Church of England. I remember his speaking much about them in 1835' (S.P. Tregelles to B.W. Newton, 29 January 1857, Manchester/JRUL/CBA 7181 [7]). This is one of SPT's many letters preserved in the Fry Collection, and now located in the Christian Brethren Archive of the John Rylands University Library, Manchester.

During those years Darby's views developed, more particularly on prophetic matters, and he began to propound ideas with which his former fellow worker, Benjamin Newton, could not agree. Darby was becoming increasingly certain that the Christian church had apostatized and was irreparably in ruins, and this conviction was accompanied by his adoption of what is commonly described today as dispensationalism. According to this theological and hermeneutical system, God's dealings with the Jewish nation must be precisely distinguished from the destiny of the church, with the result that the teaching of Christ particularly in the synoptic Gospels (before the founding of the Church) has to be perceived as being in a different category from that of later writings like the Pauline Epistles.

In the 1830s and 1840s this hermeneutic was only in its infancy and its place in Darby's thinking was far from fully fledged, but it was radically different from Newton's more traditional approach and it soon became a major issue of disagreement between these two very strong characters. Newton was particularly fearful that such a system would effectively separate the children of God into different categories, thus dividing the mind of God and his work of salvation. Almost inevitably such a fundamental disagreement on biblical interpretation was bound to exacerbate still further the element of personal rivalry between them. Newton was loath to give up his position of leadership, but bearing in mind Darby's emotional attachment to the assembly, it seems only natural that while he was away, the older man began to grow resentful of Newton's unquestioned leadership and influence over the Brethren in Plymouth.

4.1.3   Disagreements and Division

Some time in the early 1840s, without making any reference to their differences in prophetic interpretation Darby complained in some letters to Newton that the earlier principle of 'Liberty of Ministry' had been abandoned in Plymouth. He accused Newton of dominating the Plymouth assembly and, as an elder, imposing his will on its members.[12] With an increasingly confrontational exchange of letters, matters came to a head late in 1845 when

---

[12] These undated letters together with Newton's replies were formerly part of the Fry Collection but are now in the possession of Mr. Tom Chantry who has published them on his website at http://www.brethrenarchive.org/manuscripts/letters-of-jn-darby [accessed June 2019].

Darby and those who followed him separated from the Plymouth assembly in Ebrington Street and began to meet independently. Although several leading members of the assembly (like Tregelles) remained loyal to Newton and rejected Darby's criticisms, there were clearly some grounds for complaint. Shortly before Darby's withdrawal, Newton's fellow elder, James Harris, was conflicted in his loyalties to such an extent that he decided to leave Plymouth so as to avoid having to take sides, but, even so, for some time Newton enjoyed the continuing approval of many members of the church and it was only later that several of these supporters changed their mind and sided with Darby.[13]

In the course of the ensuing dispute, Newton was also accused of heresy in his exposition of Christ's humanity, and this seems to have tipped the balance, significantly reducing the number of his supporters. Although Newton retracted certain statements, which had given rise to the charge, the accusations and counter-accusations continued, further demonstrating the clashing personalities of the leaders and their differing views. In the end, Newton left Plymouth, never to live there again—an extraordinarily drastic *dénouement* for a 40-year-old man who was a Plymouthian by birth.

It was a distressing episode[14] and the depths of controversial abuse to which at times the participants sank are an unedifying spectacle. There would normally be very few reasons, in this account, to try to plumb the depths of the dispute, but it has a certain interest for us because these events occurred during a crucial stage in the unfolding career of Prideaux Tregelles.

4.1.4   SPT's Involvement with Brethren in London

Although in the early 1840s, his work in London resulted in his not being very often in Plymouth, Tregelles followed very closely events in what was

---

[13] Among these were Henry W. Soltau, James E. Batten, William B. Dyer, and Joseph Clulow, who all publicly supported Newton, as late as 25 December 1846, in their *Remonstrance Addressed to the Saints at Rawstorne Street, London, Respecting Their Late Act of Excluding Mr. Newton, from the Lord's Table, and Protest Against It* (Plymouth, 1846).

[14] The details are judiciously evaluated in Jonathan D. Burnham, *A Story of Conflict: The Controversial Relationship Between Benjamin Wills Newton and John Nelson Darby* (Carlisle: Paternoster Press, 2004), 149–203; cf. Rowdon, *Origins*, 236–61. I am well aware that, in this chapter, my account of developments at Plymouth is grossly simplified but my outline is intended to provide a meaningful context for the development of Prideaux Tregelles during these years. For fuller details the reader should consult the works by Rowdon and Burnham.

to become his hometown, and similarly in late 1845 and early 1846 when he was on the Continent, he kept in touch with domestic developments. In particular when the quarrel burgeoned in 1846 and Brethren in London and elsewhere began to take sides, Prideaux Tregelles, who had friends and connections both in Plymouth and London, felt the pain of division very acutely. Being of one mind in most things with Newton, it was distressing for him to see others distancing themselves from his mentor, for fear of appearing to condone heresy. He therefore felt, all the more, a special responsibility to clarify the issues and set the record straight as to what, as he understood it, had and had not been said and done.

The need for such clarification became very apparent a few years later when a pamphlet of some substance, entitled *A Retrospect of Events That Have Taken Place Amongst the Brethren*, was published in 1849. Although it was anonymous, the pamphlet was generally well informed and contained a perceptive critique of the unseemly controversies that had marred the recent history of the Brethren in Plymouth. The work was produced by the Baptist publisher, Benjamin Lepard Green (c.1825–1896), and the author appears to have been an outsider who hoped (in vain!) that the Brethren's 'confrontational turmoil of spirit could be calmed with a pinch of dust'.[15]

It was probably because the author was not a partisan and had 'sought to give a fair statement of the facts', that SPT reckoned it was worth his while to correct the record where he thought it to be inaccurate. His reply was a calm and considered account of the unravelling life of the Brethren in Plymouth as Tregelles had observed it in the course of five years. His *Three Letters to the Author of 'A Retrospect of events …'* is a model of careful and precise explanation[16] mingled with evident sorrow that a work so full of promise had disintegrated into such a travesty of piety. Taken together with

---

[15] Anonymous, *A Retrospect of Events That Have Taken Place Amongst the Brethren* (London: Benjamin L. Green, 1849) [Anonymous, *Retrospect of Events*]. The title page has an epigraph taken from Virgil's *Georgics*:

> *Hi motus animorum atque haec certamina tanta*
> *Pulveris exigui jactu compressa quiescent…*

('This turmoil of spirit and these great contests will be calmed by throwing a pinch of dust on them'.) Would that the sentiment had proved to be the case!

[16] Tregelles, *Three Letters*. See page 1 for SPT's respect for the author of *A Retrospect*. In his account, Tregelles is commendably frank about the irregularity of his own time in Plymouth, see pp. 4–5, 9, 21, 22, 25n. etc. Although Tregelles's support for Newton has almost inevitably resulted in critics finding him to be doctrinally guilty by association, there have been very few who questioned the reliability of his account. They may have ignored the facts that SPT adduced but they rarely challenged his accuracy.

some supplementary sources it gives us quite a good idea of the dynamics of the situation between the supporters of Newton and Darby, and the distress caused by the dispute.

At the outset, SPT gave a clear account of Newton's position as an elder and the fact that his role as such had once been approved of by Darby and others. The Brethren, as Tregelles explained the matter, had followed the principle that Ministry was 'Stated but not Exclusive'. In other words, certain Brethren were recognized as teachers and expositors of scripture but such a ministry was not confined to them and the voice of others could be heard so long as their ministry was edifying. As SPT recalled the situation, on at least one occasion, when this had not been the case, Newton had intervened in the Plymouth meeting 'to stop ministry which was manifestly improper, with Mr. J.N. Darby['s] and Mr. G.V. Wigram's presence and *full concurrence*'.[17]

It will be clear, from what we have already observed, that Prideaux Tregelles was, on most matters, of one mind with his cousin Newton. They both valued order in ecclesiastical matters and precision in biblical exposition. Tregelles must have seen the crisis in the making when Darby refrained from ministerial participation in the meetings, and though saddened, was probably not surprised when, on the eve of his departure for the continent (19 October 1845), he learnt from Newton's fellow elder, James Harris, of the latter's intention to withdraw from Plymouth.[18]

---

[17] Tregelles, *Three Letters*, 8. I have put this episode in its wider social context in 'Elitist Leadership and Congregational Participation among Early Plymouth Brethren' in Stunt, *Elusive Quest*, 200–202. Some fifteen years later, Tregelles described the pattern of ministry at Plymouth in the early days as 'modified Presbyterianism;' see 'IV. The Brethren's pathway of error in doctrine' (North Malvern, 3 September 1863) in Tregelles: *Five Letters*, 16. In fact, the phrase 'modified Presbyterian Church' was used by the Brethren's anonymous critic in 1849 (Anonymous, *Retrospect of Events*, 15) to describe the Plymouth assembly under Newton's leadership. According to my reading of their subsequent replies, neither Darby nor Wigram ever denied SPT's claim that there had been a time when they sanctioned Newton's conduct.

[18] See Tregelles, *Three Letters*, 21–22. A month before his own departure for Italy in 1845, Tregelles had unequivocally shown his support for Newton in a pamphlet opposed to the consequences of dispensationalism, insisting that 'the *essential* blessings of the redeemed' are held as a common portion of 'that communion of saints which unites those past, present and future'. *On Eternal Life and Those Who Receive It*, signed S.P.T., September 17, 1845 (n.p., n.d.), 8 [only known copy in the British Library].

It was however during Tregelles's time on the Continent that Darby actually separated from the Plymouth assembly (on 26 October) and in so doing raised a problem for the Brethren in London whose loyalties were now divided. Some like SPT's brother-in-law Frederick Prideaux were inclined to support Newton against his critics, while others, led by SPT's former employer George Wigram, took their cue from Darby and called upon Newton to attend a meeting of London Brethren to answer their questions, arising from Darby's complaints. When Newton and his supporters in Plymouth replied that such a demand was unreasonable and inappropriate, most of the London Brethren, led by Wigram excluded Newton from their fellowship.

Again, the dispute, which was conducted in a lengthy exchange of letters, is scarcely edifying and would not be worthy of our attention, were it not for the fact that it was still unresolved in 1846 when Tregelles returned from the continent. Having previously worshipped with the Brethren in Rawstorne Street, when he was working on Wigram's Concordances from 1837 to 1843, he now felt constrained to express his opinion. As might be expected, in his letter[19] to Henry Gough, one of the elders in the London assembly, Tregelles supported his cousin and argued that the disagreement was a local (Plymouth) issue which, although it was of interest to individual Brethren in London, should not have been the occasion for an ecclesiastical judgement from the assembly in London. In requiring Newton to give an account of himself before the London Brethren, it seemed to Tregelles that Wigram and Darby's other supporters had, in effect, been trying to bring Newton for trial before the London Assembly. The basis for his rejection of this course of action is of particular interest for our purposes because the letter, in which he expressed his opinion on the matter, co-incidentally gives us some valuable information about his earlier time in London of which we would otherwise be ignorant.

It was not a little ironic that the earlier episode, which provided a significant precedent in the light of which Tregelles reckoned that the London Brethren should reconsider their actions, was directly concerned with the

---

[19] The letter was addressed to Henry Gough (dated Plymouth 16 December 1846) and appeared in print as a *Letter [from] Mr. Tregelles to Mr. Gough Relative to the Exclusion of Mr. Newton from the Lord's Table in Rawstorne Street, London,* published by request [of William Blake, John Scoble, and Frederick Prideaux] (London: I.K. Campbell, 1847). Having attended the Rawstorne Street assembly he was in a position to recall the assembly's earlier practice. The only copy (known to me) of this pamphlet is in Manchester/JRUL/CBA 13813. The extracts cited below are from pp. 13–14.

conduct of George Wigram and the production of the Hebrew Concordance on which SPT had devoted so much energy a few years earlier. SPT now reminded his readers in 1846 of events with which they were familiar but of which we would otherwise have been unaware:

> In the beginning of 1844, grave charges were vehemently brought and pressed against Mr. Wigram, as to want of honesty and integrity in his transactions with Mr. Burgh about the Hebrew Concordance,

and now SPT asked his readers to remember how the Brethren had reacted when 'the charge was diffused in print, first in a periodical publication, and then by post in a circular'. Jogging their memories he retold the story:

> You [in the assembly at Rawstorne Street] (or rather we, for London was then my abode) never thought of bringing him [Wigram] for trial before the assembled body: — the truth of the charges was inquired into by most (all, I expect) of those who took any oversight in or near London; and Mr. Wigram's own explanation [to them individually] was deemed sufficient, and the evidence which he brought forward was felt by all consciences as wholly rebutting the charge; no one asked that the saints should be assembled to tell them that Mr. Wigram's character for honesty and integrity was unaffected by the injurious allegations: the statement which he drew up and printed was enough.
>
> And if any wanted farther information, I was myself a witness who could (and did) give it to many; so that the accusations passed by without leaving a stain on his [Wigram's] character. Now what would we have said if a summons had been sent to Mr. Wigram, to appear and defend himself before a democratic tribunal (or any tribunal) in Dublin, where the accusation was first made, or anywhere else? In Mr. Wigram's case no one thought of such a thing; information was indeed asked for; Sir A.T.C. Campbell, for instance, wrote from Exeter, pressing the importance of this being sent him, but I believe he used no threats of ulterior proceedings; and if he had, we should have been startled at the assumption ...

Applying the precedent to the current question, SPT emphasized that he only referred 'to the affair in which Mr. Wigram was the party charged, by way of illustrating the want of equity shown in recent acts' concerning B. W. Newton; 'I am perfectly aware how notoriously and scandalously false the charges were to which he [Wigram] was subjected, for I was cognizant personally of all the more important facts'.

Tregelles's efforts on Newton's behalf were unavailing. At a meeting convened to judge Newton in London, Henry Gough read a letter, dated 10 December 1846, in which SPT wrote 'as a Christian long in fellowship with the Christians meeting in Rawstorne Street, London', solemnly protesting 'against the character, objects, and competency for disciplinary action, of the meeting purposed to be held there tomorrow evening'.[20] It was to no effect as the London Brethren followed Darby in the matter as they did in the following year when the first charges of Christological heresy were levelled at Newton.

In the face of these accusations, although Newton soon left Plymouth permanently, Tregelles, together with other Brethren in the Ebrington Street Assembly, continued to defend him, but by now the number of members in the assembly had significantly diminished and by 1848 they had relocated to a smaller building in Compton Street where for the next fifteen or more years Tregelles was an elder in what soon came to be called an 'Evangelical Protestant Church'.[21]

Deeply wounded by the behaviour of Darby and his followers, Tregelles and others like him insisted that they were now no longer part of the 'Brethren'.

[20] The letter is quoted fully in W.B. Neatby, *A History of the Plymouth Brethren*, 2nd ed. (London: Hodder and Stoughton, 1902), 128–29, n. 1. In the same note Neatby describes SPT's letter as 'an interesting relic of a great scholar and true-hearted Christian man' and adds that 'Darby and Wigram were very angry with Tregelles for his tract on their singular proceedings' but assured his readers that SPT's 'character stands far above the reach of their intemperate imputations'.

[21] In a statement made in 1863, by Prideaux Tregelles and W.G. Haydon (elders of the church,) we learn that the Evangelical Protestant Church in Compton Street was established on 14 December 1847 when many Christians in Plymouth had 'found themselves in peculiar circumstances;' see 'Evangelical Protestant Church, Compton Street Chapel, Plymouth', *Confession of Faith and Other Papers Connected with the Settlement of the Rev. William Elliott as Pastor; Addressed to the Pastors of Christ's Churches* (London: Houlston and Wright, 1863) [Compton St Chapel, *Confession*], 19–20. See also the copy of B.W. Newton's letter to Dr. Luigi De Sanctis, 5 April 1864, Manchester/JRUL/CBA 7181 (66). For subsequent developments, see below Chapter 12, p. 6ff.

4.2   BRETHREN IN WALES

4.2.1   John Pughe and John Eliot Howard

Sometime in the mid 1840s, before he left for Italy, SPT's interest in Welsh culture seems to have been reawakened when he made the acquaintance of a Welsh Plymouth Brother, John Pughe (1814–1874) of Aberdovey.[22] We do not know the circumstances, but Pughe was a surgeon, who had previously trained at St Thomas's Hospital in London which is probably where, in the late 1830s, he first met the pharmaceutical scientist John Elliot Howard (1807–1884)—a man on whom we must focus our attention for a few moments.

Like Tregelles, John Howard had left the Quakers, in the 1830s, to join the Brethren.[23] As was the case with his father Luke Howard, the pioneer of cloud nomenclature, John's scientific interests were accompanied by a deeply romantic aesthetic awareness, and this was well exemplified in his love for what he called 'Wild Wales'. His interest in Welsh history later gave birth to his study of 'The Druids and Their Religion'[24] in which he deplored the tendency of the school boards to discourage the study of the Celtic languages. Such a combination of scientific inquiry and enthusiasm for Welsh culture had evidently put Howard on the same page as SPT's friend, John Pughe, who in addition to being a Fellow of the Royal College of Surgeons and a Medical General Practitioner, was no mean scholar of the Welsh language and, for some years, was engaged in a translation of the ancient Welsh MSS of *Meddygon Myddfai*, an account of the herbalist practitioners in Carmarthenshire during the thirteenth century.[25] Evidently, Pughe was delighted to find that the common ground which he shared

---

[22] See 'Pughe, John (Ioan ab Hu Feddyg)' in *DWB*. For fuller details, see John H. Cule, 'John Pughe, 1814–1874: A Scholar Surgeon's Operation on the Imperforate Anus in 1854,' *Annals of the Royal College of Surgeons of England* 37 (October 1965), 247–57. The article contains a photograph of John Pughe and is available [20 March 2017] online at https://www.ncbi.nlm.nih.gov/pmc/articles/PMC2311899/pdf/annrcse00219-0060.pdf.

[23] For J. E. Howard and the origins of the Brethren at Brook Street Chapel, Tottenham, see Gerald T. West, *From Friends to Brethren: The Howards of Tottenham, Quakers, Brethren and Evangelicals* [Studies in Brethren History, *Subsidia*] (Troon: BAHN, 2016), 234–41. For his enthusiasm for 'Wild Wales', see West, op.cit., 8. Cf. Stunt, *Elusive Quest*, 49–51, 260.

[24] J.E. Howard, 'The Druids and their Religion,' *Journal of the Transactions of the Victoria Institute* 14 (1881): 87–130.

[25] John Pughe [tr.], John Williams Ab Ithel [ed.], *The Physicians of Myddvai; Meddygon Myddfai* (Llandovery: D.J. Roderic, 1860). His younger brother, David William Pughe

with Howard in intellectual and professional matters was accompanied by a spiritual like-mindedness. The fact that the surgeon named his eldest son *John Eliot Howard* Pughe (1845–1880) is indicative of the friendship, and it was similarly very natural for Prideaux Tregelles, another former Quaker with a passion for Welsh literature and history to be closely associated with these enthusiasts.

4.2.2   Ebenezer Thomas, the Bard

In his youth, before he met Howard, John Pughe had lived at Clynnog, on the Llŷn peninsula, where he was well acquainted with another pious enthusiast for the ancient Welsh language and its culture, the poet Ebenezer Thomas (1802–1863) or, as he was known to the Welsh, Eben Fardd. As a young man of twenty-two, this poet had not only won a bardic prize at the Powis Eisteddfod in 1824,[26] but was also evidently in sympathy with the evangelical aspirations that would lead Pughe to associate with the Brethren. Although Fardd, in 1839, had resumed his membership with the Calvinistic Methodists, he could write in his Diary at the end of 1843:

> having been for years wishful for some Christian mode of uniting the church in love and concord which is now divided into so many sects and parties to the great detriment of the cause of the Gospel, I have at last touched upon a most perfect mode and plan, developed in the writings of the Brethren called by the World '*the Plymouth Brethren*' whose views as exhibited in their temperate and most Christian writings I am greatly taken up with.[27]

Around this time, the poet encountered and was impressed by the work of the Brethren hymn-writer Sir Edward Denny whom he described in his

---

[Dafydd ap Hu Feddyg] (1821–1862) who was also a surgeon, shared his antiquarian interests and published several works concerning the castles of North Wales; see *DWB* s.n. John Pughe.

[26] For Eben Fardd, see 'Thomas, Ebenezer [Eben Fardd]' in the *DWB*. John Pughe himself had adopted his own Bardic title of Ioan ab Hu Feddyg [John Pugh, Physician] and so admired Eben Fardd that, when the poet died, it was Pughe who wrote a biographical introduction to his final collection of poetry: Ioan ab Hu Feddyg, 'Nodion a hynodion Eben Fardd: In Memorium [sic],' in Eben Fardd, *Cyff Beuno : sef awdl ar adgyweiriad eglwys Clynnog Fawr, yng nghyd a nodiadau hynafol, achyddiaeth y plwyf, rhestr o'r beirdd a'r llenorion* (Tremadog: R.I. Jones, 1863), vi–xxiv.

[27] Extracts from Fardd's Diary quoted in E.G. Millward, 'Eben Fardd a Samuel Prideaux Tregelles,' *National Library of Wales Journal* 7 (Winter 1952): 344.

Diary as 'a very pious and agreeable Brother. I was for some quarter of an hour closeted with him and his Lady, and had a most edifying conversation on religious subjects and experimental piety'.[28]

Almost certainly it was John Pughe, the friend of his youth (and later his biographer) who had introduced Fardd to Edward Denny and the Brethren, because by now Pughe had settled in Aberdovey and was one of the ministers in the 'Christian Meeting House' in Towyn, Aberdovey, a gathering described in the religious census of 1851 as 'Brethren Meeting on Unsectarian Principles'.[29] In a letter to Pughe that he wrote, in May 1845, Eben Fardd made very clear his sympathy for the principles of the Brethren:

I feel greatly cheered by the intelligence of a few Christians in those parts [Aberdovey] being gathered in the name and love of Christ, unembarrassed by sectarian littleness and denominational interests. I greatly appreciate this movement of the Saints, and hope it will become more general and extended. As for myself, I can say that I fully coincide with you and other brethren in the view you take of Christianity; but I am sorry that, as yet, I have not sufficient courage to divest myself of my party-coloured garments.[30]

4.2.3   Eben Fardd and SPT

The shared antiquarian interests and commitment to the Welsh language and its literature that had fostered John Pughe's friendship with Eben Fardd, as well as with John Howard, was a similarly bonding element in his relationship with Prideaux Tregelles, whose earlier enthusiasm for Welsh history and civilization was easily rekindled, and it was only natural that Pughe should put Tregelles in touch with the bard of Clynnog.

Tregelles's first letter to Eben Fardd was written in July 1844 to thank the poet (whom he had not yet met) for translating into Welsh his recently

---

[28] Ibid., 344. For Sir Edward Denny there is very little information available apart from the hagiographically inclined H. Pickering [ed.], *Chief Men Among the Brethren*, 2nd ed. (London: Pickering and Inglis [1931]), 44–46. For the interesting circumstances that led to his evangelical conversion, see [Edward Denny], *Some of the Firstfruits of the Harvest* by one who has sown in tears (n.p. [1861]), 3–9.

[29] Ieuan Gwynedd Jones [ed.], *The Religious Census of 1851: A Calendar of the Returns Relating to Wales*, Vol. ii (North Wales, CA: University of Wales, 1981).

[30] Fardd, *Cyff Beuno*, xxiii.

published *The Blood of the Lamb and the Union of Saints*. It is clear from his letter to Fardd that SPT's appreciation of Welsh culture had now led to his desire to evangelize in Wales:

> I have now been for the last fortnight in Wales, going about from place to place, preaching the Gospel wherever I can find hearers, whether in English or in such imperfect Welsh as I can manage; but it is not difficult to use enough Welsh to show to persons the simple testimony of God as to what sin is ... and what the love is in which salvation has been provided for sinners.[31]

With the poet's encouragement, Tregelles travelled North to the Llŷn peninsula where they finally met. The account in Eben Fardd's journal of his first meeting with Tregelles is probably the only description that we have of our subject written by a contemporary and is therefore worthy of quotation at length:

> Aug 23 [1844] As I was just entering the Chapel at Gyrngoch to the Church Meeting held there, I was overtaken by a man wearing spectacles and hurrying on violently enquiring for Mr. Ebenezer Thomas [the English form of Eben Fardd], as he said. After a mutual recognition he signified his desire to get a place and opportunity at Clynnog to preach in Welsh as well as he could '*Faddeuant pechodau trwy yr Arglwydd Iesu Grist*' [The Forgiveness of sins through our Lord Jesus Christ]: so he worded his mission. I promised him a room on the next Sunday morning for that purpose. He was Saml Prideaux Tregelles, a native of Cornwall, but had been in London for the last ten yrs, 71/2 yrs whereof he spent every day in composing a *Hebrew Concordance* to the Bible, he also compiled a *Greek Concordance*, and is now bringing through the Press a *Hebrew Lexicon*, a proof sheet of which he showed me.[32] He appears to be a very deep Scholar, and possessing a general knowledge of the World and Literature. He has devoted himself to the Lord, teaching the way of salvation in the manner of the Brethren. (Plymouth Brethren)

Subsequent entries in Eben Fardd's Diary noted further time spent with Tregelles and his wife, the fact that his new friend's 'Welsh was very badly [sic] and disagreeable to the ear' but that 'I am happy beyond measure for

---

[31] From the Cwrt Mawr collection MS 73, letter 83, cited in Millward, *Fardd a Tregelles*, 345.

[32] This was SPT's edition of *Gesenius's Hebrew and Chaldee Lexicon to the Old Testament Scriptures, with Additions and Corrections from the Author's Thesaurus and Other Works* (London: Bagster 1847). See below Chapter 9, Footnote 22–24.

the spiritual enlightenment I have recently experienced, never in my life have I viewed the religion of Jesus with so much glory, nor did I hitherto see fully the divine simplicity and grandeur of the gospel Salvation through Christ'.[33]

Writing to the Bard from his home in Islington, London, in April 1845 a few months before his departure for Rome, Tregelles is unequivocal as to his continued involvement with the Brethren:

I had a very pleasant visit at Plymouth; I much enjoyed the intercourse which I had there with my many valued Christian friends, and I trust that thro' the Lord's blessing I found it profitable to my soul. There are many at that place who meet together simply as belonging to Christ; the Lord has graciously given them those whom the Holy Ghost has fitted to teach them, and to care for them; and there are several who preach the gospel of the grace of God to the unconverted. It is true that in the years which have now passed since they first began to meet for communion at Plymouth they have had trials and difficulties, but it has been very gracious of our God and Father to show His hand as caring for His people and giving them abundantly to prove that tho' weak in themselves they have strength in Christ their Head ...

I have seen the few last numbers of the *Dysgedydd* [a Welsh magazine *The Instructor*]; it is strange that they should *say* so much about Brodyr Plymouthaidd; they *know* evidently much less than they *say*, for their accounts are very incorrect in almost every respect: I do not wish to defend *myself*, but if the *truth of God* is concerned, I ought to value that truth, and seek to hinder it from being evil spoken of. They say that we do not preach the gospel to sinners, — the best way of answering such a charge is by being even more diligent than before in preaching it, for thus it is that those who make such accusations are left without excuse.[34]

Tregelles kept in touch with the Welsh poet for many years and several of his letters (many written in Welsh) were later published, like the one just quoted, in the Welsh magazine *Y Traethodydd [The Essayist]*. To two of these letters, in particular, we shall later refer for details of his time in Rome and later in Spain about which he wrote at some length to Eben Fardd in 1846 and in 1860.

[33] Millward, *Fardd a Tregelles*, 346, part of which is quoted (without acknowledgement) in G.H. Fromow [ed.], *Teachers of the Faith and the Future: The Life and Works of B.W. Newton and Dr. S.P. Tregelles* (London: Sovereign Grace Advent Testimony, n.d.), 31.

[34] 'Llythyrau Dr. Tregelles at Eben Fardd', *Y Traethodydd* 29 (July 1884): 286–87.

Here then, is the subject of our study, an earnest Plymouth Brother, in his early thirties, an evangelist who was ready to take his message to the Welsh, a linguist and scholar whose textual researches would shortly direct him to Italy for some months, but, strange to relate, it seems almost certain that, at this stage, Tregelles was unaware of another group of people who soon would also be of great interest to him. These were Italians—more particularly Tuscans—who would also adopt many of the ideas associated with the Plymouth Brethren just at the time when Tregelles was beginning to have second thoughts about his involvement with them. However, before we consider these folk and SPT's interest in them we must follow him in his continental quest for biblical MSS and if we are properly to understand his motives in this quest, we need briefly to examine the nature of textual criticism and why it had come to have such an important place in SPT's life and thinking.

CHAPTER 5

Textual Criticism and Its Importance for SPT: A Necessary Digression

5.1   Manuscript Transmission

In our electronic age when most writing is done on the keyboard of a computer, it is easy to forget (even if we once appreciated it) the revolution in communication, which was made possible when printing with moveable type became a feature of European civilization in the fifteenth century. Previously, ideas had been transmitted either through the spoken word (oral transmission) or, for some four and half thousand years, through pictures and words inscribed on something solid like stone or written in ink by hand (manuscript transmission). The spoken word is peculiarly evanescent and the recorded preservation of sound for posterity has only been possible during the last hundred and fifty years, but manuscript transmission of ideas and information was also very fragile in its own way. The life of a manuscript text was, at maximum, only as long as that of the material on which it was written unless another accurate copy was made.

Let us take a specific example. When, in about 50 BC, Julius Caesar (or a scribe to whom he may have been dictating) wrote the account of his campaigns in *De Bello Gallico* (*The History of the Gallic War*), that script was the *only* copy in existence until, we may suppose, perhaps five other scribes reproduced the original text, at which point—such is the unreliability of the average copyist—there could already have been six different versions of Caesar's account, albeit the variations would probably have been only minimal.

© The Author(s) 2020   53
T. C. F. Stunt, *The Life and Times of Samuel Prideaux Tregelles*,
Christianities in the Trans-Atlantic World,
https://doi.org/10.1007/978-3-030-32266-3_5

Fifteen hundred years later, with the invention of printing the dynamics of the writing process were radically changed. In AD 1500, if the proofs were properly checked for accuracy, hundreds of *guaranteed identical* copies of the written text used by the typesetter, could be produced, of which at least some would probably survive *even if no-one wanted to read them*. This was in stark contrast to the earlier situation.

If, at the turn of the first century, Caesar's adopted son and heir had *not* been victorious and had not emerged as the great Emperor (Caesar) Augustus and if, in consequence, his father's military and political reputation had been eclipsed and of only a short duration, then the motivation for scribes to copy the text of his *De Bello Gallico* would have been very much less. Our suppositional six copies of the history might never have been recopied, and like many other works of antiquity, the text might not have survived. To take a case in point: Of the sixteen books of *The Annals* of Tacitus (a brilliant historian writing about one hundred and fifty years *later* than Caesar) at least four are no longer extant and for our knowledge of the remainder we have only a very slender line of transmission, depending on MSS from the ninth and twelfth centuries. With Caesar's *History* the line of transmission is less fragile but hardly copious. The earliest MS in existence today, containing the text of *De Bello Gallico*, was written in France during the ninth century and is preserved in the University Library of Amsterdam. We cannot say how many copies of the original were made in the course of the intervening eight hundred years but for it still to be extant in the year 900 suggests not only that some people wanted to read his account, but that scribes were ready to make copies.[1]

When we turn to consider the transmission of the Christian scriptures written in Greek in the first century, we are dealing with a significantly different situation. As the Christian faith spread across the Greek and Latin speaking civilization of the Mediterranean, the number of believers who wanted to read (or have read to them) the Christian scriptures grew rapidly and therefore many more copies were made than of the works of Caesar (let alone Tacitus!) and they were made on a variety of materials. The most fragile of these was papyrus—a material which only survived in dry climatic

---

[1] For details of the earliest surviving MSS of Caesar's work, see V. Brown, 'Manuscripts of Caesar's *Gallic War*', in Scuola speciale per archivisti e bibliotecari dell'Università di Roma [ed.], *Palaeographica diplomatica et archivistica: Studi in onore di Giulio Battelli*, Vol. 1 (Rome, 1979), 105–57. For *The Annals*' slender line of transmission, see C.W. Mendell, *Tacitus: The Man and His Work* (New Haven: Yale University Press, 1957), 294–97, 325.

conditions like those of Egypt or Qumran, near the Dead Sea, where writings on papyrus have been recovered, dating from the time of Christ and earlier.[2] Elsewhere, for the writings to have survived, they could be written on skins of varying quality, and as they were treasured and valued as sacred scriptures, the original Greek text was repeatedly copied and recopied over a period of many hundreds of years *with the numerous variant readings that inevitably occur in the copying process.*

5.2   The Printing Revolution

By the nineteenth century, scholars were becoming aware of the considerable number of old MSS of the Greek New Testament, which were lurking in monastic and royal libraries, and how numerous were the variant readings contained in them, but in the sixteenth century the scholars, who wanted to produce a printed copy of the biblical text, had access to only a few MSS. Nevertheless, their choice of which MS to copy, would be responsible for the printed text, which, for the next three hundred and fifty years, would be reproduced repeatedly and would in turn be used as the basis for vernacular translations circulated by the million. Strange as it may seem, the scholars of the day were probably unaware of how critical their choices would be in deciding the words of the Bible for more than a dozen generations.

When the Basel publisher Johann Froben persuaded the Dutch scholar Erasmus, in 1513 to prepare the first printed edition of the Greek New Testament he was anxious for their work to appear before the edition of Cardinal Ximenes Cisneros, which was currently under production in the Complutense University of Madrid.[3] Erasmus was therefore in a bit of a hurry and his sources were limited to the materials readily at hand. The Dominican monks of Basel made three codices (MS books) available for Erasmus to use. They were written in minuscule, as opposed to the older uncial (majuscule) script, two of them dating from the twelfth and one from

---

[2] It is only in the last 150 years that archaeologists have been acquainted with the considerable corpus of extant New Testament papyri, so this dimension of the subject never confronted SPT. For a fascinating survey of other locations for New Testament texts with which Tregelles would have also been totally unfamiliar, see P.M. Head, 'Additional Greek Witnesses to the New Testament (Ostraca, Amulets, Inscriptions and Other Sources),' in Ehrman and Holmes *The Text*, 429–60.

[3] In fact the Complutensian polyglot was printed before Erasmus's edition of the Greek New Testament (*Novum Instrumentum Omne*) but its publication was delayed for several years.

the fifteenth century.[4] For the Book of Revelation he borrowed from a fellow scholar, Johannes Reuchlin, another twelfth-century MS (in minuscule script), which unfortunately lacked the last six verses. In a famous lapse of scholarly principle, in the final passage where his MS source was incomplete (Rev. xxii. 16–21), Erasmus translated these verses back into Greek, from the Latin Vulgate—in effect inventing the Greek text that was missing![5]

As Tregelles was keenly aware, it was a poor selection of MSS that was used by Erasmus for a pioneer project of such importance, and the consequent unreliability of this first printed edition of the Greek New Testament had far-reaching consequences. For the next hundred years and more, the subsequent editions of the Greek New Testament, produced by Stephanus (in Paris and Geneva) and the brothers Elzevir (in Leiden), followed Erasmus in essentials and made minimal attempts to establish an older or more authentic text. What soon came to be called the *textus receptus* was more or less the basis for Luther's German translation and, similarly, for the English translations of Tyndale and Coverdale, and indeed the Authorised Version of 1611.

It would be unfair to suggest that the translators were unaware of the poverty of their text, but the fact remains that only occasionally did they add footnotes, which drew attention to their reservations about the text they

---

[4] These are now in the Basel University Library.

[5] The Reuchlin MS (now in the University Library of Augsburg) was lost for some two hundred and fifty years but its rediscovery in the Œtingen-Wallerstein Library, Mayhingen, Bavaria, by Franz Delitzsch in 1861, was a source of immense excitement to SPT who wrote of the discovery to Newton in January 1862: 'The one Greek MS of the Revelation which Erasmus used (having borrowed it from Reuchlin) has come to light after having been lost for three centuries ... The guesswork use which Erasmus made of the MS, and the false readings which he introduced from the commentary annexed, or from the Vulgate turned into Greek, or from his own supposed correction — and which still hold their place in the common text gives us a most important proof how needful it is to recur to MS authority in that book especially. It is really strange that this had not been done up to my ed[ition] of 1844. I am particularly glad that this MS has come to light: it takes away all possible grounds for defending many false and troublesome readings. We can now say positively that there is nothing known which contains them [Erasmus's inventions]' (SPT to B.W. Newton, Plymouth, January 3, 1862, Manchester/JRUL/CBA 7181 [22]). For a similar comment written when he was examining the MS in Erlangen, see below Chapter 12, Footnote 49. For his published account and collation of the MS (25 September 1862), see Tregelles, 'A Few Notes on Codex Reuchlini of the Apocalypse, Together with a Collation of Its Text with the Common Editions,' in *Handschriftliche Funde von Franz Delitzsch*, Vol. 2 (Leipzig: Dörffling und Franke, 1862), 1–16.

were translating.[6] The great French Protestant scholar Theodore Beza is a good example. Not only was he familiar with a sixth-century (and in places very unusual) Codex,[7] which he presented to the University of Cambridge and which is consequently named after him, but he also acquired from the monastery of Clermont another sixth-century Codex, which was later purchased by Louis XIV and found its way to Paris. In the later sixteenth century, Beza published several editions of the Greek New Testament but in spite of his familiarity with much earlier MSS like the Codices Bezae and Claromontanus, his text differed very little from that of Stephanus and further contributed to the almost universal adoption of the *textus receptus* based on the late MSS used by Erasmus (and the few lines that he composed himself!).

5.3   The Beginnings of Modern Biblical Textual Criticism

There were several later scholars who published editions of the Greek text and among them were two seventeenth-century English churchmen who drew their readers' attention to other MSS containing texts differing from the *textus receptus*. In 1657, a Greek New Testament edited by Brian Walton,[8] contained footnotes with variant readings from the recently acquired

---

[6] Thus in Rev. xxii. 14 Erasmus rejected the older MSS reading which proclaimed as 'blessed' πλύνοντες τὰς στολὰς αὐτῶν (they who wash their robes) because the MSS didn't include the phrase 'in the blood of the lamb'. Instead he followed the Vulgate and referred to the 'blessed' as οἱ ποιοῦντες τὰς ἐντολὰς αὐτοῦ (they who do his commandments). This was therefore the basis for Luther's translation in 1522 ('seine gebote halten') as also for Tyndale's ('that do hys commaundementes') and the similar translation of the English Authorised Version (1611). Likewise in Rev. xxii. 19b, both Tyndale and the AV translators again followed Erasmus who, translating back from the Clementine Vulgate into Greek, had used the phrase ἀπὸ βίβλου τῆς ζωῆς (out of the book of life) instead of ἀπὸ τοῦ ξύλου τῆς ζωῆς (from the tree of life). In this instance, however, the AV translators gave 'from the tree of life' as a marginal alternative.

[7] The Codex Bezae was taken from the monastery of St Irenaeus when the Huguenots sacked Lyons in 1562 and Beza presented it to Cambridge University in 1581. See Robert C. Stone, *The Language of the Latin Text of Codex Bezae: With an Index Verborum* (Eugene, OR: Wipf and Stock, 2009), 9.

[8] Brian Walton [1600–1661] was consecrated Bishop of Chester by Charles II in 1660 but in the preface to the early copies of his New Testament published during the interregnum, he mentioned the encouragement he had received from Oliver Cromwell—an acknowledgement that was eliminated in copies printed after the restoration of Charles II.

fifth-century Codex Alexandrinus[9] and in 1707, although the text published by John Mill, the Principal of St Edmund Hall, Oxford, was a reissue of the 1550 *textus receptus* of Stephanus, the editor also provided the reader with variant readings from seventy-eight MSS in the Bodleian Library and elsewhere.[10] Another notable aspect of Mill's work was his use of quotations from the early fathers as evidence for what the text had been in their day. For example, none of the older MSS of Matthew's Gospel gives Jesus as the first name of Barabbas, the prisoner released by Pontius Pilate, so it might be concluded that this detail was a later addition. However, an editor like Mill, who was familiar with the writings of the early fathers, would know that the learned Origen discussed his anxiety about this particular reading, which must therefore have been current in *some* third-century MSS. The *textus receptus* still reigned supreme but textual critics had begun to gather the evidence with which they could question it.

In the eighteenth century, two German scholars stand out, as textual critics who seriously addressed the question of how to evaluate the reliability of MS readings. Johann Albrecht Bengel [1687–1752] suggested that MSS could be classified into two families, reckoning that while an Asiatic or Byzantine tradition contained an inferior text, there was a better and earlier text found in an African or Alexandrian family of MSS. Bengel is also always credited with being the first to formulate the principle that, as copyists like their text to make sense, a more difficult reading is probably more reliable than an easy one.[11] A few years later, a second German scholar Johann Jakob Griesbach [1745–1812][12] formulated another principle of textual criticism (with which not everyone agreed) that shorter readings are more

---

[9] The four volumes of this fifth-century uncial MS were given in 1627 to the Stuart monarchy by the patriarch of Constantinople, Cyril Lucar, and became part of the Royal Library which George IV gave to the nation in 1823 with the result that in SPT's day the MS was in the British Museum.

[10] John Mill [1645–1707] worked on his Greek New Testament for some thirty years, dying just two weeks after its publication.

[11] Bengel's principle was enunciated as '*Proclivi scriptioni praestat ardua*' [the difficult reading takes precedence over the easy one]. It was to be found in his *Prodromus Novi Testamenti recte cauteque ordinandi* ['Preface for a New Testament whose text is to be decided rightly and cautiously'], which was published as a supplement to his edition of St John Chrysostom, *De Sacerdotio* (Stuttgart, 1725), xii. To be fair, it appears that Erasmus had understood the principle some two hundred years earlier, see J.H. Bentley, 'Erasmus, Jean Le Clerc and the Principle of the Harder Reading', *Renaissance Quarterly* 31:3 (1978): 318.

[12] During some forty years, Griesbach published three editions of the Greek New Testament as well as other works, in one of which he propounded his own synoptic hypothesis that

reliable as copyists are more inclined to add words than to remove them. He also developed a more complex theory of MS families in which the Constantinopolitan or Byzantine text was treated as a combination of the earlier Alexandrian and Western type of text. In theory, he treated the later (Constantinopolitan) text as inferior and yet in cases of uncertainty he too seems to have fallen back on the *textus receptus*.

Possibly the greatest (but also the most quarrelsome) eighteenth-century scholar of the Greek text of the New Testament was the Master of Trinity College, Cambridge, Richard Bentley [1662–1742]. Unfortunately, his many other interests and contentious polemics prevented him from bringing to completion his planned edition of the Greek New Testament. His textual collations and research, however, were far-reaching, and in his *Proposals for printing a New Edition of the Greek Testament* (1721), it is apparent that he was planning to replace the *textus receptus* with a text based on the oldest Greek MSS. Tregelles had immense admiration for Bentley and his textual principles and more than once reckoned it was worth his while to spend time in the Library of Trinity College, working on Bentley's papers and correspondence, which are preserved there.[13]

5.4   The Overthrow of the *Textus Receptus*

It was only in the nineteenth century that the hegemony of the *textus receptus* was finally broken even though its shackles still held captive the almost universally used Authorised Version of 1611. In 1838 when Prideaux Tregelles first conceived the idea of producing an edition of the Greek New Testament, his plan was to produce an eclectic text, based principally (but not exclusively), on ancient MSS and ancient patristic readings. He recognized his debt to the methodology of previous scholars like Bengel, Bentley and Griesbach but ironically at this stage he seems to have been unaware of the scholar who, on SPT's later admission 'led the way in casting aside the so-called *textus receptus*, and boldly placing the New Testament wholly and entirely on the basis of actual authority'.[14] This was

---

Matthew's gospel was written before that of Luke and that Mark's work was later making use of the first two.

[13] For Bentley's optimistic self-confidence with regard to the text of the New Testament, see J. Sheehan, *The Enlightenment Bible: Translation, Scholarship, Culture* (Princeton: University Press, 2005), 46–49; cf. below Chapter 6, Footnote 6.

[14] This tribute to Karl Lachmann is taken from Tregelles, *Account*, 103.

the German classical scholar Karl Lachmann [1793–1851] who in 1831 finally produced a text that was based solely on the oldest available MSS together with readings quoted by Irenaeus and Origen. Ignoring the large number of later MSS, which, in the opinion of many of his critics, seemed to validate the *textus receptus*, Lachmann followed in the steps of Richard Bentley and applied the methods he himself had used when editing the works of classical authors like Catullus.

Unfortunately in the first edition of his Greek New Testament, Lachmann provided no *Prolegomena* and if his readers wanted to understand his aims and principles of textual choice, they were briefly referred to an explanatory account that he had published previously in a scholarly German periodical, with the result that Tregelles, who only later learnt to read German, was unaware, in the earliest stages of his work, of the similarity between his and Lachmann's approach.[15]

His later visit to Berlin in 1850 was therefore a time of special importance for SPT as he was able to meet the older scholar and discuss 'many points connected with New Testament criticism. It was', he said, 'very interesting to hear *from* [Lachmann] *himself* an explanation of his plan etc., in his Greek Testament … I entreated Lachmann to publish his Latin collations, — little thinking how soon this scholar was to be taken from us'![16]

It was the overriding principle of giving precedence to the ancient MSS that made the nineteenth century a truly fruitful field for New Testament textual studies and in this Tregelles was a real pioneer. Inevitably, there was a conservative rearguard, which sought to justify the continued respect for the *textus receptus* on the grounds that it was effectively a 'majority text' based on the superior number of MSS, which contained it. It would be wrong to claim that Tregelles was unique in his rejection of the idea of a majority text or in his vision of making the *textus receptus* a thing of the past. As we have noted, Lachmann anticipated him and as we shall discover later, Tregelles was working in parallel with other scholars who took a similar approach, but he publicly enunciated the principle in 1839, sometime before other more famous scholars like Tischendorf. His desire to establish a text, that was as ancient as possible, is sufficient to explain the decision of this pious and somewhat retiring scholar to set out in 1845

---

[15] SPT's lengthy account of his earlier misunderstandings concerning Lachmann's first edition makes clear his admiration for Lachmann's pioneering achievement (ibid., 97–117).

[16] Ibid., 163–64.

for the Vatican archives and thence to other European libraries with a view to establishing the texts of all the known ancient Greek MSS of the New Testament.

CHAPTER 6

Roman Frustrations and European Research

6.1   Codex Vaticanus and the City of Rome

The man who set out for Rome in 1845 was a scholar with a passion for history and literature, and for whom detailed biblical studies had been his principal pre-occupation for the best part of ten years. His collations of the Greek text of the New Testament were already extensive and eminently accurate,[1] but until now however, apart from those that had found their way into print, Tregelles had only examined MSS in the UK. His decision to travel on the continent in 1845 was an indication of his growing awareness of a challenge that no-one else in England seemed ready to tackle—the need to establish a scholarly and reliable text of the Greek New Testament based on the earliest MSS.

Probably the oldest biblical MS known at the time was the Codex Vaticanus, which, as its name suggests, was (and still is) in the papal library in Rome, and this was going to be the principal scene of SPT's endeavours for several months, but he was by no means the first student of scripture who

---

[1] Tregelles's explanation of his method of MS collation is admirable: 'I procured many copies of the same edition of the Greek New Testament so that all the MSS. might be compared with exactly the same text. When a MS. was before me, I marked in one of these copies every variation, however slight; I noted the beginning of every *page, column* and *line*, so that I can produce the text of every MS., which I have collated, *line* for *line*. This gave a kind of *certainty* to my examinations, and I was thus prevented from hastily overlooking readings'. Tregelles, *Account*, 155.

© The Author(s) 2020   63
T. C. F. Stunt, *The Life and Times of Samuel Prideaux Tregelles*,
Christianities in the Trans-Atlantic World,
https://doi.org/10.1007/978-3-030-32266-3_6

wanted to establish the text of this ancient uncial MS. It had been listed in the Vatican Library catalogue as early as 1481 and had long attracted a great deal of interest, but SPT's desire to collate it for himself arose from the inadequacy of the work of his predecessors, whose accounts of the MS were often at variance with each other. To appreciate his motives and the long line of scholars in whose steps he was following, we must briefly consider the efforts of these predecessors, details of whom are sometimes hard to discover.

6.1.1   The Work of Predecessors

Soon after the publication, in 1516, of his edition of the Greek New Testament, Erasmus asked his friend, Paulus Bombasius,[2] the prefect of the Vatican Library, to provide him with the text of the Vatican MS for I John v. 7 (which in fact is omitted in that MS) and some time later, in the 1530s, he was in correspondence with a Spanish scholar, Juan Ginés de Sepúlveda[3] concerning other variant readings in the MS.

In 1669, another Vatican librarian and Hebrew scholar, Giulio Bartolocci,[4] closely examined the MS and made a collation which was preserved in the Royal Library of Paris where it was discovered in 1819 by Johann Scholz.[5] In the early eighteenth century, important textual research was undertaken by Richard Bentley,[6] the Master of Trinity College, Cambridge, whose papers Tregelles had closely examined in the summer of

---

[2] For Paolo Bombace (1476–1527), a true renaissance scholar, who was killed in the sack of Rome, see the article by Elpidio Mioni in *Dizionario Biografico degli Italiani* (Rome: Istituto della Enciclopedia italiana, 1969) [*DBI*], 11.

[3] Juan Ginés de Sepúlveda (1494–1573) is better known for his defence of Spanish conquests in America. His letters concerning the Vatican MS are quoted and evaluated by SPT in his re-written and revised edition (1856) of *An Introduction* [originally by T.H. Horne] *to the Textual Criticism of the New Testament, with Analyses, of the Respective Books, and a Bibliographical List of Editions of the Scriptures in the Original Texts and the Ancient Versions* (London: Longmans, 1856) [Tregelles, *Introduction*], 108–10 and in an addendum, at pp. xv–xvii. For SPT's account of Bombasius, see Idem, p. 158.

[4] Giulio Bartolocci (1613–1687) is better known for the four volumes of his *Bibliotheca Magna Rabbinica* (Rome 1675–1693) and other Hebrew studies; see also Giovanni Garbini art. s.n. in *DBI*, 6 (1964).

[5] For details of Johann Augustin Scholz, see below Footnote 65.

[6] For the very contentious career of Richard Bentley (1662–1742), see the article by R. C. Jebb in the *Dictionary of National Biography* rather than the disjointed account by Hugh de Quehen in the *ODNB*. Tregelles admired Bentley's progressive attitude towards textual

1845 prior to his continental researches.[7] For many years, Bentley had been preparing an edition of the Greek New Testament, which in fact was never published, but in the process he acquired a collation of the Roman codex, made by Apostolo Mico,[8] a Greek *scriptor* in the Vatican Library. In the interests of accuracy, Bentley's nephew checked some of Mico's readings and later secured the services of another *scriptor*, the Abate Rulotta,[9] to collate the corrections, made by a later hand, in the MS. These collations (made for Bentley) were later prepared for publication by a German scholar Carl Gottfried Woide[10] as an appendix to the second edition of his text of the Codex Alexandrinus.[11] A further (somewhat hasty) collation had been made in 1781 by a Danish scholar Bishop Andreas Birch[12] and was published in a series of volumes in Copenhagen (1788, 1798 and 1801). With the exception of Bartolocci's collation, Tregelles was familiar with all these readings of the MS but there was an overriding problem: the variations were just too numerous.

criticism; see Tregelles, *Account*, 57–68; cf. S.P.T., 'Tischendorf's Greek Testament,' *JSL* 5 (January 1850): 37–39, and *passim*, 40–52. See also above Chapter 5, Footnote 13.

[7] 'I spent a great part of the summer of 1845 at Cambridge, and I was for most days in the Library of Trinity College, to which the Rev Mr Carus kindly procured me admission'. SPT, Plymouth, 29 December 1848, to C. Wordsworth (London/LPL, MS 2143 f 373v). Cf. *infra* Chapter 10, Footnote 20.

[8] Apostolo Mico (died 1726) was a native of Corfu and had been a chaplain in the Scuola Greca in Venice.

[9] We learn the name and nothing more about this elusive man from a letter written by a rather shady German antiquarian 'wheeler-dealer', Baron Philipp von Stosch (1691–1757), see [Christopher Wordsworth, ed.], *Correspondence of Richard Bentley, Master of Trinity College, Cambridge*, Vol. 2 (London: Murray, 1842), 706.

[10] For Charles Godfrey Woide (1725–1790), as he was known in England, where he was an assistant curator of the British Museum, and for some fascinating details of his scholarship and work on the collation of the Vatican Codex obtained by Bentley, see John Nichols, *Literary Anecdotes of the Eighteenth Century, Containing Biographical Memoirs ... 9 vols.*, Vol. 9 (London: Nichols, 1815), 10–13.

[11] Published posthumously by Henry Ford of the Clarendon Press, as C.G. Woide, *Appendix Ad Editionem Novi Testamenti Græci e Codice MS. Alexandrino ... quibus subjicitur Codicis Vaticani Collatio* (Oxford, 1799).

[12] The collation work of Andreas Birch (1758–1859) under the patronage of the King of Denmark was usefully discussed by John Scott Porter, a Presbyterian scholar from Belfast, in *Principles of Textual Criticism, with Their Application to the Old and the New Testaments* (London: Simms and M'Intyre, 1848), 259, 278–79, 474n. There are fuller details of Birch in Frederik Nielsen's article in C.F. Bricka [ed.], *Dansk Biografisk Lexikon*, Vol. 2 (Copenhagen: Hegel, 1888), 280–82.

In addition to the inquiries of this wide range of scholars, general interest in the Vatican codex was further increased when Napoleon invaded Italy and many of the treasures of the Vatican, including the ancient codex itself, were taken to Paris. When the learned Professor Hug[13] of Freiburg was given a prolonged holiday for the sake of his health he spent the winter months of 1809–1810 in Paris, where he was given permission by the French Emperor to borrow the Vatican MS from the Imperial Library, but instead of preparing a collation, he spent most of his energies, analysing the uncial script and comparing it with the writing on the first-century papyri that had recently been recovered from the excavated remains of Herculaneum, near Pompeii.[14] Other scholars also had plans[15] to consult the Vatican Codex in Paris, and with the defeat of Napoleon, there even appear to have been 'strenuous representations' that the MS 'might be transferred to the British Museum', where it would have been a companion for the Codex Alexandrinus, but in the negotiations for the 1815 settlement, the British Foreign Secretary, Lord Castlereagh, respected the principle of 'legitimacy' and honourably insisted that the MS should be restored to the papal library,[16] with the result that it was back in the Vatican in 1845.

Having attracted the attention of so many scholars for some three hundred years, the Vatican MS was a document celebrated by textual critics, but Tregelles was only too well aware that their collations were far from

[13] For Johann Leonhard Hug (1765–1846), Professor of Oriental languages and Biblical studies at Freiburg University, and his time in Paris, see Adalbert Maier, *Gedächtnissrede auf Joh. Leonh. Hug bei dessen akademischer Todtenfeier in der Universitäts-Kirche zu Freiburg am 11. März 1847 gehalten* (Freiburg: Poppen, 1847), 13–14.

[14] For his account of the Vatican Codex (published by the University of Freiburg which had recently become part of the newly created Grand Duchy of Baden), see Io. Leonardus Hug, *De Antiquitate Codicis Vaticani commentatio qua Albertinae Magni Ducatus Zahringo Badensis* (Freiburg: Herder, 1810). Available at https://books.google.com/books?id=TXNYAAAAcAAJ&printsec [accessed June 2017]. John Scott Porter (vide supra n. 12) 'gratefully' owned Hug as one of 'my masters in the art of Criticism', from whom he seems to have gleaned some personal details, op. cit., 223n, 278–79.

[15] The Rev. Henry Harvey Baber, the Keeper of Printed Books in the British Museum, was travelling in February 1815 and hoped 'to procure a sight of the Vatican MS at Paris on his way home [from Munich] that he may collate it with the Alexandrine Codex', B. Madan [ed.], *Spencer and Waterloo: The Letters of Spencer Madan, 1814–1816* (London, 1970), 78.

[16] 'The Public Libraries of Paris and London,' *The British Review, and London Critical Journal* 20 (December 1822): 472; cf. Christopher M.S. Johns, *Antonio Canova and the Politics of Patronage in Revolutionary and Napoleonic Europe* (Berkeley and Los Angeles: University of California Press, 1998), 178–80.

unanimous. In his opinion, it was a MS of such importance that a totally accurate reading was essential for his projected New Testament text. Not surprisingly therefore, Rome was his first destination when, with his wife, he left England on Monday 20 October 1845.[17]

6.1.2   The Journey to Rome

As we saw earlier, he was leaving, in Plymouth, a church that was in turmoil. In spite of all the excitement and new experiences of his time on the continent, Tregelles was far from forgetful of the situation of his friends in Plymouth—indeed, a letter, which he wrote from Rome to one of his patrons, Lord Congleton (a leader among the Brethren), is as much concerned with developments in Plymouth as with the writer's experiences in Rome.[18] However, he was primarily engaged in a mission of textual scholarship and everything else had to be a subsidiary concern.

Travelling from England to Rome in 1845 was a tedious business, taking the best part of a month.[19] The journey through France to Marseilles, with a few days break in Paris and in Avignon, took two weeks by coach and by boat on the rivers Saone and Rhône, but inevitably there were locations of special interest for an enthusiastic student of history and language. Taking the old Roman road from Boulogne, across the plains of Picardy, Tregelles noted with some excitement that they passed between the site of the battle of Crécy[20] on their left and the port of St Valéry, on their right where William of Normandy had assembled his fleet at the mouth of the Somme for the invasion of England in 1066.[21] Similarly fascinating for the historian was the night spent on board a river ferry just north of Avignon,

---

[17] Tregelles, *Three Letters*, 21.

[18] S.P. Tregelles to Lord Congleton, 18 January 1846 (formerly in the Fry Collection, on the Isle of Wight, where I transcribed it in 1962, but now in the possession of Mr. Tom Chantry, and accessible on line at http://www.brethrenarchive.org/manuscripts/letters-of-sp-tregelles/). For the full text see my Appendix of Unpublished Materials.

[19] For the route and chronology of SPT's journey, my principal source is his letter (March 1846) to Eben Fardd written and published in Welsh in *Y Traethodydd* (1853), 367–71, and kindly translated for me, many years ago, by Mrs. Olwen Wonnacott. Her English translation is included below in the Appendix of Unpublished Materials.

[20] Scene of the English victory in 1346, early in the Hundred Years War.

[21] Not to be confused with St Valéry-en-Caux, some miles SW on the coast, also in Normandy.

at Roquemaure, where, Tregelles, taking his cue from recent scholarship,[22] reckoned that Hannibal had crossed the Rhone, in 218 BC.

Following their arrival in Marseilles, they spent a further week on board a Mediterranean ship, with a delay in Toulon, because of bad weather, and after brief stops in Genoa and Leghorn (from where they took the train[23] to visit friends in Pisa), they travelled overland from Civitavecchia, arriving in Rome in mid-November.

6.1.3   *Frustrations in the Vatican*

Exciting as it was for SPT to find himself in a city steeped in thousands of years of history, he was very conscious that this was not a holiday and that his expenses were being paid for by patrons, like Benjamin Newton, John Eliot Howard and Lord Congleton, who were sponsoring his research, but his mission proved to be far from straightforward. This earnest and very Protestant scholar must have felt somewhat isolated when he ventured into the Vatican.[24] He had come to Rome with a letter of introduction from the Roman Catholic Bishop Nicholas Wiseman[25] to Doctor Thomas Grant,[26] the Rector of the English College at Rome, but although Wiseman appears to have been in favour with the Papacy, the introduction proved to be, in Tregelles's own words, 'utterly useless'.[27]

---

[22] Tregelles would have known Livy's account (*History of Rome*, 22) and that of Polybius (*Histories*, 3) but he was evidently, also familiar with the work of the Swiss scholar, Jean-André De Luc [junior], *Histoire du passage des Alpes par Annibal: dans laquelle on détermine d'une manière précise la route de ce général, depuis Carthagène jusqu'au Tésin, d'après la narration de Polybe, comparée aux recherches faites sur les lieux...* (Geneva: Paschoud, 1818), 49, where De Luc identified Roquemaure as the site of the crossing.

[23] This was the only part of the journey taken by train—still very much a new mode of transport!

[24] For an excellent account of both the Codex and also of the Vatican Library as described by a British observer some thirty years later, see Hugh Macmillan, *Roman Mosaics, or Studies in Rome and Its Neighbourhood* (London: Macmillan, 1888), 360–79.

[25] For Nicholas (later Cardinal) Wiseman (1802–1865) who was, at the time Bishop, Coadjutor to the English Vicar-apostolic, Thomas Walsh, and President of Oscott College, see *ODNB* s.n. art. by Richard J. Schiefen.

[26] Thomas Grant (1816–70), appointed as Rector in 1844, had previously been secretary to Cardinal Acton and was later Bishop of Southwark. See *ODNB* s.n. art. by Michael Clifton. It was only at a later stage that Wiseman and Grant came into serious disagreement.

[27] Tregelles, *Account*, 157.

Challenged by the bureaucracy of the Vatican, Tregelles was greatly helped by the many efforts on his behalf made by Cardinal Acton[28] to whom in his letters and published work SPT pays repeated tribute, emphasizing that he 'has really been very kind and has taken a great deal of trouble for me'. The Cardinal's first approach was to the prefect of the Vatican Library, Gabriele Laureani,[29] whose rather unhelpful response was that the sole 'access his regulations permitted ... amounted to only seeing the MS in his [Laureani's] hands'.[30] In a lecture given a few years later (after Laureani's death), Tregelles suggested that the prefect was one of the chief villains in the frustrating series of 'promises, which came to nothing, and delays of a most wearying kind'. As Tregelles recalled, it was 'Monsignor Laureani, the *primo custodè*, [who] acted on secret orders that he had received and took no notice of the apparent permission that had been given'.[31]

Cardinal Acton then promised to approach Cardinal Lambruschini,[32] the Secretary of State to the Pope, but this application, as Tregelles explained in his letter to Lord Congleton, covered a period of two months having been hindered by the state visit of the Russian Tsar Nicholas I, during which Acton served as an interpreter for the Pope.[33] This was followed by the celebrations of Christmas, and finally by Acton having been very

[28] Cardinal Charles Januarius Edward Acton (1803–1847), an uncle of the historian Lord Acton. From the late 1820s, he had been a respected Papal diplomat, despite his youth. By 1845 when he gave so much help to Tregelles he was already a dying man. See *ODNB* s.n. art. by Thompson Cooper, rev. R. Ashton; cf. Charles S. Isaacson, *The Story of the English Cardinals* (London: Elliot Stock, 1907), 238–41.

[29] For Gabriele Laureani (1788–1849), see Philippe Boutry, *Souverain et Pontife: recherches prosopographiques sur la curie romaine à l'âge de la restauration: 1814–1846* (Rome: École française de Rome, 2002) [Boutry, *Souverain et Pontife*], 712–13.

[30] SPT to Lord Congleton 18 January 1846 (see above Footnote 18).

[31] S.P. Tregelles, *The Historic Evidence of the Authorship and Transmission of the Books of the New Testament: A Lecture Delivered Before the Plymouth Young Men's Christian Association, October 14, 1851* (London: Bagster, 1852) [Tregelles, *Historic Evidence*], 82.

[32] For Cardinal Luigi Lambruschini, see G. Monsagrati, 'Lambruschini, Luigi,' *DBI*, 63 (2004). On the death of Pope Gregory XVI in 1846, Lambruschini (1776–1854) was a strong candidate, to be his successor, but eventually lost out to Mastai Ferretti, Pius IX. Lambruschini was a very conservative prelate who must not be confused with his nephew, the liberal minded Abbot Raffaello Lambruschini (1828–1873) of San Cerbone in Tuscany, whom we shall encounter in Chapter 8 [Footnote 16].

[33] [Nicholas Patrick] Cardinal Wiseman, *Recollections of the Last Four Popes and of Rome in their Times* (London: Hurst and Blackett, 1858) [Wiseman, *Recollections*], 479–80.

unwell. In January, however, the Cardinal's efforts on Tregelles's behalf seemed to be prospering. Having obtained Lambruschini's approval in principle, Acton indicated that the application 'must be mentioned to the Pope and this [he] has engaged to do, not exactly as making an application from me but making it his [Acton's] own request'. At last it looked as if the project could now go ahead, and on 19 January 1846, Tregelles could write to Lord Congleton: 'This morning I saw Cardinal Acton and he gave me the Pope's answer: *no objection is made, and the formal permission to collate the MS will be sent*'.

Unfortunately, Tregelles had underestimated the opposition with which he was contending, because the formal permission never materialized. Further efforts on his behalf from Cardinal Acton[34] as well as friendly contacts with the famous hyperpolyglot, Cardinal Mezzofanti,[35] and an Irish priest, Joseph Nicholson (later Archbishop of Corfu),[36] were unavailing. In a final attempt to resolve the deadlock, Tregelles even had a personal conversation with the Pope himself. It must have been a strange encounter, and writing to his Welsh friend Eben Fardd, Tregelles felt the need to justify his having done so, his reasoning being that

> I thought it would not be right for me to leave untried any lawful means of achieving my object, and then, since an opportunity arose, I made the best of it. The pope[37] looks a strong, active old man, of 81; his eyesight good

[34] Tregelles, *Account*, 157.

[35] Cardinal Mezzofanti (1774–1849) was said to have been able to speak some forty languages and dialects. George Fox Tregelles referred to Mezzofanti when he claimed that SPT 'remembered that his eminence was reputed to know a marvellous variety of languages, so Tregelles addressed him in Welsh:- "Pa fodd yr ydwyt heddyw?" (How art thou today) to which the other replied: - "Yr ydw yn lled dda, diolch i ti" (I am very well thank thee.)' (G.F. Tregelles, 'Life of a Scholar,' 450). Mezzofanti's knowledge of Welsh is confirmed in C.W. Russell, *The Life of Cardinal Mezzofanti with an Introductory Memoir of Eminent Linguists, Ancient and Modern* (London: Longman, Green, Longman, Roberts and Green, 1863), 320. A slightly different account of the encounter with SPT, in which it is said that Mezzofanti took the initiative, can be found in T. Mardy Rees, *A History of the Quakers in Wales and Their Emigration to North America* (Carmarthen: Spurrell and Son, 1925), 244. Here the author adds the detail that Mezzofanti was 'taught Welsh in exchange for Italian by a notable Welsh portrait painter, Thomas Brigstocke of Carmarthen, when an art student in Rome'.

[36] For some idea of SPT's curious conversations with Nicholson (1805–1855) an Irish Carmelite priest 'who spent several months under the same roof with me at Rome', see below Chapter 8, Footnote 33.

[37] Gregory XVI was a very conservative Pope who despised modern inventions of any kind, considering such things as gaslighting to be but a step towards a more bourgeois and therefore

enough to read writing without glasses, his voice strong and clear. He seems to be striving to entertain his visitors, by talking to them about a great variety of topics.

Sadly it was all to no avail and in March 1846 he received a final and absolute refusal from Cardinal Lambruschini. Six years later, Tregelles gave a vivid picture of the obstructionist conduct that he encountered:

> It is true that I often *saw* the MS., but they would not allow me to use it; and they would not let me open it without searching my pockets, and depriving me, of pen, ink, and paper; and at the same time two *prelati* kept me in constant conversation in Latin, and if I looked at a passage too long, they would snatch the book out of my hand. So foolishly and meaninglessly did the papal authorities seek to keep this precious MS. to themselves.[38]

Needless to say this account, which he repeated almost *verbatim* in a letter (29 November 1855) to *The Times*, some four years later, appealed greatly to the anti-catholicism prevalent in England at the time, but there is an *addendum* to the episode about the details of which we cannot be so sure. In an oft-repeated embellishment of the story, several writers claimed that SPT, desperate to have some record of the manuscript but, deprived of his note-books, heroically made notes on his shirt-cuffs or/and his fingernails. The origin of this version of the story is hard to identify. One raconteur, speaking in Falmouth soon after the scholar's death, claimed that he had the story from a friend of SPT.[39] The earliest allusion to the incident seems to have been made during the last years of SPT's lifetime in 1868 when Henry Robert Reynolds, one of the editors of the congregational *British Quarterly Review* admiringly claimed that 'the Englishman was a match for the Romans and contrived to bring away some pencil-marks on his thumb-nail'.[40] As we noted earlier, SPT had a formidable

---

liberal society. He used a French pun to condemn the railways when he called them *le chemin d'enfer* [the road to Hell]. Tregelles met him about six months before his death in June 1846. He was born in September 1765, so in fact he was only 80 years old.

[38] Tregelles, *Historic Evidence*, 84, cf. *The Times*, 29 November 1855.

[39] R.N. Worth, 'A Cornish Valhalla', lecture delivered 13 September 1881 [in the Polytechnic Hall, Falmouth] in *The Royal Cornwall Polytechnic Society, 49th Annual Report* (Falmouth, Truro, 1881), 229–30.

[40] 'The Great Vatican MS of the New Testament,' *British Quarterly Review* 47 (April 1868): 346; cf. 53 (January 1871): 95. For the attribution to Reynolds, see *The Wellesley Index*, 4.

memory and we may assume that on returning to his lodgings he noted various readings he had made during his several 'sightings' of the MS. One such observation enabled him to declare, with certainty, that he had 'examined the Vatican MS.1209 in this passage [Matt xvi.18] and it does read with the common text'.[41]

Whatever the subterfuges to which Tregelles may have resorted, the intransigence of the authorities was clear. In due course, it emerged that the real opposition was coming from 'those in charge of the Vatican Library', and more specifically from Cardinal Angelo Mai himself,[42] who had already prepared an edition of the Codex and was not going to let another scholar steal his thunder. On the other hand, Tregelles reckoned that Mai was more direct and less 'slippery' than other officials. 'He told me in civil words that he would never consent to any person using the MS but himself as long as he could help it: — it pleased me much more to have to do with a plain spoken person than with those who say one thing and mean another'.[43] In fact, SPT's respect for Mai's scholarship was such that he took the trouble to go to the Cardinal's residence in the Palazzo Altieri where he found Mai's agent, Don Domenico Mostacci from whom he purchased 'the chief

---

[41] S. Prideaux Tregelles, 'Matthew xvi.18,' *Christian Annotator* 1 (8 July 1854): 174. He was rejecting the claim (based on Granville Penn's conjecture in *Annotations to the Book of the New Covenant* [1837], 151) that the first words of the Dominical charge to Peter in the Vatican uncial MS were CYEIΠAC [Thou hast said] rather than a contraction of CYEIΠETPOC [Thou art Peter].

[42] Cardinal Angelo Mai (1782–1854) was the custodian of the Vatican Library and Secretary of the Sacred Congregation for the Propagation of the Faith [*Propaganda Fide*]. The fullest English account of his career is in Salvador Miranda, *The Cardinals of the Holy Roman Church*, available on line at https://webdept.fiu.edu/~mirandas/bios1837.htm#Mai [accessed 31 May 2019]. Mai's initial claim to fame came with his discovery of the text of Cicero's *De republica* in a palimpsest under a later work of St Augustine in the Vatican Library. His most useful work was in MS elucidation rather than textual criticism.

[43] S.P. Tregelles, Florence, 13 April 1846, to B.W. Newton (consulted in 1962 in the Fry Collection, on the Isle of Wight, but recently acquired by Mr. Tom Chantry and accessible on line at http://www.brethrenarchive.org/manuscripts/letters-of-sp-tregelles/). The full text of the letter is included below in the Appendix of Unpublished Materials. In his published account (1851) of his Roman difficulties Tregelles made no complaint about Cardinal Mai, but as we noted earlier (see Footnote 29) reserved his criticism for the prefect Laureani. 'I obtained an interview with the late Pope ... and he, in word, graciously gave me permission; but he referred me to Mgr. Laureani, who was already my hindrance'. Tregelles, *Historic Evidence*, 84.

works which the Cardinal had edited and published'.[44] He also went out of his way publicly to declare, at a later date (1859), that although there were errors in Mai's published text of the Greek New Testament, they were editorial slips or printers' misprints, but *not* deliberate falsehoods. Almost certainly, however, Tregelles's experiences in the Vatican contributed to Mai's subsequent reputation in England for 'a want of liberality in permitting others to share his advantages'. Years later, in his *Recollections*, Cardinal Wiseman noted that it was commonly said, that Mai 'shut the Vatican to scholars, especially from foreign countries, who wished to collate manuscripts for some particular work'. Although Wiseman went on to testify that Mai's behaviour towards him [Wiseman] had been completely otherwise, he seems to have forgotten that he [Wiseman] was a Roman Catholic and that his own encounter had been much earlier and therefore with a younger man.[45]

Some fifteen years later, when Mai's edition was finally published, a lengthy anonymous assessment, which was, in fact, written by Tregelles, appeared in the *Edinburgh Review*,[46] In the opening sentence of what was his last magisterial word on the Cardinal's work, SPT quoted Professor De Wette of Basel[47] who had once walked with him 'through the gallery of the Vatican Library [and] designated it "as a magnificent mausoleum for dead books"'. It was a judgement that tallied with SPT's own frustrating experiences.

[44] Letter from S.P. Tregelles (2 February 1857) to O.T. Dobbin, on 'The Vatican Codex,' *JSL* 5 (April 1857): 162; cf. SPT's further letter (10 November 1858) when he affirmed that he possessed 'more than *forty large vols*' of Mai's publications in *JSL* 8 (January 1859): 461.

[45] 'If I have to speak from personal experience, I can only say that I never either felt or observed this failing. I ever found him, not merely obliging, but extremely kind, at all times; and was permitted to examine, to collate, and to copy or trace any manuscripts that I required, or wished to study. And I have generally seen the great reading-room of the library crowded with scholars busy upon codices. Mere idlers, or persons who came with no definite object, it is very probable that he would not encourage; but I should doubt if any great classical work has been published in our time, which is deprived of the advantages derivable from Roman manuscripts, in consequence of such a refusal to examine them, or if ever any scholar properly recommended, experienced a rebuff. Like most persons, who, working hard themselves, exact full labour from those subject to them, Mai had his murmurers in the library itself; but time has fully justified his exaction of vigilance and industry from them' (Wiseman, *Recollections*, 501–502). It is hard to imagine that the Cardinal felt that the critical edition of the Greek New Testament, in which SPT was engaged, did not qualify as a 'great classical work'.

[46] *Edinburgh Review* 112:227 (July 1860): 256

[47] For Wilhelm Martin Leberecht De Wette (1780–1849), see below Footnote 68.

6.1.4   Other Activities in Rome

We should not assume however that Prideaux Tregelles was inactive between these conversations and interviews in the Vatican.

For a start, it appears that he finalized the proof-reading of his English edition of Gesenius's *Hebrew and Chaldee Lexicon*, the preface of which is signed 'S.P.T., ROME, February 24th, 1846'.[48] There were other matters too, which occupied his attention. Bearing in mind his passionate interest in history, we would not expect him to have neglected the monuments of the city in which he was so frustratingly detained. One of his less predictable quests was when he visited the church of Sant'Onofrio, the official church of the Order of the Holy Sepulchre, where Torquato Tasso (1544–1595) spent the last years of his life before he was buried there. Tregelles tells us that it was to pay respect to the memory of the sixteenth-century poet that he went to see the church.[49]

Five years later in 1851, when Tregelles was lecturing on the early transmission of the New Testament and emphasizing how reliable were Eusebius's sources of information, he recalled another unusual visit that he had made to a Church in Rome:

> In the popedom of Sixtus V (1585-90), was born Giovanni-Battista Altieri. When very old he became Pope, in 1670, under the name of Clement X.: he died in 1676. Now, in March, 1846, I visited at Rome the convent of Santa Francesca Romana [the 'Monastero delle Oblate di Santa Francesca Romana' located in the Via del Teatro di Marcello, near the Piazza Venezia]; the abbess of this convent was a princess of the Altieri family, then aged almost 100. This abbess had known several in her own family, very aged of course when she was young, who had been acquainted with their kinsman, Pope Clement X. In conversing with the old abbess of these things, it seemed as if I was

---

[48] 'I finished the proof sheets, &c. of the Lexicon while in Italy'. S.P. Tregelles, 'Letter to Professor Samuel Lee,' *Churchman's Monthly Review* (April 1847): 315; Tregelles, *Gesenius's Lexicon*, vi. See above Chapter 4, Footnote 32 and below Chapter 9, Footnote 22–24.

[49] Sant'Onofrio is in the Trastevere district of Rome, and Tasso's wildly romantic epic about the First Crusade and the deliverance of Jerusalem in 1099 (*Gerusalemme Liberata*) gave him a natural connection with the Order of the Holy Sepulchre. For Tregelles's visit, see Waring, *Recollections of Iolo Morganwg*, 199.

transported back two centuries and more. Here were links of connection, which carried me back into the reign of Queen Elizabeth.[50]

What led Tregelles to this place is not clear. It may have been after his visit to Cardinal Mai's offices in the Altieri Palace (about half a mile away), but, whatever the circumstances, the irrepressible historian emerges once more, collecting oral tradition and putting it in a meaningful context.

His interest in some other sites is more easily explained. Most of the tourists visiting the monastery and church of Sta. Maria del Popolo were attracted by Raphael's Cappella Chigi with its sculpture of Jonah and the Whale by Lorenzetto, but Tregelles went there primarily to see the place where, as an Augustinian monk, Luther had lodgings when he went to Rome in 1510.[51] Similarly unsurprising was SPT's visit to The Holy Staircase [*La Scala Sancta*] opposite the Lateran Basilica, where he could observe pilgrims climbing on their knees and where, it was often claimed, Luther stopped his climb half way up on remembering that 'the just shall live by faith'.[52]

In contrast to the circle of like-minded, evangelical Christians, whose friendship Tregelles had enjoyed back in England, his social contacts in Rome were more circumscribed, and finding himself in what he considered to be the seat of papal idolatry[53] the scope for 'edifying Christian fellowship' was diminished. Although he claimed, when writing to Fardd in March

---

[50] S.P. Tregelles, *Historic Evidence*, 65. In this account, SPT's phenomenal memory appears momentarily to have let him down when he gave Pope Clement X [Emilio Bonaventura Altieri] the names of his brother Cardinal Archbishop Giovanni-Battista Altieri.

[51] S.P. Tregelles, 'Dr. Tregelles' Letters from the Continent,' *JSL* 12 (October 1850): 455. That SPT's interest was primarily in Luther's experience is apparent from his mistaken attribution of Lorenzetto's sculpture to Raphael.

[52] Ibid. In fact, Luther's visit to Rome in 1510 was some years before he gained the assurance of Romans i.17. The realization (of the just living by faith) that is supposed to have come to him halfway up the 'Holy Staircase' is almost certainly a legend invented by Luther's son Paul. It is clear from Luther's own account that the question that troubled him on reaching the top of the 'Holy Staircase', was whether perhaps the climb had been a complete waste of time; R.H. Bainton, *Here I Stand: A Life of Martin Luther* (Nashville: Abingdon, 1978 [1950]), 36. For an excellent discussion of Luther's early development, see Alister E. McGrath, *Luther's Theology of the Cross: Martin Luther's Theological Breakthrough* (Oxford: Blackwell, 1990).

[53] In his letter to Eben Fardd (vide supra n. 19), he writes: 'I had often heard of the idolatry of Rome, but before coming here and seeing for myself, I had not realized it existed to such an extent. There are in the city hundreds of churches and in every one carved figures and pictures of the saints (especially of the Virgin Mary) and even of the persons of the Trinity!'

1846 that 'a number of Englishmen were staying in Rome this winter, some pleasant friends, many of them in addition attractive Christians', this must be taken along with his observation to Lord Congleton in January that 'We have not found out many Christians here yet'.

Among the few whose acquaintance he did make was an Irish physician, whom SPT had consulted professionally, James Trayer,[54] 'a nice Christian person', who was lodging with a Church of Ireland minister, William Lawrenson,[55] and his wife, 'both Christians of a very nice spirit'. The clergyman 'has a scripture exposition at his house every Wednesday morning; I was there twice, and it was quite refreshing'. Usually, however, SPT was working in the library at the time but, as he explained to Lord Congleton, 'Mrs Tregelles generally goes'. They had also 'been introduced to a family named Gell, Christian friends of Mrs. Galton's, a father and son both evangelical clergymen[56] ... we have spent one evg with them very happily'.

From these few details, it is clear that Tregelles and his wife were glad to frequent the company of evangelical Christians, but in so doing they were far from abandoning their Brethren identity. In another part of his letter, SPT explains that they have especially appreciated the arrival of Mrs. Galton, who had brought them news from Lord Congleton and who appears to have been associated with the Brethren as, she 'and her maid break bread with us in our room in this pension where we are lodged, each Lord's day'.

Such times of evangelical fellowship were, however, only breaks from SPT's scholarly programme. More in accordance with the overall purpose

[54] Dr. James John Trayer [1815–1877] later Medical Officer of the Bagenalstown dispensary, County Carlow.

[55] Rev. William Robert Lawrenson [c.1802–1877, also sometimes spelt Laurenson], matriculated from Oriel College, 12 February 1819 aged 17; BA 1824 (*Al Oxon. 1715–1886*, iii. 825). He was Prebendary of Howth from 1852–1874.

[56] Rev. Philip Gell [1783–1870], Minister of St John's, Derby and his wife, Elizabeth. Their son Frederick (1820–1902), a Fellow of Christ's College, Cambridge, was later (1861–1898) Bishop of Madras and subscribed to receive two copies of SPT's Greek New Testament; see J.A. Peile [ed.], *Biographical Register of Christ's College, 1505–1905* ... 2 vols., Vol. 2 (Cambridge: University Press, 1913), 467–68. In a later amicable exchange on prophetic subjects, Philip Gell refers to SPT as 'my learned friend, Dr Tregelles' (*Christian Annotator* 2 [8 December 1855]: 376) and SPT addresses Gell as 'my valued Christian friend' (ibid., 3 [19 January 1856]: 32).

of his original project was his prolonged series of visits to the *Biblioteca Angelica*[57] where he spent some time

> collating an ancient MS[58] containing the Acts and the Epistles: access to this was refused me at first, but a letter from Cardinal Acton removed all difficulties; and from that time on each day when the library has been open I have been always there by 8 o'clock in the morning; there are often plenty of monks and priests there — a strange sort of sight to meet.[59]

At least in the face of enforced delays and times of waiting that were outside his control, SPT was able to redeem the time with some useful textual work. It was also the occasion of his making the acquaintance of the Abate Francesco Battelli with whom he developed an unusual friendship and a brief postal correspondence on his return to England.

A copy of a letter that he later addressed to Battelli was known to SPT's sister-in-law, when she wrote her account of his life and it affords us an interesting glimpse of Tregelles in an unusual context:

> I often remember the kindness I received from you when I was at Rome and the conversations which we then had together, especially the day when we were both glad to avoid the confusion of the Carnival and sought more quiet scenes and thus met near the Colosseum and how we walked together conversing on subjects of the deepest interest, afterwards returning to the city by the town and the Piazza dei Santi Apostoli. Ever since the conversation of that day, I have had my heart filled with earnest desires for your real and everlasting blessing …

Such were some of the endeavours of SPT to build a bridge across the theological gulf that separated him from a friendly scholar of the Roman Church.[60]

---

[57] Founded by Angelo Rocca in the seventeenth century, this was now the public library of the Augustinians.

[58] This was a ninth-century MS known in Tregelles's day as the 'Codex Passionei' but now usually referred to as the 'Codex Angelica'.

[59] SPT to Lord Congleton 18 January 1846 (see above Footnote 18).

[60] Cambridge, MA/AHTL, Prideaux, MS Life [p. 12]. The Abate Francesco Battelli with his brother Dominico was later one of the editors of the Vatican tri-weekly newspaper *L'Osservatore Romano* (1849–1852); see Giulio Battelli, '*L'Osservatore Romano* degli anni 1849–1852,' in *Strenna dei Romanisti: Natale di Roma* (Rome: Editrice Roma, 2002), 17–30. For further details of the exchange between SPT and Battelli, see below Chapter 8, Footnote 59.

6.2   OTHER EUROPEAN LIBRARIES

6.2.1   The Journey Home: Florence to Basel

After these frustrating months in Rome, Tregelles spent several further weeks collating MSS in other continental libraries, and it would be a mistake to assume that the impediments that he encountered in the Vatican Library were typical. When he arrived in Florence in April 1846, he immediately went to the Laurentian (or 'Medicean') Library[61] where the eighth-century Codex Amiatinus of the Latin Vulgate is preserved.

> After my annoyances at Rome I feared delays here; but on the contrary as soon as I had told my errand every facility was afforded me for doing all I want; the monstrous MS (so heavy that it takes two men to lift it) was brought to me, and my convenience about light, desk, &c consulted in a way that I never knew the like in any library in England.[62]

Similarly co-operative were the services of Count Giovanni Galvani,[63] the librarian of the ducal palace in Modena, who arranged for Tregelles to collate the Codex Mutinensis. Equally helpful were the Venetian librarians in the Biblioteca San Marco, Dr. Giuseppe Valentinelli and Signor Andrea Baretta 'who kindly afforded the fullest access to all that I wanted … [and] gladly I acknowledge this courtesy'.[64]

---

[61] Curiously Tregelles gave a Welsh address when he signed the library's Visitors' book as 'Saml Prideaux Tregelles, Neath Abbey, Glamorgan, Pays de Galles, 6e Avril 1846'; (Florence/BML, *Album dei visitatori della Biblioteca Laurenziana*, Vol. 2). The entry in the library's *Registro dei studiosi 1826–1863* indicates that he worked on the Codex Amiatinus for over a month, after which, on May 15, he consulted the 'Codex Siriaco' (the Rabbula Syriac Gospels).

[62] S.P. Tregelles (Florence) to B.W. Newton (Plymouth) 13 April 1846 (see above Footnote 43). SPT may perhaps have appreciated the irony of his receiving superior treatment in an Italian Library when he was reading a MS written about a thousand years earlier in Anglo-Saxon Northumbria.

[63] For Count Giovanni Galvani (1806–1873), linguist and philologist, see Antonio Masinelli, *Notizie intorno alla vita ed alle opere del conte commendatore Giovanni Galvani di Modena* (Modena: Tipografia pontificia ed arcivescovile, 1874). He does not appear to have been directly related to Luigi Galvani of Bologna, the pioneer of bioelectromagnetics.

[64] Tregelles, *Account*, 158. He contrasted his Venetian experience with the unfriendly reception given by the Benedictine monks of San Marco to the French scholar, Bernard de Montfaucon.

It had been just before Tregelles left England in autumn of the previous year that the Roman Catholic Professor Johann Augustin Scholz[65] had informed him of a previously unknown uncial MS of the Gospels, which had recently found its way to Munich. In June therefore, this was the next stop on SPT's itinerary, and again he found what a sorry exception the intransigence of the Vatican had been in the world of scholarship. Dr. Maurus Harter,[66] a Benedictine monk, was the under-librarian of the University Library, which had recently been relocated to Munich by King Ludwig I of Bavaria. Tregelles found Harter very obliging in the arrangements he made for his English visitor to consult the rather mutilated Codex Monacensis of which 'some of the leaves have become brown, while the ink has faded to a sort of yellow'. SPT particularly appreciated Harter's readiness to let him use the MS outside the library and evidently reckoned that this was a collation that should be recorded for posterity as he noted in red ink on a paper fly-leaf of the MS: 'Textum Evangeliorum hujus Codicis contulit Samuel Prideaux Tregelles mensibus Jun. et Jul. MDCCCXLVI'. He was touched too by Harter's concern at seeing Tregelles (whose eyesight in any case was not the best) struggling to read one of the almost obliterated pages, and by Harter's sympathetic advice: '*Parce oculis tuis*'.[67]

The final port of call before Tregelles could return home was the city of Basel (with its eighth-century Codex Basiliensis), and here he seems to

---

[65] The Roman Catholic oriental scholar, Johann Martin Augustus Scholz (1794–1852) was Professor of exegesis at the University of Bonn (for his earlier travels, see below Chapter 10, Footnote 5). SPT readily acknowledged the help he had received from Scholz before leaving for Rome (Tregelles, *Account*, 159) but in 1848 he confided to Christopher Wordsworth that Scholz 'does not appear to me to possess a high degree of critical acumen'; SPT, Plymouth, 29 December 1848, to C. Wordsworth (London/LPA, MS 2143 f.372).

[66] For Maurus Aloysius Harter (1777–1852), see s.n. art. by P.A. Lindner in *Allgemeine Deutsche Biographie*.

[67] 'Spare your eyesight'; Tregelles, *Account*, 158. The tenth-century Codex Monacensis may have been damaged in its removal from the ancient university at Ingolstadt to Landshut in 1800, from where in 1827 it was transferred to Munich. SPT's note in red ink can be seen at https://commons.wikimedia.org/wiki/File:Cod._Monacensis,_two_notes_on_paper_flyleaf_-_Tregelles_and_Bruder.jpg [accessed 18 June 2019].

have developed a mutually appreciative friendship with Wilhelm de Wette[68] who had, for more than twenty years been Professor of Ethics and Theology at the University and whom SPT had met in Rome a few months earlier. The profundity of de Wette's biblical learning combined with his very urbane manners seems to have made a great impression on SPT who again appreciated being allowed to consult the Basle Codex outside the University Library—a convenience for which de Wette made the necessary arrangements, albeit with 'the collator and the MS ... alike secured by lock and key'.[69] Although Tregelles took a very different line from the Professor when it came to the reliability of scripture, he was evidently charmed by de Wette, whose dismissive verdict on the Vatican Library (as we noted earlier) coincided with his own sufficiently for him to quote it in the *Edinburgh Review* more than ten years later.[70]

By the time Tregelles was back in England, his overall objective of establishing the Greek Text of the New Testament, according to the most ancient MSS, had come very much more clearly into focus, though it would inevitably involve further travel abroad for the collation of numerous other MSS. Distracted, as he undoubtedly was, by ecclesiastical developments among the Brethren at Plymouth, his textual labours had now clearly become his prime concern, and establishing the text of the Codex Vaticanus was still at the top of the list of his priorities. Accepting that he had been thwarted in his desire to collate the MS, he nevertheless had the satisfaction that he had been able to make a mental note of certain readings, and he now had a context into which he could place the records of others who had studied and made a record of their observations.

---

[68] For Wilhelm Martin Leberecht De Wette (1780–1849), see J.W. Rogerson, *W.M.L de Wette, Founder of Modern Biblical Criticism: An Intellectual Biography* (Sheffield: JSOT, 1992). Although evangelicals like Christian Friedrich Spittler (and Tregelles) were critical of his rationalism, de Wette's charm and earnest piety often won them over (Rogerson, op. cit., 214). The Professor was, in SPT's words 'one whose name the writer of this review cannot mention without expressing the deep sorrow, which his death has occasioned him. Dr. De Wette was one whose personal kindness and urbanity were as remarkable as his extensive learning: — it is indeed *deeply* to be lamented that his learning and abilities were so applied. It may be questioned how far the greater divergences of others (e.g. the Tubingen school) may not have caused a reaction in Dr. De Wette's mind towards sounder apprehensions of Scripture' [S.P. Tregelles], 'Davidson's Introduction to the New Testament,' *JSL* 4 (October 1849): 354n; but see below Chapter 9, Footnote 54–57.

[69] As cheerfully described in SPT's anonymous account in the *Edinburgh Review* 112:227 (July 1860): 257.

[70] See above Footnote 46 and below Chapter 9, Footnote 58.

6.2.2   Paris, Cholera and a German Itinerary

The subsequent efforts of Tregelles were unremitting. Following his return, having worked, in 1847 on the Codex Harleianus and the Curetonian Syriac Gospels in the British Museum, he still had hopes of collating the Vatican Codex. In January and February 1849, apparently undeterred by the Republican revolution of Mazzini and Garibaldi in Rome, he was corresponding with Dr. Christopher Wordsworth[71] about his 'Roman project' stressing that 'if I were to go now [February] I should I think, go alone, for my wife could not bear an expeditious journey nor yet the coming on of warm weather in Italy',[72] In the end, it seems that he decided that a second attempt would be fruitless.

In fact, it was to Paris that he travelled in 1849 to work in the Royal Library (now the *Bibliothèque Nationale*) where he collated the Codex Claromontanus and transcribed Bartolocci's collation of the Codex Vaticanus which Scholz had discovered thirty years previously, but SPT's further intention of collating the ninth-century Codex Cyprius was thwarted by his falling victim to the outbreak of cholera which necessitated his wife travelling to Paris to bring him home in July for convalescence. In a letter to Newton, he vividly described the effects of the disease:

> I am still very feeble in body and mind and my limbs and body still feel the effects of the spasms and cramps: but I am not as weak as when I wrote you last; that was only the second time that I had taken a pen in my hand: once before I wrote a few lines to my dear Mother ... the condition of many of the poorer convalescents is very sad: they are discharged from the hospitals where they have been *well* cared for, and they have no means of procuring the great quantity of nourishment which they need to recruit their debilitated frames ... the general destitution, however, of the poor of Paris is grievous.[73]

---

[71] Christopher Wordsworth (1807–1885) nephew of William, the poet, had been the Headmaster of Harrow (1836–1844) and was now a Canon of Westminster (1844–1869). He would later be the Bishop of Lincoln (1869).

[72] S.P. Tregelles, Plymouth, 12 January, and Kingsbridge, 21 February 1849 to C. Wordsworth (London/LPL MS 2144 f.14, 29). As late as January 1850, he still envisaged the possibility: 'Mgr Laureani, the Primo Custode of the Vatican is dead, perhaps Signor Molto the Secondo Custode may be a more practicable person' (LPL MS 2144 f.98).

[73] S.P. Tregelles (Paris) to B.W. Newton (Bayswater, London), July 1, 1849; formerly in the Fry Collection but recently acquired by Mr. Tom Chantry and accessible

Shortly before his return to England, in spite of physical weakness, Tregelles was focused as ever on his textual work and visited the celebrated bookshop of the Frères Firmin-Didot to purchase copies of the latest two editions of Tischendorf's Greek New Testament. As he was crossing the Île de la Cité on his way to the shop on the left bank[74] of the Seine, the convalescent SPT may have wanted to sit down for a few moments or he may have been acting on one of those impulses that are liable to beset the historically minded traveller. No matter the motive—he seized the opportunity to visit (probably, not for the first time) the cathedral of Notre Dame. To his surprise, he found himself in the middle of a commemorative service for the soul of the late Archbishop Affre—an occasion that profoundly impressed him, in spite of what he considered to be its superstitious character. Just a year earlier during the revolution of 1848, the prelate had tried to intervene to stop the bloodshed of the revolutionary June days in Paris, but had been shot by the insurgents. SPT had little time for the ceremony itself but, as a man who had recently faced the prospect of death at the hand of the cholera, he was nonetheless deeply moved. 'The whole scene and the occasion, and the deep sorrow of the kneeling multitude, and the chanted dirge, were intensely striking and solemn'.[75]

Undeterred, in the following year, Tregelles returned to Paris to complete his work and from there, accompanied by his wife, he travelled to Hamburg and other German cities. Calling on Karl Lachmann in Berlin and Constantin Tischendorf in Leipzig, he was able to discuss with them specific details of textual criticism and compare notes on variant textual readings.[76] From there he returned to England by way of Dresden, Wolfenbüttel and Utrecht, in the last of which cities the inquisitive historian once

on line at http://www.brethrenarchive.org/manuscripts/letters-of-sp-tregelles/three-page-letter-to-bwn-dated-1st-july-1849/. My annotated copy of the text is included below in the Appendix of Unpublished Materials.

[74] For many years, the Imprimerie-Librairie Firmin-Didot was located on the Quai des Augustins, but in the early nineteenth century had moved a few blocks away to the Rue Jacob.

[75] Samuel Prideaux Tregelles, 'Tischendorf's Greek Testament,' *JLS* 4 (October 1849): 211n.

[76] For his time with Lachmann, see above Chapter 5, Footnote 15–16; for his visit to Tischendorf in Leipzig, see below Chapter 10.

again got the better of SPT, when he took time to converse at length with the Jansenist Archbishop van Santen of Utrecht.[77]

Collating MSS in each of the cities he visited, Tregelles was now well on the way to acquiring the materials for his *magnum opus*, a prospectus of which he had issued in 1848. Regretfully he had to recognize that a detailed reading of the Vatican Codex had eluded him and he could not know that in a few years time his task would be further complicated by Tischendorf's sensational discovery of the Codex Sinaiticus. Nevertheless, he had laid some solid groundwork providing a position from which he could pursue his ultimate object.

---

[77] His account of the interview appeared as 'The Jansenists and Their Remnant in Holland, a Chapter in Church History,' *JLS* 7 (January 1851): 34–82. It was later in the year published in book form by Bagster in London; cf. *infra* Chapter 7, Footnote 7.

An Embarrassed Advocate of Brethren in Italy

7.1   Tuscan Protestants and Plymouth Brethren

Although Tregelles was in Rome and Northern Italy for several months of
1845 and 1846, he was probably unaware that in the late 1840s, a number of spiritually dissatisfied Italians in Tuscany were beginning to show
an interest in Protestantism.[1] We shall consider these developments more
closely in the next chapter, but at this point, we shall confine our attention
to some of these Tuscan Italians who in due course came to be regarded as
part of the Brethren movement. Some of these folk had previously worked
abroad for a while. Encouraged by Swiss and British visitors,[2] they soon

---

[1] The starting point for any consideration of nineteenth-century Italian Protestantism is
Giorgio Spini's pioneer work *Risorgimento e Protestanti* (Naples: Edizioni scientifiche Italiane,
1956), the theme of which has recently been revisited in an essay with the same title by
Eugenio F. Biagini, in S. Maghenzani, G. Platone [eds.], *, Riforma, Risorgimento e Risveglio:
Il Protestantesimo italiano tra radici storiche e questioni contemporanee* (Turin: Claudiana,
2011), 77–96. For the part played in Italian Protestantism by the Brethren (or *Fratelli*),
Spini's account must be supplemented with Domenico Maselli's *Tra Risveglio e Millennio:
Storia delle Chiese Cristiane dei Fratelli, 1836–1886* (Turin: Claudiana, 1974). The linguistic
insularity of the British and their ignorance of this subject are well demonstrated by the fact
that in English, we are effectively confined to a single, slender and verging on the simplistic
volume by Daisy D. Ronco, *Risorgimento and the Free Italian Churches, Now Churches of the
Brethren* (Bangor: University of Wales, 1996).

[2] For the part played in this movement by Swiss visitors, see my 'L'influenza del *réveil*
svizzero prima dell'Unita d'Italia,' in Maghenzani, *Riforma*, 105–13.

© The Author(s) 2020
T. C. F. Stunt, *The Life and Times of Samuel Prideaux Tregelles*,
Christianities in the Trans-Atlantic World,
https://doi.org/10.1007/978-3-030-32266-3_7

began to meet in private houses to read the scriptures together. From time to time, several of them, including Count Piero Guicciardini,[3] an aristocratic descendant of the Renaissance historian of that name, attended the Swiss Church in Florence where some services were held in Italian—ostensibly for Swiss immigrants from the south-eastern cantons of Switzerland where Italian was widely spoken. As an aristocrat, Guicciardini was something of a social exception, but some of these crypto-Protestants were professionals and well-educated, while others were more often artisans and domestic servants of humbler social status.

Among the foreign visitors who gave encouragement to these Tuscan groups were some Christians who were connected with the Brethren in England. One of the earliest Brethren had been Anthony Norris Groves of Exeter whose ideas, as a freelance missionary in India, were an important influence on the thinking of two military officers, George and Arthur Walker whose parents lived for some years in Florence. These members of the Walker family took a friendly and supportive interest in the Tuscans meeting for Bible study and were closely associated with Count Guicciardini.[4]

Another link with the Brethren was established by a member of the assembly in Plymouth, Miss Eliza Browne who, for reasons of health, had travelled to Madeira and then, in 1850, settled in Florence, where she immediately took an interest in the little gatherings of Italian Protestants who very soon had to meet in secret.[5] She may have been a stepdaughter of B.W. Newton's fellow elder in the Plymouth assembly, James Lampen

[3] For Guicciardini's unusual Christian pilgrimage, the best account is still Stefano Jacini, *Un Riformatore Toscano dell'Epoca del Risorgimento: Il Conte Piero Guicciardini (1808–1886)* (Florence: Sansoni, 1940), but reference should also be made to D.D. Ronco, *"Per me, vivere e Cristo": La vita e l'opera del Conte Piero Guicciardini nel centenario della sua morte 1808–1886* (Fondi, Italy: Unione Cristiana Edizioni Bibliche, 1986) and to Lorenza Giorgi, Massimo Rubboli [eds.], *Piero Guicciardini, 1808–86: Un Riformatore religioso nell'Europa dell'Ottocento* (Florence: Olschki, 1988), in which several of the essays are in English.

[4] For the Walker family in Florence, see Alessandra Pecchioli, 'Giulia Baldelli: Una prima breve panoramica delle famiglie Walker, Baldelli e Tommasi,' in A. Pecchioli [ed.], *La Chiesa 'degli italiani': All'origine del Evangelismo risvegliato in Italia* (Rome: GBU, 2010), 207–22. For George Walker, see also Stunt, *Elusive Quest*, 226–28.

[5] Anna Shipton, *The Upper Springs and the Nether Springs; or, Life Hid with Christ in God* (London: James Nisbet, 1882), 165–66. Cf. M. Newlin, *Memoir of Mary Anne Longstreth by an Old Pupil* (Philadelphia: J.P. Lippincott, 1886), 108.

Harris, being probably a daughter of his wife by her previous marriage.[6] Eliza Browne was definitely acquainted with Prideaux Tregelles, who presented her with a copy of his little book on the history of the Jansenists, endorsed with the inscription: 'Eliza Browne with the author's Christian regards, Plymouth May 17. 1852'.[7] Indeed, it is highly likely that it was through his contacts with her, that Tregelles began to take an interest in the Tuscan movement of which, he had probably been ignorant when working on the Codex Amiatinus in Florence in 1846. That Eliza Browne remained in close touch with her Plymouth friends is apparent from the letters that she wrote from Florence to Henry Soltau and his wife, who in the 1840s had also been members of the Plymouth assembly. Many years later, their son, William Soltau, published a selection of her letters and they provide a valuable contemporary account of the difficulties faced by the nascent Tuscan Protestant movement.[8]

7.2   PERSECUTION AND ITS CONSEQUENCES

In a subsequent letter to the Bible Society, Tregelles observed that

> at Florence Bibles were sold when I was there [in 1846]; it was however generally done *quietly*, so as not to disturb the peace and if a person asked for a Bible he was generally told to come *after 8 in the evg*. At Florence I met with *no* hindrance in the distribution of Tracts, and deeply did this cause me to regret that I then had no portions of the word of God to put into the people's hands.[9]

[6] In 1814, Sophia Elizabeth Robertson of Plymstock married Captain Henry Reddish Browne who died in Calcutta (June 1825). In 1829, she married James L. Harris, who was, for some years, the editor of the *Brethren magazine* the *Christian Witness*. This explains Eliza Browne's ability to identify the names of the anonymous authors in her copies of their works, which are preserved in the Biblioteca Nazionale in Florence and in the library of the Brethren assembly of Via Vigna Vecchia, also in Florence; see Timothy Stunt, 'Understanding the Past in the City of Florence,' *Harvester* (September 1983): 70.

[7] S.P. Tregelles, *The Jansenists: Their Rise, Persecutions by the Jesuits and Existing Remnant— A Chapter in Church History* (London: Bagster, 1851). Copy in the writer's possession.

[8] W. Soltau, 'The Story of the Madiai,' *Sunday at Home* (1904): 446–53. This source appears to be unknown to any of the authors who have discussed the origins of the Italian *fratelli evangelici*. For Henry Soltau's involvement with the Brethren in Plymouth, see Stunt, *Elusive Quest*, 170–73.

[9] S.P. Tregelles (Plymouth, 29 November 1848) to the BFBS (Cambridge/CUL BSA/D1/2 Tregelles 29/11/1848).

That however had been in 1846 when the Tuscan authorities had turned a blind eye to these crypto-Protestants who were questioning Roman Catholic dogma during what might be called 'the lull before the storm'. There were high hopes and expectations of the revolution in 1848, but these were dashed in the summer of 1849 when the Grand Duke of Tuscany, supported by Austrian troops, regained control and very soon, more repressive measures came into force. Italians in Florence were now forbidden to attend the Swiss Church, and people who were found reading the Bible with friends in their homes were arrested and either sent into exile or condemned to imprisonment and hard labour. The link with Plymouth is again apparent in the fact that when Count Guicciardini was forced to go into exile, he went to England where he spent much of the winter of 1851 working on an edition of the Diodati Italian translation of the Bible, together with George Walker, the former military officer whose family lived in Florence and who was now a leader in the Brethren assembly in Teignmouth not far from Plymouth.[10]

An English translation of the account of Guicciardini's arrest, imprisonment and exile was published in 1852 and included the text of his statement of faith, which, at the time of his departure for exile in England, he addressed to the Tuscan Christians with whom he had been associated. This included the following counsel:

> I believe that true Christians ought to break bread and drink wine together, in remembrance of the death of the Lord Jesus, until he come again, and as a testimony of their common faith in the expiatory sacrifice accomplished by him. (1 Cor. xi. 23–26; Acts xi. 42–46; xx. 7)

> … Go from house to house breaking bread. So did all the disciples and the faithful in apostolic times. In order to do this there is no need of furniture, forms, or special persons. It is well to know this in seasons of difficulty and persecution, like the present, in which the true Church is not permitted to have an external organization.[11]

---

[10] Stunt, *Elusive Quest*, 228.

[11] *Religious Liberty in Tuscany in 1851: or Documents relative to the Trial and Incarceration of Count Pietro Guicciardini and others, exiled from Tuscany by decree of 17 May 1851*. Tr. from the Italian (London: Nisbet [1851]), 17, 18. This early persecution suffered by Guicciardini and his companions is given a fuller context in Maselli, *Tra Risveglio*, 52–68.

There were some decidedly anticlerical overtones in this advice, to which the translator of the English edition took exception, and in the preface, he bluntly stated that 'Count Guicciardini is understood to incline towards the views of the Plymouth Brethren; indeed, the latter clauses of his confession leave no doubt upon the subject', at which point the editor went on to criticize the Count for his 'unscriptural and absurd' tenets. Such indeed was the editor's indignation that he went out of his way to complain that 'the spiritual socialism of the Plymouthian system' coincided 'with the strong republican character and tendencies of the large masses of the Italian people, and with the ancient Ghibelline spirit of the Florentines in particular' which, he claimed, was calculated to do much mischief.[12]

7.3   TREGELLES TAKES UP THE DEFENCE

The accusation that Guicciardini was a Plymouth Brother would often be made (and as often be denied by his followers) but this is perhaps its earliest appearance in print, and it is of particular interest for our purposes, as the booklet in which it appeared was reviewed in the *Journal of Sacred Literature* by one of the Journal's regular contributors on biblical and textual subjects—none other than Prideaux Tregelles, though the review appeared anonymously over the initials L.M.[13] It was a review that Tregelles probably found difficult to write, and this may explain its anonymity. His consistent support of B.W. Newton in the Plymouth controversies had made many of the Brethren suspicious of him with the result that by 1851–1852, as we noted earlier, the distrust had become mutual and he was beginning to dissociate himself from the Plymouth Brethren as such, and the congregation in Compton Street of which he was a member was on the point of re-inventing itself as a 'Free Evangelical Church'.

Nevertheless in his review, Tregelles insisted that in a time of persecution (comparable to the situation of the church in the first century), it was perfectly reasonable for Guicciardini to advocate 'going from house to

---

[12] *Religious Liberty*, 4.

[13] [S.P.T.] L.M., 'Review of Books: *Religious Liberty in Tuscany in 1851*,' *JSL* NS 1 (January 1852), 464–68. That it was written by Tregelles is apparent from the occurrence of several sentences concerning Florence and Savonarola (464, 468) which he later used in his introduction to S.P. Tregelles [ed.], *Prisoners of Hope: Being Letters from Florence Relative to the Persecution of Francesco and Rosa Madiai...* 2nd ed. (London: Partridge and Oakey, 1852), 1–2, 16–17; vide infra Chapter 8, p. 106, Footnote 28.

house to break bread' with no need for 'apparatus, forms or special persons', which Tregelles identified as 'the very things on which the Romanist relies, as rendering the mass valid'.[14] In his review, Tregelles claimed that the translator of the Italian pamphlet, who was so critical of Guicciardini, 'appears to be a Scotch minister (now we believe in Turin)', but even if he (Tregelles) had serious reservations about the Brethren in Plymouth, his attitude to ecclesiastical order was still sufficiently anticlerical for him to dismiss the Scots minister's criticisms of Guicciardini which, he felt, were latently favouring the Roman Catholic church and therefore betraying the simple faith of the Tuscan believers.

SPT's concern for historical accuracy emerges very clearly when he chides Guicciardini's critic for confusing the Ghibelline [Imperial] and the Guelf [Papal] parties of fifteenth-century Italy, as in fact Florence had been a Guelfish city. SPT then went on to suggest that instead of denigrating 'the spiritual socialism of the Plymouthian system' as the heir of 'the ancient Ghibelline spirit of the Florentines', the writer would have done better to draw a parallel between the pro-papal Guelfs and the zeal of the persecuting authorities in the nineteenth century. As a historian, he similarly may have enjoyed reminding the clerically inclined 'Scotch minister' that in the early days of the Reformation, the Christians in Geneva 'met in a garden [where] … a simple carpenter handed the bread and wine round to his brethren'.[15]

---

[14] [S.P.T.], 'Review of *Religious Liberty*,' 466. In a footnote, Tregelles explained that he was using 'a MS translation previously in circulation' where instead of the word *furniture* the translator used *apparatus*. Tregelles evidently preferred this as it was a literal translation of the Italian word *apparato* in Guicciardini's original letter, the text of which can be found in full in Jacini, *Riformatore*, 301–308; for *apparato*, see p. 307.

[15] [S.P.T.], 'Review of *Religious Liberty*,' 467. Tregelles is referring here to the occasion in April 1533 when the followers of Guillaume Farel first celebrated the Lord's Supper in the garden of Étienne Dada, just outside Geneva. Guérin Muète, who distributed the bread and wine, is variously described as *un bonnetier*, a hat-maker, a hosier, a stocking weaver or a 'dealer of knitwear'. Tregelles's reference to him as a carpenter is strange. He could not have consulted the contemporary account by François Bonivard and Anthoine Froment in *Les Actes et gestes de Genève* which was not published until 1854. It is possible that he had access to the second volume of Merle d'Aubigné's *Histoire de la Réformation* published in the 1840s, but more probably, he used the English translation of Jacob Spon's *Histoire de … Genève* where Guérin Muète is referred to as a 'capmaker' (Isaac [sc. Jacob] Spon, *History of the City and State of Geneva, from Its First Foundation to This Present Time* [London: White, 1687], 96). SPT's handwriting was often appalling, and it is possible that the Editor misread 'capmaker' in the contributor's MS as 'carpenter'. For a recent discussion of the episode in 1533, see Christian Grosse, *Les rituels de la cène: le culte eucharistique réformé à Genève* (Geneva: Droz, 2008), 106–108.

It is evident therefore that whatever second thoughts Tregelles may have been having about the ways of the Brethren at Plymouth, his original attraction to their non-clerical simplicity remained unchanged in the early 1850s.

These years, in Italy, were critical ones in the development of a radical Protestant movement many of whose natural leaders, albeit of a humbler social status than Guicciardini, were obliged, like the Count, to go into exile.[16] Deprived of such devoted and single-minded men, the leadership of the movement was increasingly precarious in those years. At times, they were helped and encouraged by the few Waldensians, who were still in the region after the banishment of their pastors Malan and Geymonat in March 1851, and they were also given discrete assistance by Maxwell Hanna and Robert Stewart, the ministers of the Free Scots Churches in Florence and Leghorn.[17]

Tregelles was well aware of the difficulties with which these crypto-Protestants had to cope, and his book, *Prisoners of Hope*, gave to the English public one of the earliest accounts of the sufferings of Francesco and Rosa Madiai, a humble Tuscan couple condemned to imprisonment and hard labour for privately reading the scriptures with Arthur Walker, the friend of Count Guicciardini.[18] We shall look more closely at this work of Tregelles in the next chapter,[19] but, as suggested earlier, one of SPT's main sources of information for his book was his old Plymouth friend Eliza Browne. She had taken a close interest in the Madiai couple and their tribulations, but she was not alone in giving assistance to the clandestine Tuscan Protestants, because late in the summer of 1851 she was joined by two other Englishwomen, Miss Emily Weston and Miss Charlotte Johnson.

---

[16] The list of exiles who settled for the next few years in Piedmont or Malta included the following future leadersof the *Fratelli* (Brethren): Angiolo Guarducci, a banking accountant, Cesare Magrini, a calligrapher, Carlo Solaini and Sebastiano Borsieri, cigar makers and Fedele Betti, a waiter; see [Jean-Pierre] Meille, 'Prospects of the Gospel in Italy,' in E. Steane [ed.], *The Religious Condition of Christendom ...* read at the Conference held in Paris, 1855 (London: Ev. Alliance, 1857), 2: 369; cf. *Evangelical Christendom: Its State and Prospects* 9 (1 September 1856): 296–98.

[17] J. Wood Brown, *An Italian Campaign; or the Evangelical Movement in Italy 1845–1887. From the Letters of the Late R.W. Stewart, D.D., of Leghorn* (London: Hodder and Stoughton, 1890), 68–78. Cf. Norman L. Walker, *Chapters from the History of the Free Church of Scotland* (Edinburgh: Oliphant, Anderson & Ferrier, [1895]), 191.

[18] Tregelles, *Prisoners*. For Arthur Walker, vide supra Footnotes 4, 10.

[19] For further discussion of the Madiai case, vide infra Chapter 8, Footnotes 24–27.

7.4   PLYMOUTH SISTERS TAKE THE LEAD

Although an American writer a few years later could claim, somewhat romantically, that the Tuscan 'band of the faithful ... were secretly nourished ... after the banishment of their former guides by ... earnest maiden ladies of the English sect of Plymouth Brethren',[20] the judgement of Dr. Robert Stewart, the Scots minister in Leghorn was rather different. He regarded all three of these women with considerable suspicion, and his biographer echoed his hostile complaint when he said that 'they held more or less strongly these peculiar opinions' which he designated 'a plague of Plymouthism'.[21] The opinion of Maxwell Hanna, the Scots minister in Florence, was similarly severe when he referred, in April 1852, to the women's beliefs as 'that sort of spiritual Radicalism called Plymouthism, or whatever the name of that levelling system may be'.[22] In condemning them so decidedly, the ministers were assuming that the ladies' attachment to the Brethren meant that they had no time for orderly church government and that they were therefore encouraging ecclesiastical disorder among their Tuscan *protégés*.

There was, perhaps, a certain degree of irony that, at this stage, the fairer sex was able to play such an important part in the early Italian development of a movement, which would soon become almost a byword for ecclesiastical male chauvinism, but in fact, the situation was a little less straightforward. As we noted earlier, Eliza Browne was on good terms with Tregelles, and similarly, Emily Weston is mentioned as a respected friend in Tregelles's correspondence with Benjamin Newton. The original conflict at Plymouth between Newton and Darby, as we noted earlier, had been concerned with precisely the question of order and discipline in the assembly—the very issue that alarmed the two Scots ministers. Both Newton and Tregelles were most emphatically of the opinion that teachers and elders in the assembly should be recognized and have the authority to intervene in moments of disorder or, taking a position which might be

[20] Anonymous, 'The Italian Reform Movement,' in *The American Quarterly Church Review and Ecclesiastical Register* 15 (July 1863): 240.

[21] Brown, *Letters of Stewart*, 81.

[22] F.J. P[akenham], *Life Lines; or God's Work in a Human Being* (London: Wertheim, Macintosh, and Hunt, 1862), 145.

described, in Tregelles's phrase, as a 'modified Presbyterianism'.[23] Eliza Browne's approach appears to have been in line with their thinking, as indeed Maxwell Hanna seems to have recognized, when he reconsidered his earlier generalization and wrote in December 1852:

> I do not think [Eliza] B[rowne] is infected with Plymouth ideas, beyond what is safely tolerable; and indeed I have not much fear of that system, if people are really seeking to know the "mind of the Spirit".[24]

In fact, it was Miss Charlotte Courtenay Johnson (1799–1869) or, as she was known to the Italians, Signorina Carlotta, who was the real focus of his disapproval. She was older than the other two ladies and had probably sided with Darby in the late 1840s.[25] In contrast to Hanna's mild opinion of Miss Browne, his criticism of Miss Johnson, a few months later, was more severe, reckoning that it was scandalous that she 'held a meeting, at which she presided, expounded, and did all but break the bread' and he went on, 'these Plymouth ladies would try the patience of a Saint sometimes!'[26]

Actually, it was to Hanna that the anonymous verdict in the *North British Review* was attributed:

> In Florence, even women have presided in meetings and dispensed the Lord's Supper, taking all the duty except the simple breaking of the bread ... It is impossible to engraft a spiritual Bloomerism on the Church of Apostles and Prophets.[27]

---

[23] Tregelles later gave a full presentation of his position on such issues in his *Pastoral relations*, Part iii. 'Original Establishment' (Plymouth, December 1862) and Part iv. 'The Present Formation' (North Malvern, August 1863) (London, 1862–1863). For 'modified Presbyterianism', vide supra Chapter 4, Footnote 17.

[24] Pakenham, *Life Lines*, 147.

[25] See G. Spini, 'Nuovi documenti sugli Evangelici toscani del Risorgimento,' *Bolletino della Società di Studi* Valdesi 78 (December 1960), 89–90. Her full name and age are given on her gravestone in the Protestant cemetery of Florence. Wood Brown gives her name as *Johnstone*, and this led to Dr. Luigi Santini confusing her with Maria Johnstone (1770–1857) who is also buried in the same cemetery. L. Santini, *The Protestant Cemetery of Florence called 'The English Cemetery*,' (Florence: K.S. Printing House, 1961) 11, 22.

[26] Pakenham, *Life Lines*, 148. According to Stewart's biographer, on one occasion Johnson 'assembled some of the converts at her villa and actually dispensed the bread and wine of Communion to them with her own hands'. Brown, *Letters of Stewart*, 82.

[27] [R.M. Hanna], 'Protestantism in Italy,' *The North British Review* 20 (November 1853): 79. Bloomers were the newly fashionable (1851) female clothing of supposedly 'emancipated' women.

It was certainly an anomalous situation, which later gave rise to recrimination. In April 1861, a letter from Prideaux Tregelles appeared in the *News of the Churches* with the text of a letter he had received from Cesare Magrini, one of the Brethren leaders, categorically stating that in their meetings ladies had never been allowed to dispense the Lord's Supper.[28] In the next issue, the magazine's correspondent disputed the claim, saying that it *had* happened, even if it was no longer the Brethren's practice, to which (albeit with some embarrassment) Tregelles replied, again repeating Magrini's claim that the Tuscan brethren did not sanction the practice.[29] In a further rejoinder, the correspondent claimed to 'know positively that Miss J[ohnson] did dispense the sacrament in 1853' when Magrini had been in exile in Genoa and therefore would not have been present. He also observed that Miss Browne had not sanctioned what was done and, he added, 'to her credit' she 'rose and left the room'.[30]

7.5   TUSCAN DIVISIONS AND SPT's WITHDRAWAL

So, not by choice but out of loyalty to his earlier ecclesiastical principles, Tregelles had now found himself reluctantly involved in yet another 'Brethren' dispute—but this time in Italy. In the later 1850s, there was developing a division among the Tuscan Protestants, who would soon be known as Brethren (or *Fratelli*). The larger group, who were known as the *Arno* party (because they met in the Casa Schneidorf on the *Lung'Arno*), were identified with Carlotta Johnson, who was assisted by a former Roman Catholic priest Bartolomeo Gualtieri,[31] and their meetings had very little doctrinal or liturgical regulation. The *Corso* party was a much smaller group meeting on the Via del Corso and was associated with Eliza Browne. She appears to have been a less forceful character, though she wanted the Brethren to have recognized ministers and deacons. The numbers of her following dwindled and in due course, some of them, like Luigi De Sanctis, reverted to the more structured ministry of the Waldensians, while most of the others were reconciled to the *Arno* party. Some twenty years later,

---

[28] Letter from Magrini sent to Tregelles (Florence) published in *News of the Churches* 8 (18 February 1861): 88–89.

[29] Ibid., 174, Letter from Tregelles (Plymouth, 18 June 1861).

[30] Ibid., 198, 113.

[31] Gualtieri had converted to Protestantism in 1858. 'Chronique religieuse' in *L'observateur catholique*, 7 (October–March 1859): 273.

an American Episcopalian recalled, perhaps a little mischievously, that the two parties had been known as the *Carlottini* and the *Elisabettini*.[32] It was probably a part of their story that the Brethren (*fratelli*) in Italy preferred to forget.

The awkwardness of SPT's position was apparent in his letter to the *News of the Churches* when he cautiously reserved his judgement saying that he was not ready to discuss whether he was in full agreement with Magrini and the Fratelli.[33] His reluctance arose from the fact that although he had earlier taken up the cause of the Tuscan Protestants when they were struggling for survival in the face of dominant Roman Catholicism, Tregelles and the assembly in Compton Street, Plymouth were now completely detached from the Brethren whose Christology and soteriology he would soon systematically criticize in a series of letters in 1863.[34] It is noticeable that in his correspondence from November 1857 onwards, and in his later publications the disparaging use of the words *Brethrenism* and *Brethrenite* indicates his disapproval of their sectarianism and underlines his disillusion with the movement. By 1864, the note of despair and even scorn is palpable in one of his final comments on the curious way in which the Protestant scene had evolved in Italy. Writing to Newton in April he observes:

Some years ago this *same* correspondent of the News of the Churches (as the periodical was then called) charged all in Italy who did not hold Infant Baptism, or who did not regard that as almost a term of fellowship, with Brethrenism. In this way he helped to make them such: so that there were labourers whom Count Guicciardini refused to help because they were *not* brethrenized, while the Foreign Aid Committee [of the Evangelical Alliance] would not do it on the grounds that they were brethrenized ...[35]

We have now followed our subject from his early youthful enthusiasm in Plymouth, through his attempts to combine his faith with his fascination with Welsh culture by engaging in Welsh evangelism, to his instinctive

[32] W.C. Langdon, 'The Possibilities of Italian Reform,' *Andover Review* 5:26 (February 1886): 167. For a Methodist's account of the Brethren in Italy, see T.C. Piggott, T. Durley, *Life and Letters of Henry James Piggott of Rome* (London: Epworth, 1921), 88–90.

[33] S.P. Tregelles, Letter (Plymouth, 18 June 1861) in *News of the Churches* 8 (1861): 174.

[34] Tregelles, *Five Letters*, vide infra Chapter 12.

[35] S.P. Tregelles (Plymouth, 15 April 1864) to B.W. Newton; Manchester/JRUL/CBA 7181 (66).

desire to be allied with persecuted crypto-Protestants in Tuscany—a series of positions, which would leave him disillusioned and disappointed. For a significant segment of SPT's life—in fact, for about twenty-five years— his maturing ecclesiastical convictions repeatedly side-tracked this gifted scholar from devoting himself entirely to his textual researches. Possibly it gave his life a human dimension that his other work lacked—a measure of relief perhaps from the tedium of textual *minutiae*. It may have been the conscientious response of a good pastoral teacher who recognized some of the needs of his fellow-believers. Perhaps there was even an element of dilettantism resulting from his enthusiasm for almost any line of linguistic and historical enquiry. There are some indications that it was only in the later 1850s, when he had extricated himself from the Brethren and their quarrels that Tregelles was able to do justice to the extensive dimensions of the textual task, which he had set himself.

However, before we revert to a more chronological account of his later life, we need to consider some of the more prevalent aspects of SPT's thinking and some of the positions that he adopted toward those with whom he disagreed. These will include his attitude to Roman Catholicism, his convictions concerning the authority of scripture and his developing relationship and confrontation with his impulsive scholarly contemporary, Constantin von Tischendorf. Only when we have examined these thematic issues, shall we be in a position to understand the last decades of his life.

CHAPTER 8

Tregelles and Roman Catholicism

8.1 Introduction

In much of his writing, we discover just how strongly Tregelles rejected anything associated with Roman Catholicism. In some instances, this reflects a typically British attitude, which originated in the sixteenth and seventeenth centuries. With the Henrician reformation and the sale of former church lands after the dissolution of the monasteries, a significant element of the land-owning population had acquired a vested interest in the country remaining Protestant. The Revolution settlement of 1689 not only confirmed the removal of the Roman Catholic James II from the throne, and the establishment of the Anglican Church, but also enacted measures discriminating against Roman Catholics so that they could not hold public office or sit in Parliament. So deeply rooted was the traditional fear of Catholicism that even today, the nearest the British have to a national day is in November when they celebrate the failure of a Roman Catholic, Guido Fawkes, to blow up the Houses of Parliament. Indeed, for many years the Gunpowder Plot of 1605 was linked with the Defeat of the Spanish Armada in 1588 as part of a divine 'Double Deliverance' from Catholicism.[1]

The Act of Catholic Emancipation, which enabled Roman Catholics to sit in Parliament, was only passed in 1829 the year in which Prideaux

---

[1] Well exemplified in the numerous prints of 'God's Double Deliverance' (Amsterdam 1621) an etching by Samuel Ward, a 'preacher of Ipswich'.

© The Author(s) 2020   97
T. C. F. Stunt, *The Life and Times of Samuel Prideaux Tregelles*,
Christianities in the Trans-Atlantic World,
https://doi.org/10.1007/978-3-030-32266-3_8

Tregelles and his widowed mother moved to Wales. When, a few years later, the Tractarian movement seemed to be advocating the re-introduction of a Roman Catholic liturgy and ecclesiastical ritual into the Anglican Church, and some of its protagonists (including John Henry Newman) converted to Catholicism, popular opposition became more vocal. Five years after Tregelles returned from his abortive Roman project, the re-establishment of a Roman Catholic hierarchy of bishops and archbishops in the UK in 1851 provoked violent protests in November with effigies of the Pope and Cardinal Nicholas Wiseman being placed on the bonfires to accompany Guy Fawkes.[2]

In reality, these manifestations were part of a 'phobia' with comparatively little substance to it. From an examination of seventeenth- and eighteenth-century diaries, we know that politicians, who publicly gave voice to wildly anti-Catholic opinions, were often on good terms socially with their Roman Catholic neighbours, entertaining them in their homes like any other friends. Writing about the late seventeenth century when anti-Catholicism was at its most vocal, John Miller could claim that 'when the Catholic question did not dominate politics most Protestants were prepared to leave alone the attenuated minority of Catholics in their neighbourhood' and that they were 'more tolerant in practice than in theory'.[3] Similarly, the historian of anti-Catholicism in the eighteenth century, Colin Haydon, makes the point that 'the image of the cruel, dangerous Papist was projected [by Protestants], not on to Catholic neighbours, but on to faceless Catholics, Catholics abroad or at a distance', and he recognizes that 'stereotypes are suspended by personal contact'.[4] The phenomenon is not dissimilar to the situation today with racist prejudice where the *animus* is frequently directed against an abstract identity while making an exception of personally known individuals. In the mid-nineteenth century, an

---

[2] Owen Chadwick, *The Victorian Church Part 1, 1829–1859*, 3rd ed. (London: A & C Black, 1971 [1966]), 294–95. However, it is evident from the chapter 'Bonfires, Revels and Riots,' in D.G. Paz, *Popular Anti-Catholicism in Mid-Victorian England* (Stanford University Press, 1992), 225–66, that the religious issue was often merely a pretext for lawlessness and hostility to the police.

[3] John Miller, *Popery and Politics in England 1660–88* (Cambridge, 1973), 63; cf. J.P. Kenyon, *The Popish Plot* (London: Heinemann, 1972), 6.

[4] C. Haydon, *Anti-Catholicism in Eighteenth-Century England, C. 1714–80: A Political and Social Study* (Manchester University Press, 1993), 11–12. He cites a good example in the respectful treatment of Edward Weld, a Catholic gentleman of Lulworth Castle in Dorset during the Jacobite scare of 1745.

unknown Roman Catholic wearing a monk's habit might easily find himself threatened, and Catholic chapels were sometimes stoned, but individual laymen, known to be Roman Catholics were less likely to be the victims of premeditated popular anti-Catholicism.

Such an atmosphere in British society at large may help to explain why anti-catholic writings were often given a favourable reception, but there was more substance to the anti-Catholicism of Tregelles than that of the popular 'phobia' of his day. Born into a Quaker family, SPT grew up in circles where sacramental religion of any sort was regarded with disdain. Quakers sat lightly to the observance of any ritual (including baptism and Holy Communion) and for them the Latin liturgy and vestments of Roman Catholicism epitomized the sacramentalism of which they were so critical. Similarly, in a Society whose quarterly and annual assemblies gave an opportunity for the expression of individual opinions before the meetings voted on resolutions put to the community, Quakers had little time for clerical diktats and the official persecution that, even in the nineteenth century, often accompanied papal authoritarianism. With such Quaker attitudes, Tregelles had been familiar, all his life, but with his evangelical conversion in 1835, his disdain for the Roman Church acquired a further dimension.

8.2   A PROTESTANT EMPHASIS ON SCRIPTURE

The evangelical movement had its roots in the Protestant Reformation with its emphasis on the supreme authority of scripture (*sola scriptura*) in matters of doctrine and practice, and its insistence on justification by faith alone (*sola fide*) as the basis of salvation. In a previous chapter, we noted SPT's acknowledgement that, at the time of his evangelical conversion, certain key works had given his thinking a Reformed orientation, and not only is this Protestant dimension repeatedly apparent in his writings but it is also an inescapable element in his criticism of Roman Catholicism. As early as 1844, he (and his wife who was fluent in Spanish) had discussed with Spaniards how best the Bible should be translated into their language[5]

---

[5] 'I went through this whole question with Spaniards [whether the Greek λόγος should be translated in Spanish as *verbo* or *palabra*] twelve years ago'. In 1844, SPT's home was in London but these conversations could well have taken place in Plymouth where 'the intercourse [with Spaniards] every summer is pretty habitual'. S.P. Tregelles (Plymouth) to B.W. Newton, 11 and 20 April 1856 (Manchester/JRUL/CBA 7181 [4, 5]).

and more than once Tregelles went into print, trouncing the Bible Society for their use of the Spanish translation of the Vulgate made in 1793 by the Roman Catholic, Felipe Scio[6] rather than the translation made by Cipriano de Valera (1569) based on the work of Juan Pérez and Casiodoro de Reina.[7] In fact, he extended his criticism to the Bible Society's French and Italian Bibles, approving the French translation of the Swiss Protestant Jean-Frédéric Ostervald rather than that of the Jansenist De Sacy, and similarly strongly criticizing Martini's Italian translation as compared with that of Diodati.[8]

The errors which SPT found in the Roman Catholic versions were mainly the result of the translators working from the Latin Vulgate, and he adduced several instances where the Catholic translations favoured the idea of a sacramental priesthood, as well as what he considered to be Roman idolatry, and undue reverence for the Virgin Mary. Three examples of his perception of Roman sacramentalism must suffice. In many places where in the English versions the Greek verb *metanoein* (μετανοεῖν) was translated as *to repent*, the Catholic versions gave the translation as *to do penance*.[9] In Ephesians, chapter four the *mystery* (μυστήριον) of marriage was translated as *sacrament*, and, particularly glaring, was Martini's translation of the Greek phrase *leitourgountes to Kurio* (λειτουργοῦντες τῷ Κυρίῳ) in Acts xiii.2 as *offering sacred mysteries to the Lord*, rather than Diodati's *publicly serving the Lord*.[10] In these and other instances, SPT reckoned that the Bible Society had capitulated to a Roman Catholic interpretation of scripture.

---

[6] Phelipe Scio de San Miguel, *La Biblia Vulgata Latina traducida en Español, y anotada conforme al sentido de los santos Padres y expositores Cathólicos* (Valencia, 1791–1793).

[7] [S.P. Tregelles], *Valera's Spanish Bible of 1602. Appeal to Protestant Christians Respecting the Reprinting of This Version*, prefatory note signed B.W. N[ewton] (London: Houlston and Stoneman, 1856).

[8] S.P. Tregelles, *The Versions of Scripture for Roman Catholic Countries: An Appeal to the British and Foreign Bible Society* (London: Wertheim and Macintosh; Plymouth: W. Brendon, 1856). In his letter, Tregelles wrote 'It is now [October 1855] about eighteen years [sc. c. 1837] since I first endeavoured to draw the attention of those concerned to the condition and character of the Romish versions' (p. 6). Antonio Martini [1720–1809] had been the Archbishop of Florence whereas Giovanni Diodati [1576–1649] was Beza's successor in Geneva as Professor of theology, two centuries earlier.

[9] In Italian *fare penitenza*, rather than *ravvedersi*.

[10] *Offerivano al Signore i sacri misteri* (Martini) rather than *facevano il publico servigio del Signore* (Diodati).

8.3   VARIETIES OF CATHOLICISM ENCOUNTERED IN ITALY

The months in Rome, spent by Prideaux Tregelles in 1845–1846 only served to confirm his disdain for what he considered to be 'Popish superstition' and 'priestcraft'. We find him observing a parish Sunday school where there is no priest teaching the children but 'a sharp-looking girl, with a shrill voice and commanding manner who acts as a sort of monitress, and after her, the young children repeat a great deal by rote… I never found them occupied with anything but *Litanies* addressed to the Virgin Mary'.[11] He indignantly notes the 'idolatry' of the 'carved figures and pictures of the saints (especially the Virgin Mary) and even of the Trinity!' and despises the right foot of the brass figure of St Peter, which had to be restored 'because much of it had been kissed away'. Similarly, we can feel the scorn in his account of the notice that he observed in the Arcibasilica di San Giovanni in Laterano 'which says that the indulgences of this church are so many that only God Almighty can count or remember them'.[12] Three years later in a letter addressed to the British and Foreign Bible Society he wrote of these days: 'I saw the condition of the people, ignorant of the gospel of Christ, without the word of God, and almost every channel obstructed thro' which light could reach them. I had with me some gospel tracts [but] at Rome I was obliged to use them *very cautiously*'.[13]

For Tregelles, these abuses were not recent accretions to the Roman Catholic faith but rather were they an essential part of an historic system that had been corrupt for centuries. A few years later, Tregelles described how in 1849 he found himself working in the *Bibliothèque du roi* in Paris, at a desk next to the French scholar Emmanuel Bénigne Miller (1812–1886) who was transcribing the newly discovered text of Hippolytus's *Philosophumena*, which contained some scandalous details of the life of Pope Callixtus I (died AD 223).[14] There is something almost prurient in Tregelles's

---

[11] Tregelles, *Historic Evidence*, 87.

[12] Quotations taken from SPT's letter to Eben Fardd (Rome, March 1846); see below Appendix of Letters. Tregelles refers to the *arcibasilica* as 'the cathedral of Rome'.

[13] S.P. Tregelles (Plymouth, 29 November 1848) to the BFBS (Cambridge/CUL, BSA/D1/2 Tregelles 29/11/1848) but, see above (Chapter 7, Footnote 9) for his easier experiences in Florence.

[14] For an early discussion of Emmanuel Miller's discovery which was published in Oxford in 1851, see C.C.J. Bunsen, *Hippolytus and His Age; or the Doctrine and Practice of the Church of Rome Under Commodus and Alexander Severus…*. 4 vols., i. *The Critical Inquiry: In five letters to Archdeacon Hare* (London: Longman, Brown, Green, and Longmans, 1852) where

account of how he was thus able to read the 'historic statements there recorded relative to the flagitious deeds of that Pope'.[15] Events in Tuscany would very soon reinforce SPT's conviction that the Roman Church was both historically corrupt and the sworn enemy of Protestant truth. It is important however to be aware that SPT's perception of the situation was incomplete. When he was in Florence in 1846, Prideaux Tregelles was probably unaware of the extent to which the situation in Tuscany differed from that of Rome and the Papal States; much of the nascent Protestant movement in Tuscany to which we referred in the last chapter was likewise unknown to him. Those developments, however, originated in a Roman Catholic environment, which was very much more liberal than that of the Papal States and this gives them a fascination all of their own. At this point, in seeking to give a balanced account where SPT's perception was very one-sided, a digression is warranted and this is all the more needful as there are virtually no details of this brief flowering of progressive Catholicism with its Protestant consequences, available to English readers.

In the earlier decades of the nineteenth century, the government of the Grand Duchy of Tuscany had a very independent policy with regard to the Roman Catholic Church—a tradition going back to the eighteenth century when the Austrian authorities had kept the Papacy and its decrees at arm's length. Under the enlightened influence of the Habsburg Emperor Joseph II, the offices of the Inquisition had been abolished and there was even a decree in force requiring only the scriptures in Italian to be read at meals in the monasteries. In such an enlightened atmosphere, some liberal Roman Catholics took a still more independent and critical position towards the church, and even considered the possibility that Catholicism might abandon the decrees of the Council of Trent. If Tregelles had been aware of this progressive and questioning element in Catholicism, some of his judgements might have been less severe, but in any case this period of 'enlightenment' was soon to be silenced.

the author acknowledges that it was SPT, in early June 1851, who introduced him to Miller's work and had assured him [Bunsen] of the enthusiastic interest of the elderly President of Magdalen College, Dr. Martin Routh (1755–1854), Bunsen, op. cit., 1: 9.

[15] S.P. Tregelles [ed.], *Canon Muratorianus. The Earliest Catalogue of the Books of the New Testament* ... (Oxford: Clarendon Press, 1867), 63n.

Liberal spirits like Raffaello Lambruschini[16] (1788–1873), the solitary educational pioneer of San Cerbone in the Val d'Arno, Lapo de' Ricci[17] (1782–1843), and Baron Bettino Ricasoli[18] (1809–1880) began as social reformers (fascinated by the challenge of making agricultural and educational techniques more effective) but they soon found themselves criticizing the church and its authoritarian policies. One of this enlightened circle was Count Piero Guicciardini whom we encountered earlier. He with other like-minded reformers had been able in the 1840s to spend time with Swiss Protestants[19] like Matilde Calandrini,[20] Jean-Pierre Vieusseux[21] and Charles Eynard,[22] who had made Tuscany their home, as well as with English ex-patriots like Captain Montague Walker and his sons Arthur de

[16] For the contrasting opinions of Raffaello Lambruschini, (1828–1873) of San Cerbone, and his very conservative uncle, Luigi Lambruschini, whom we encountered in an earlier chapter, see V. Gabbrielli [ed.], *Gino Capponi — Raffaello Lambruschini, Carteggio (1828–1873)* (Florence: Spadolini-Le Monnier, 1996), 91–92, n.2.

[17] Lapo de' Ricci (1782–1843) was one of the editors of the progressive *Giornale Agrario Toscano*. He was a nephew of the reforming Jansenist Bishop of Pistoia, Scipione de' Ricci (1741–1810). It was he who encouraged his *protégé*, Salvatore Ferretti, who was preparing for the Catholic Priesthood, to attend the Swiss Church, in the belief that such an encounter with Protestants would prepare him for an active part in the spiritual renewal envisaged by liberal Roman Catholics. In the event, Ferretti became a Protestant and found his way to England where he edited *L'Eco di Savonarola*; see S. Ferretti, 'La mia conversione,' in *L'Eco di Savonarola* (1847), 215.

[18] Bettino Ricasoli (1809–1880) Count of Brolio, the 'Iron Baron'. An austere and highly moral aristocrat, famed for pioneering the advanced viticulture in Tuscany with the production of Chianti. As a politician, he favoured unification with Piedmont and succeeded Cavour as Italy's second Prime Minister.

[19] For the role of the Swiss *réveil* in these developments, see T.C.F. Stunt, 'L'influenza del *réveil* svizzero prima dell'Unità d'Italia,' in Maghenzani, *Riforma*, 105–13.

[20] For Matilde Calandrini (1794–1866), see *DBI* 16 (1973); V. Gabbrielli [ed.], *Carteggio: Lambruschini – Vieusseux I, (1826–1834)* (Florence: Spadolini-Le Monnier, 1998), 212, n.17; D.D. Ronco, *La fede e l'opera di Matilde Calandrini (dalle lettere a Gian Pietro Vieusseux)* (Bangor: University of Wales, c.1995).

[21] For Jean-Pierre Vieusseux (1779–1863), see R. Ciampini, *Gian Pietro Vieusseux: i suoi viaggi, i suoi giornali, i suoi amici* (Turin: Einaudi, 1953). Anthony Trollope's brother, Tom, wrote an excellent appreciation of Vieusseux's unique place in Florentine life, which appeared in his brother's magazine. 'Giampietro Vieusseux, The Florentine Bookseller,' *The Saint Pauls Magazine* 2 (1868): 727–35.

[22] For Charles Eynard (1810–1876) historian and biographer, see T.C.F. Stunt, *From Awakening to Secession*, 373; Alville, *Anna Eynard-Lullin et l'époque des congrès et des révolutions* (Lausanne: Feissly, 1955), 295–96.

Noé and George Walker.[23] As we observed earlier, the régime of the Grand Duke of Tuscany in the 1830s and 1840s had been ready to turn a blind eye to this fraternization of Italians with Protestant foreigners which is why Tregelles found he 'could use [his gospel tracts] more openly' in Florence than in Rome.

However, after the short-lived revolution of 1848, Tuscany was subjected to a harsher régime. Acting hand in glove with the Roman Catholic hierarchy, draconian measures were imposed on any Italians who might be accused of Protestant heresy. However liberal the previous régime might have been, the situation now tallied precisely with SPT's critical view of Catholicism, as soon became apparent in the case of Francesco and Rosa Madiai, which would become something of an international *cause célèbre*.

8.4   The Madiai Case in Tuscany and SPT's Reaction

As we noted earlier, Count Guicciardini was forbidden to attend services in the Swiss Church and was arrested in May 1851 with some like-minded friends for reading the scriptures. The penalty was six months imprisonment but this was commuted to exile—a punishment that would subsequently be a recurring phenomenon but *not* for people of humbler social origins for whom the option of exile was not feasible. The events of the following August would provide a notorious case in point.

Francesco and Rosa Madiai were a middle-aged couple who earned their living by letting furnished lodgings in a house in the Piazza Santa Maria Novella, where, today the Florence railway station is located. Their clients were chiefly families from England and other countries, coming to Italy for short periods. Francesco, the son of a Tuscan yeoman, was a courier and in 1840 had visited his brother in the United States, where, dissatisfied with Catholicism, he had been attracted to the Episcopalian Church. Soon after his return, he married Rosina Pulini, who, having resided for many years in England, had a much better command of English than her husband, but who still reluctantly attended the Roman Church. Reading the Bible together in English, they became increasingly disillusioned with the 'careless and scandalous manner of performing religious worship, by the open and shameless profligacy of the priests and by the blind superstitions of the

[23] For the Walker family, see above Chapter 7, Footnote 4.

people'. In or about the year 1849, they finally abjured the Roman faith and began regularly to attend the Italian services in the Swiss Church.[24]

They were quiet and respectable people living a simple life, and in 1849 they had joined with a Swiss gentleman in having meetings for Bible study in their house. However, when their Swiss friend left Florence he suggested that they discontinue the meetings because of the increasingly hostile political developments in Tuscany, but so many wished to come that they continued the meetings for a while. In the summer of 1851, they resolved to give them up and on 17 August the Madiai were deliberately absent from their home to ensure that such a meeting would not take place. That evening Arthur de Noé Walker came to their house and while he was waiting for their return, two other Italian Protestants joined him. They were conversing together when four police officers arrived and arrested them for reading the Bible. On searching the house, they found two Bibles and another one in Walker's pocket, but then Francesco Madiai arrived and the four men were taken to jail. Walker was released, and the Italian friends chose to go into exile rather than face imprisonment.[25] About ten days later, Rosa Madiai was arrested[26] and in due course (June 1852) she and her husband were condemned—Francesco to fifty-eight months of hard labour in Volterra, Rosa to forty-five months in the house of correction in Lucca.

In a country like Britain where freedom of worship had been established for over a century, the narrative of these events was shocking to say the least and confirmed all the anti-catholic prejudice to which we referred earlier. It certainly tallied with the negative opinions of Prideaux Tregelles, with regard to the Roman Church. It is not clear exactly how he came into possession of the Madiai correspondence, but it was probably facilitated by his acquaintance with Eliza Browne, who had previously been a member of the Brethren assembly in Plymouth, but, who, from late in 1850, was living

---

[24] Sarah Senhouse [ed.], *Letters of the Madiai and Visits to Their Prisons* by the Misses Senhouse (London: Nisbet, 1853), 4–6, cf. 111. For a recent account of the Madiai, see Laura Demofonti in *DBI* 67 (Rome: Treccani 2006), s.n.

[25] The Italian friends were Francesco Manelli and Alessandro Fantoni; *L'Eco di Savonarola* 9:5 (1 October 1856): 149

[26] In most accounts, the couple are described as being arrested on the same day, but according to Pietrocola-Rossetti, Rosa Madiai was arrested eight days later, and the account based on Eliza Browne's letters gives her arrest as ten days later; see T. Pietrocola-Rossetti, *Biografia di Rosa Madiai* (Florence: G Pellas, 1871), 10; Soltau, *Story of Madiai*, 447.

in Florence, where she had immediately taken an interest in the problems of the secret meetings of Italian Protestants.[27] As a fellow member of the Plymouth assembly, Tregelles would have known about her work. What is clear is that when, in 1852, Tregelles edited his account together with some of the Madiai's letters in a small book entitled *Prisoners of Hope*, the Madiai were still in prison and his was the first published account of these events. Although subsequent writers often failed to acknowledge their dependence on his work, Tregelles was the pioneer in bringing the sufferings of the Madiai to the attention of the British public.

Of course, it could be argued that the problem lay with the secular authorities rather than the Roman Church itself, but Tregelles was adamant that it was the church that was responsible for the persecution:

> But what causes the possession of the word of God to be regarded as a *criminal* charge? The dogmas of Rome as taught by the priests (Jesuits probably) to the Tuscan authorities. If any Romanist disclaims persecution, it goes no farther than himself; he is in that respect a dissenter from his church. So long as Rome recognises the decree of the Lateran council under Innocent III *requiring* the temporal powers to persecute "heretics" — so long as she authorizes "Instructions to Theological Candidates" hinting not obscurely (by *condemning the contrary as heresy*) "that it is according to the mind of the spirit to burn heretics," — and so long as every Roman Bishop swears that he will *persecute and oppose all heretics*, so long shall we be justified in charging on Romanism as a system, and on its priests as the ministers of that system, the persecutions which are carried out by the secular authorities which profess that religion.[28]

Effectively therefore from Tregelles's standpoint, the Roman Church was the instigator of governmental persecution, and this was much the position he would later take with reference to the opposition encountered by Protestants in Spain.

---

[27] See above Chapter 6, pp. 64–65, Footnotes 5–7.

[28] Tregelles, *Prisoners*, 15–16.

8.5   The Social Consequences of Faith: Two Viewpoints

To appreciate more fully SPT's attitude to Catholicism at this time, we must consider once more some of his experiences in Rome itself in 1845–46. To put these in a wider context, it is perhaps appropriate to look first at another English scholar, with a totally dissimilar background, who arrived in Rome less than a year after Tregelles left the city.

John Henry Newman[29] had been a Fellow of Oriel College, Oxford where he had followed his conscience in a completely different direction from SPT. Moving away from his earlier evangelicalism to become, as the Vicar of the University Church of St Mary, the eloquent exponent of Tractarian Churchmanship, he shocked his many admirers by his evident attraction to the Roman Catholic Church into which he was received in October 1845 ten days before SPT set out for Rome. In consequence, about a year later, Newman himself arrived in Rome late in 1846 to study for the Roman priesthood in the *Collegio di Propaganda*.

There is a dearth of social detail in Tregelles's letters and they tell us nothing about such things as the weather, clothing, his accommodation or new culinary experiences, Instead, he is more preoccupied with matters of piety, scholarship, and observations of historical interest. In contrast, John Newman shares with his family and friends back in England a host of thoughts about Roman life—the lethally cold weather, his hotel ('a palace of filth'[30]) the condition of the streets, and the habits of the people, and curiously it is here that one of his observations casts a revealing light on some of SPT's attitudes.

After three months in Rome where, in contrast to England, the population was overwhelmingly Catholic, Newman declares:

> I do not like the people of Rome — one is struck at once with their horrible cruelty to animals — also with their dishonesty, lying and stealing apparently without any conscience — and thirdly with their extreme dirt ...

---

[29] The literature on John Henry Newman (1801–1890) is immense and I shall refer below to his published *Letters and Diaries*, but there is probably no better overview of his extraordinary career than Ian Ker, *John Henry Newman: A Biography* (Oxford: Oxford University Press, 2009 [1988]).

[30] C.S. Dessain [ed.], *Letters and Diaries of John Henry Newman* (London: Nelson, 1961), 11: 267.

and yet, a sentence later he reckons that

> they really have faith in a most uncommon degree... and I observe *every where* a simple certainty in believing, which to a Protestant or Anglican is quite astonishing but though they have this they show in a wonderful way how it is possible to disjoin religion and morality.

In a telling comment a few lines later, he concludes:

> ... the same people, who have a sort of instinctive conviction of the unseen world, which is strange to an Englishman, have not that *living* faith which leads to correctness or sanctity of character.[31]

If one compares Newman's comment with an experience of SPT in Rome a year earlier, one might easily conclude that, Newman's verdict could really have been that of Tregelles himself.

In a book written a little later, Tregelles gives some account of the figure of the Holy Bambino of Aracœli, which was kept in the Franciscan church of Sta Maria on the Capitoline Hill (*il Campidoglio*), and a history of which was published in 1797 with the *imprimatur* of the archbishop of Larissa, and of the Master of the Holy Apostolic Palace.[32] SPT then recalls a conversation about the book that he had in Rome with an Irish priest, Francis Joseph Nicholson (1805–1855), who was later appointed to be the Roman Catholic Archbishop of Corfu:

> In 1845 I bought this little book, and on its being shown to a native of the British Isles, a scholar and a gentleman, then a priest and now [1852] a bishop in the Romish Church, who spent several months under the same roof with me at Rome, he said that no one was bound to *believe* the narration as a fact. I asked what then might the "Conlicenza de' Superiori" mean: he replied that it was by no means a sanction of the book as authentic, only an approval of it as not unedifying, *just like Æsop's fables*. The misfortune, however, is

---

[31] Letter to his sister Jemima Mozley, 26 January 1847; C.S. Dessain, *Letters and Diaries*, 12: 24.

[32] Pier Gio[vanni]. Vincenzo Giannini, *Notizie istoriche sopra la miracolosa imagine di Gesú bambino che si venera nella ven. Chiesa presbiterale di S. Maria in Aracœli di Roma: con alcuni divoti esercizi per conseguire le grazie che si domandono: coll'aggiunta di varie notizie, e savie riflessioni sopra la nascita del medesimo divin redentore* (Rome: Puccinelli, 1797).

that this and similar "not unedifying" books *claim* to be true narratives —
that they pass current as such with the people at large, and if not true, they
are irreverent in the extreme. It would be well if they were half as edifying
as Æsop. It is only from such books that thousands learn all their ideas of
religion, such as they may be. What a thought it is, that foolish and profane
tales are approved as "not unedifying", while the Scriptures (of which the
[first century] *Romans* were taught "whatsoever was written aforetime was
written for our learning") are utterly proscribed![33]

It seems that starting from completely opposite poles, Tregelles and Newman had come to the same verdict—albeit a rather *British* one—namely that
the accretions of Roman dogma and tradition might be attractive for uneducated folk but could not produce what Newman described as 'the *living*
faith, which leads to correctness or sanctity of character'. For that, Tregelles
would have insisted, biblical teaching, free from legend, was essential. This
was very much his view of the matter when, a few years later he was taking a similarly 'British' interest in Spanish Protestantism. Interestingly, he
now focused on a cultural difference that was not unlike the distinction
Newman observed between English and Italian attitudes.

8.6   A Spanish Dimension

Soon after the Plymouth Brethren came into existence, their interest in
Spain as a mission field had been aroused by one of their most respected
leaders, Robert Cleaver Chapman of Barnstaple, who, as early as 1834, had
travelled from Santander to Madrid and on towards Lisbon, distributing
scriptures and testifying to his faith.[34] In Plymouth itself, Spanish-speaking
sailors whether from Spain or from South America were regular visitors, and
both SPT and his wife who, as we noted before, was fluent in Spanish, took a
great interest in them. In the reports of the Spanish Evangelisation Society,

---

[33] S.P. Tregelles, *Remarks on the Prophetic Visions in the Book of Daniel*...new ed. (London: Bagster, 1852), 209n. For an amusing and not uncritical account of Francis Joseph
Nicholson (1803–1855), a curiously Protean character, and his diplomatic activities in Rome,
see J.P. Flint, *Great Britain and the Holy See: The Diplomatic Relations Question, 1846–1852*
(Washington, DC: Catholic University of America Press, 2003), 14–15 and *passim*.

[34] K. Eaton, *Protestant Missionaries in Spain, 1869–1936: 'Shall the Papists Prevail?'* (Lanham, MA: Lexington Books, 2015) [Eaton, *Protestant Missionaries*], 69. Chapman made
two further visits in 1838 and 1839 before his more systematic Brethren work in Spain with
George Lawrence beginning in 1863.

(established in Edinburgh in 1855), there were regular contributions from 'a Lady in Plymouth' who evidently was SPT's wife Sarah Anna.[35]

In 1855, a Wesleyan missionary magazine gave an account of evangelistic work among emancipated Cuban slaves who lodged in the disused Plymouth workhouse before continuing their journey to Nigeria,[36] and John Kitto's biographer noted that 'our friend Dr. Tregelles and his lady, with others, were very attentive to them'.[37] Writing to Newton in the following year Tregelles described some of the people with whom he and his wife sought to share their faith in their home in Portland Square:

> hardly a week passes without our seeing Spanish speaking people — Spaniards, blacks, mulattoes, from Spain, the West Indies or Mexico. There is often *much* that is interesting as to these people, and much to lead to prayer that the seed may not be [sown] in vain.[38]

Indeed, it is in this context that we can better appreciate SPT's concern, which we noted earlier, for a good Spanish translation of the scriptures, free from what he considered to be the 'Popish' errors of the Vulgate. Typical of the evangelistic endeavours of Prideaux and Sarah Anna were their efforts in June 1857 when the Duke and Duchess of Montpensier spent a little time at the Royal Hotel in Plymouth on their way to London.[39] Sarah Anna's report gives us the details:

[35] Extracts from the annual reports were later incorporated into Mrs. Robert Peddie, *The Dawn of the Second Reformation in Spain: Being the Story of Its Rise and Progress from the Year 1852* (London: S. W. Partridge, 1871) [Peddie, *Second Reformation*]. For the reports from 'a lady correspondent in Plymouth', see pp. 41 [1855], 58–59 [1856], 89–90 [1857]. Mrs. Peddie [Maria Denoon *née* Young] had edited the *Spanish Evangelical Record* and seems to have been one of its chief financial supporters. SPT described some of the work in which he and his wife were engaged among Spanish speakers in Plymouth in a letter to Eben Fardd written in July 1856 later published in *Y Traethodydd* 29 (July 1884): 289–90 where the date is misprinted as 1836.

[36] *The Wesleyan Missionary Notices Relating Principally to the Foreign Missions Under the Direction of the Methodist Conference*, 3rd series, 2 (October 1855): 173–75.

[37] John Eadie, *Life of John Kitto, DD., FSA.*, (Edinburgh: Oliphant, 1857), 35n.

[38] SPT, Plymouth to B.W. Newton, 20 April 1856 (Manchester/JRUL/CBA 7181 [5]).

[39] After the Republican Revolution in 1848, the Duke, who was the youngest son of the overthrown, Orleanist French, king Louis Philippe, and the Duchess, a daughter of the Spanish King Ferdinand VII, had gone to live in Spain. In 1857, they were visiting the Duke's widowed mother at Claremont House in Surrey which Queen Victoria had made available to the French King and Queen in exile (*London Gazette*, 23 June 1857).

The Duke and Duchess de Montpensier spent a day here this week, and several Spanish servants with them. I wrote a Spanish note to the Duchess, asking leave to present her with the Gospels of Luke and John, and a little prayer-book, and put a tract into each book. This parcel and note my husband gave to one of the Spanish attendants to present to her. The next morning we gave some of the Gospels to two of the Spanish men-servants, just as they were all leaving, for which they expressed 'muchas gracias'.[40]

But of even greater interest was the news reaching them from Spain itself where there seemed to be encouraging signs of Protestant activity. As early as April 1856, SPT had written to Newton:

I strongly believe that Seville is a far better place than Madrid for any general [evangelistic] work in Spain. I believe that a few persons more of the class of our town missionaries if such could be found might do much in Spain — more as to intercourse than those who would take a higher social place: I wish that Brown[41] the town missionary here whose knowledge of Spanish makes him so useful could be sent to the North of Spain for a few months.[42]

SPT's interest in the challenges faced by Spanish Protestants was not a momentary phenomenon. In May 1860 when his plan of going to St Petersburg in Russia (where he had hoped to consult the newly discovered Codex Sinaiticus) didn't materialize, he announced to Newton:

Sarah Anna and I therefore propose to carry out what was before our plan; that is to go to the South West and not to the North East, to go towards the Pyrenees and to visit at least some of the places in Spain in which something is doing and in which S.A. has so long been interested.[43]

Some fifteen years had elapsed since their journey to Rome in 1845 and with the rapid progress in railway construction, they were now more easily

---

[40] Peddie, *Second Reformation*, 89.

[41] William Thomas Brown (1821–1899), formerly a clerk at the Methodist Mission House, 'had learned Spanish and used it among Spanish sailors in the Port of London'. In 1872, he went to Barcelona where for a decade he distributed scriptures and gathered a little Methodist society; John Pritchard, *Methodists and Their Missionary Societies* (London: Routledge, 2013), 220. A Spanish observer described him as 'intellectually poor and lacking linguistically'; quoted in Eaton, *Protestant Missionaries*, 134, n.51.

[42] SPT, Plymouth, to B.W. Newton, 11 April 1856, (Manchester/JRUL/CBA 7181 [4]).

[43] SPT, Plymouth, to B.W. Newton, 5 May 1860, (Manchester/JRUL/CBA 7181 [20]).

able to travel south in France by train to Bayonne from where they took the stagecoach into Spain and continued their journey via San Sebastián, Burgos and Valladolid to Madrid.[44] After a day in Toledo, they travelled further south to Granada where Tregelles, on the last day of June, began to write a long letter (finished in Seville) to his Welsh friend Eben Fardd, giving some details of his Spanish travels.[45]

Inevitably, given SPT's passionate interest in all things historical, he is fascinated by the traces of Imperial Spain and the pervasive influence of the Moors. His letter abounds with references to the Moorish palaces like the Alhambra of Granada and the Alcazar in Seville. He is hugely impressed by the cathedrals of Toledo and Seville and he even attempts to describe the low columns and arches, 'like some very thick forest', in Córdoba cathedral. On the other hand, Tregelles is under no illusions and does not forget for a moment that these are but outward manifestations of a religion, which has no time for his own faith. His accounts of the Protestant meetings that they attended are brief and cautious (and in Welsh) to ensure that his letter will not betray details that must remain secret.[46] The conspiratorial tone is unmistakable:

> But what is more worthy of note in Granada is its Protestant Church; a *secret* body of folk, those who by the mercy of God have received Christ into their hearts. It would be dangerous to tell of them. We must give thanks and pray for them. We are the first foreigners to visit them. It is necessary for them to worship in secret (sometimes at night) and it is difficult for them to obtain copies of the Scriptures. One evening we attended a meeting of some of them and heard a magnificent sermon (on Gal[atians]. i.9) given by a gifted young man, spiritual and humble. It would be difficult to forget such a meeting,

[44] One is not surprised to learn from his sister-in-law that SPT travelled the extra twenty miles to visit Alcala where the Complutensian polyglot of the Greek New Testament was produced by Cardinal Ximenes and published in 1514, Cambridge, MA/AHTL, Prideaux, MS Life [p. 26].

[45] Unless otherwise indicated my account of SPT in Spain is based on this letter, the text of which (together with some of his other letters to Eben Fardd) was published much later in the Welsh magazine, *Y Traethodydd* [*The Essayist*] 29 (July 1884): 292–93. Because of its intrinsic interest, I have reproduced the entire letter in my appendix of original letters. [[The double square bracketed paragraphs]] were originally in Welsh but I have given them in the English translation with which Mrs. Olwen Wonnacott most kindly provided me some fifty years ago.

[46] The need for secrecy may be reflected in the fact that no letters from SPT in Spain, to Newton have survived. Perhaps he reckoned it was safer not to write to him.

doors and windows shut and each one careful that no *zealous* papist should know the time and place of their meeting. Persecution again in Spain!

A few days later, in Málaga he attended a meeting of some eighty people and heard an impressive sermon from a young preacher, Manuel Matamoros,[47] who a few months later would be arrested and condemned to serve a long sentence of hard labour.

SPT's later movements in Spain are hard to establish and we cannot be sure when he returned to England. We know that in January 1861 he visited Edinburgh to attend a meeting of the Protestant Alliance and share his findings with the Committee of the Spanish Evangelisation Society,[48] but before leaving Spain he had also managed to visit Gibraltar.[49] We also know that at one stage Sarah Anna suggested that the Spanish evangelist Matamoros would do well to get in touch with William Greene, an English Protestant engineer who, having worked on the Spanish railways, was fluent in Spanish. Greene later published a life of the long-suffering Matamoros, in which he claimed that Tregelles and his wife had visited Barcelona in September, but it is unlikely that they would have spent so long abroad, bearing in mind that SPT was not engaged in any textual labours in Spain.[50]

In fact, it was in September 1860 that Matamoros was arrested and the sequel to SPT's visit was depressingly painful. After many procedural delays, the Spaniard and his fellow evangelist José Alhama were condemned to serve nineteen years hard labour—a sentence that was reduced on appeal to eight years, but the decision still provoked widespread European protests orchestrated by the Evangelical Alliance with the result that the punishment was finally commuted to exile where Matamoros died a few years later. Identifying with the protests, Tregelles was prepared, having spent some time

---

[47] Manuel Matamoros–Garcia (1834–1868). 'One of these meetings [in Málaga] was witnessed by Dr. and Mrs. Tregelles, at which there were about ninety-seven present...' William Greene, *Manuel Matamoros: His Life and Death. A Narrative of the Late Persecution of Christians in Spain, Compiled from Original Letters and Other Documents*, 3rd ed. (London: Alfred Holness, 1889), 11.

[48] Peddie, *Second Reformation*, 66.

[49] SPT, Plymouth to B.W. Newton, 29 January 1864 (Manchester/JRUL/CBA 7181[62]), vide infra, Appendix of Unpublished Letters, No. 7, note 5.

[50] See Greene, *Matamoros*, 11–12. Following the advice of Mrs. Tregelles, Matamoros did write to Green from Barcelona in September 1860 but Greene may have wrongly assumed that it was then and there that SPT and his wife had met Matamoros (p. 11).

with the accused, to testify in a public hearing in London, on their behalf.[51] However, his attitude to Catholicism had changed somewhat from what it had been fifteen years earlier in the Tuscan context.

8.7   DISAPPOINTMENT

The object of his indignation was now more specifically the intolerance of the government. Certainly, he still treated Roman Catholicism as a persecuting church, but as events took their course, one gathers from his correspondence that he was becoming increasingly disillusioned with the Spanish themselves. Even in his earlier letter to Eben Fardd he had observed: 'The people of Spain seem to be divided between fanatical Roman Catholics, and people altogether indifferent: but both agree in disliking and opposing the truth of the gospel', and in the years that followed, his disillusion increased.

In quite a short time, both SPT and his wife reluctantly concluded that several of the Spanish Protestants had feet of clay. He doesn't explain in his letters how they disappointed him, but evidently they were inconsistent in their stories. Sarah Anna corresponded at some length with Nicolas Alonzo, a Spanish Protestant who had escaped to England by way of Gibraltar.[52] When his conduct proved to be questionable, SPT sought for a while, albeit in the condescending tone of an English Victorian, to defend him:

> I cannot form so unfavourable a judgment of Alonzo as you [Newton] do: I quite hope that his recent letter to Sarah Anna is the beginning of a better tone of feeling. I understand something of the defects of the Spanish character; and I think that a kind of secluded life was not the best for meeting or curing those defects. I have not any reason to believe that he has been acting a part;

---

[51] As it was reported, 'Both [Matamoros and Alhama] are personally known to Dr. Tregelles, the well-known Biblical critic, who, with several other gentlemen, has presented a memorial upon the subject to her Majesty's foreign secretary... To the facts thus stated in the memorial, Dr. Tregelles added that the law of Spain inflicts, as the punishment of apostasy, or worshipping contrary to the principles of the church of Rome, eight years' imprisonment with hard labour'; *Sunday at Home* 8 (1861): 80. Cf. a similar report of the Deputation to Lord John Russell: 'Dr. Tregelles, of Plymouth, said he had spent a great portion of the last summer [1860] in Spain, and had had much personal intercourse with Matamoros and Alhama, and could bear warm testimony to their Christian character...' *The Bulwark or Reformation Journal* (1 January 1861): 190.

[52] For Alonzo's later work in Spain, see *Christian World: Magazine of the American & Foreign Christian Union* (June 1869): 166; *Evangelical Christendom* (July 1869): 249.

tho' he may have given abundant proof that he has been in various things activated by perversity, self-will, and that kind of concealment, which is part of a Spaniard's pride. I do not seek to excuse any of these things; they are however very different when found in any who have had the advantage of English Christian training thro' life, from what they are in a young man who has had none of these benefits and who thus has to learn every thing in new circumstances.'[53]

At which point, we may be forgiven for hearing an echo of John Henry Newman's patronizing British complacency and sense of superiority towards the Italians in Rome.

Eighteen months later SPT's opinion of Alonzo has changed for the worse, and he is no longer able to defend those for whom he had once been an advocate:

> It may become a needful duty to let others see what Alonzo's conduct and character really are, so as to stop the evil if possible: but I fear lest this would be in vain;

and in an even more surprising change of tune SPT indicates that his admiration for Matamoros, expressed in his earlier letter to Eben Fardd is similarly a thing of the past, explaining that he has 'lost all confidence in Matamoros's veracity and uprightness'.[54]

8.8   CHANGING ATTITUDES

It is evident however, that these changes in SPT's feelings were accompanied by a view of the Roman church that was also being modified. He still considered Catholicism to be a persecuting church, and he was deeply disturbed by the swingeing punishments imposed on Matamoros and Alhama, but his disappointment seems to have been primarily with what he considered to be 'Spanish' behaviour. A further factor in his thinking was that his contacts with Roman Catholic scholars and his consequent awareness of

---

[53] SPT, Plymouth to B.W. Newton, 7 May 1863 (Manchester/JRUL/CBA 7181 [49]).

[54] SPT, Plymouth to B.W. Newton, 5 October and 19 December 1864 (Manchester/JRUL/CBA 7181 [77, 80]).

their intellectual integrity and devotion to the pursuit of truth were beginning to take effect. This in turn affected his relations with some English-speaking fellow Protestants. Inevitably, there were then (as there are now) ultra-conservatives who regarded textual criticism as an insult and betrayal of their loyalty to the sacredness of Holy Scripture, but Tregelles was used to this and could cope with such a reactionary response to his work.

Far more worrying for SPT was the obstinacy of the Bible Society, which continued to circulate the old Roman Catholic translations with all the errors to which, as we noted earlier, SPT had repeatedly drawn their attention. Not only was the society adamant in doing this, but they also clung to the old principle of issuing the biblical text 'without note or comment'. This gave rise to a richly ironical situation. As the Catholic scholarly authorities were finally recognizing some of the mistranslations of the Latin Vulgate and began issuing new editions of the Bible in which there were notes drawing attention to these errors, the Bible Society insisted on continuing to issue the old texts, replete with the mistakes but *they refused to include the notes of correction provided by the publishers*. The note of despair in Tregelles's letter to Newton late in 1863 is palpable:

> It ought to be distinctly known that Martini, Scio and De Sacy [the Italian, Spanish and French translations, authorized by the Catholic church] *without* the notes are much worse than with them: for they all correct in the notes the readings from the Vulgate. Scio continually protests against the errors of the Latin Papal Vulgate, and Martini gives the reader a table of places to be corrected by the Greek. Of course the Bible Soc^y gives none of these additions to the text. But I quite think that Rome will revise its Vulgate sooner than nominal Protestants will on principle reject the Romish versions. [Carlo] Vercellone[55] is now publishing at Rome under the Pope's sanction a collation of old Latin MSS of the Vulgate, so as to form if possible an effective revision. The notes are quite definite as to false readings; … and this work will do more than all Protestants together have ever done [?to enable?] the Vulgate to be what Jerome left.

The reader senses that SPT felt some justifiable satisfaction when he quotes (not without some relish!) from Vercellone's preface:

> Quid dicemus de Novi Testamenti textu? quem innumeri scriptores a Laurentio Valla et Johanne Millio ad Constantinum Tischendorfium, Tregellium

---

[55] Carlo Vercellone (1814–1869).

et Lachmannum variis lectionibus paene obruerunt? Nonne uberrimos inde fructus eruditi omnes fatentur exstitisse?[56]

We should perhaps note that there is elsewhere an interesting parallel to his approval of Vercellone's honesty. In several of his letters, SPT wrote strongly dissenting from the suggestion that Cardinal Mai's had deliberately falsified parts of the text in his edition of the Codex Vaticanus.[57] Bearing in mind that Mai's obstinacy had contributed to the fruitlessness of Tregelles's Roman experience, his subsequent defence of the Cardinal's integrity is a testimony to SPT's scrupulous fairness in matters of scholarship. Although he clearly still had no brief for the Roman Catholic Church, in the course of his researches he had discovered a significant number of its members whose friendship and scholarly help he valued.

There is something very touching in SPT's concern for the souls of his fellow scholars. When writing to ask Signor Francesco del Furia of the Laurentian Library in Florence to check a reading in the Codex Amiatinus, Tregelles concluded his letter with his prayer that the librarian would be blessed in 'une espérance qui peut être fondée sur les mérites de Jésus Christ, l'adorable fils de Dieu qui est mort que nous serions sauvés par son précieux sang'.[58] We should perhaps note that this concern for the other party's salvation was not uniquely confined to Tregelles as he discovered when a Roman Catholic scholar expressed a similar concern for SPT's eternal welfare. The Abate Francesco Battelli, whom SPT had got to know, when working in the Augustinian Library in Rome, was evidently troubled that Tregelles was outside the pale of what the priest considered to be the true church and this worried him so much that he later gave fuller

---

[56] 'What shall we say of the text of the New Testament? Which countless scholars from Laurentius Valla and John Mill to Constantine Tischendorf, Tregelles and Lachmann have almost demolished with their variant readings. Will not all men of learning acknowledge the very rich fruits that have come into existence from these sources?' [My own translation]. SPT, Plymouth to B.W. Newton, 12 December 1863 (formerly in the Fry Collection, but missing from Manchester/JRUL/CBA; Xerox copy in the author's possession). The passage in Latin, cited by Tregelles is from *Variae lectiones Vulgatae Latinae editionis Bibliorum editionis quas Carolus Vercellone sodalis Barnabites digessit.* Vol. I, Complectens pentateuchum (Roma: Iosephum Spithöver, 1860), 1 [Prolegomena] XVI [accessed October 2017 at https://archive.org/stream/bub_gb_Omx9sz2I0sEC]

[57] SPT, Plymouth, 27 October and 10 November 1858, letters to the Editor of *The Record;* reprinted in the *Journal of Sacred Literature* 8 (January 1859): 458–61.

[58] SPT (30 November 1852) to F. del Furia, (Florence/BNC Carte del Furia 82 cccxliii, 4).

expression to his concern in a lengthy letter, in which he raised the question whether there was any hope of their meeting again, among the redeemed, in the next life. Needless to say, Tregelles replied with a full explanation of his understanding of 'the way of salvation' accompanied by his prayer that the Spirit of God would lead his correspondent in the way of truth.[59] Evidently, there had been, on both sides, a search for common ground.

While recognizing SPT's single-minded and sometimes aggressive disdain and rejection of Roman Catholicism, we do well to remember that his hostility mellowed somewhat with the passage of years and that it was directed primarily at what he considered to be the evils of the *system* and was far from personal. It is clear that he appreciated the many kindnesses shown to him by numerous scholars and was the last person to confuse Roman Catholic individuals with the institution of which their circumstances had made them a part.

[59] As indicated above in Chapter 6, the only surviving account of this episode is in Cambridge MA/AHTL, Prideaux, MS Life [pp. 11–13]. SPT acknowledged Battelli's help in Tregelles, *Account* 157. The fact that the abbé framed his concern in the way he did suggests that in their earlier conversation SPT had raised the theme of his early tract, *The Blood of the Lamb and the Union of Saints*; (see above Chapter 4, p. 37, Footnote 7).

CHAPTER 9

Tregelles and Scripture

9.1 Quaker Positions and Reformation Attitudes

In his youth and as a young man, SPT's view of scripture was inevitably strongly influenced by the religious world of his upbringing, but the Quaker attitude to the Bible was somewhat ambiguous. They respected the scriptures as a divine source of moral guidance, but gave comparable weight to the part played by the Holy Spirit in directing the believer's understanding of truth and moral conduct. Naturally, therefore they emphasized the need for the student of scripture to be enlightened by the Spirit of God if he or she were to profit from their reading. Such an ambivalent approach could leave the door open to forms of scepticism, which we noted earlier, where some members of the Society of Friends questioned the morality of parts of the Old Testament and, as Tregelles recalled, sought to explain away miraculous episodes.[1]

On the other hand, the recurrent concern of the biblical writings with the history of the Near East and the world in the midst of which the Jewish people and early Christians found themselves, gave to the scriptures a dimension that a man with SPT's passionate interest in history, could not ignore. His questionings prior to his evangelical conversion, as to the fate of Edom and the historicity of the prophetic judgements on that civilization, are an indication of the close examination he had given to the

---

[1] Vide supra Chapter 3, Footnotes 1 and 3.

© The Author(s) 2020
T. C. F. Stunt, *The Life and Times of Samuel Prideaux Tregelles,*
Christianities in the Trans-Atlantic World,
https://doi.org/10.1007/978-3-030-32266-3_9

historical records provided in the Bible.[2] A further element in his attitude to scripture was the fact that, as we also previously observed, from the time of his conversion, SPT's doctrinal convictions were grounded in the teaching of the sixteenth-century reformation. This, coupled with his long-standing opposition to papal Catholicism, meant that for the rest of his life the Reformers' motto, *sola scriptura* was typical of his thinking.

However, while asserting the authority of scripture, the Reformers had often been far from precise as to what they understood by the inspiration of scripture and they were surprisingly free from dogma on the subject. Indeed in the case of Luther, one could argue that his view of scripture was decidedly eclectic if not capricious. Famously, he declared the *Letter of James*, to be 'an Epistle of Straw', and equally dismissive was his early opinion that the Holy Spirit could not have produced the last book in the bible.[3] There is a comparable subjectivity in his conclusion that when, in the early chapters of *Genesis*, Moses omitted any mention of the creation and fall of the angels, he seemed 'to be forgetting himself'.[4]

One may be similarly surprised to find that Calvin, in spite of his insistence on the authority of scripture, had no difficulty in admitting that Matthew was mistaken in attributing to Jeremiah a prophecy, which in fact was from Zechariah,[5] or that Luke was wrong about the burial place of Jacob.[6] It was only in the early eighteenth century when the sceptical materialism of philosophers like Thomas Hobbes and Baruch Spinoza seemed to have encouraged some Christian scholars, like Jean Le Clerc (1657–1736) and Jean-Alphonse Turrettini (1671–1737) to concede that parts of the Bible might be unreliable, that others felt the need to define

[2] Vide supra Chapter 3, Footnotes 8–13.

[3] 'I can in no way detect that the Holy Spirit produced it [the book of Revelation] ... My spirit cannot accommodate itself to this book'. E.T. Bachmann [ed.], *Luther's Works, Vol. 35: Word and Sacrament I* (Philadelphia: Fortress Press, 1960), 399. It was a verdict that he later revised. Of James he said: 'there is nothing of the nature of the gospel about it'. Ibid., 362.

[4] J. Pelikan [ed.], *Luther's Works Vol. 1: Lectures on Genesis Chapters 1–5* (Saint Louis, MO: Concordia, 1958), 22.

[5] Matt xxvii.9. 'The passage itself plainly shows that the name of Jeremiah has been put down by mistake instead of Zechariah ...'. J. Calvin, *Commentary on a Harmony of the Evangelists Matthew, Mark, and Luke*, trans. W. Pringle (Edinburgh: Calvin Translation Society, 1845), 3: 272.

[6] Acts vii.16. 'It is manifest that there is a fault ... wherefore this place must be amended'. J. Calvin, *Commentary Upon the Acts of the Apostles*, trans. C. Fetherstone, ed. H. Beveridge (Edinburgh: CTS, 1844), 1: 265.

more precisely what they meant when they claimed that the scriptures were inspired.

9.2   INSPIRATION: SUPERINTENDENCE OR VERBAL INERRANCY?

An important scholar who set out to do this was the dissenting minister, Philip Doddridge (1702–1751) whose dissertation[7] on the subject identified three categories of inspiration. In his exposition, he identified 'elevated' inspiration by which God's spirit could enable writers to use sublimely poetic language, though this was not necessarily confined to the biblical authors. Then, there was the inspiration of 'immediate suggestion' by which the writer was 'first the auditor, and then, if I may be allowed the expression, the secretary of God'.[8] This, Doddridge maintained, was the highest level of inspiration when the Spirit of God was effectively dictating the words to the writer and it was most obviously exemplified in the prophetic writings and the Book of Revelation.

The more general variety of inspiration (and the most basic of the three), which covered all the sacred writings, was what Doddridge called 'Divine Superintendency'. The individual writer employed his natural gifts of learning and understanding, but the Spirit of God was ultimately in control to ensure that the reader would be given the truth. Needless to say, there was more to his analysis than such a simplified outline has indicated, but this was Doddridge's basic position on inspiration and, for quite a while, it was sufficient for many scholars. But, however, judicious Doddridge may have been, there were still many Christians whose caution made them hesitant to be too dogmatic on such a mysterious subject.

It was only in the early nineteenth century with the establishment of the British and Foreign Bible Society and the widespread distribution of the scriptures worldwide, that the issue of inspiration emerged as a leading topic of debate. When it was discovered that, in some of its European translations, as a conciliatory gesture to Roman Catholicism, the Bible

---

[7] P. Doddridge, 'A Dissertation on the Inspiration of the New Testament as Proved from the Facts Recorded in the Historical Books of It', in *Works in Ten Volumes* (Leeds: Edward Baines, 1803), 4: 168–94. For an excellent account of Doddridge and his work, see Robert Strivens, *Philip Doddridge and the Shaping of Evangelical Dissent* [Ashgate Studies in Evangelicalism] (London: Routledge, 2016).

[8] Doddridge, *Works*, 4: 173.

Society had included the apocryphal writings of the Old Testament, the issue of inspiration began to come more prominently to the fore, as people asked themselves more precisely how *were* the biblical writings inspired and in what way were they superior to the works in the apocrypha. In consequence, even though many Anglican Prayer Books had included the apocrypha together with the canonical scriptures, a number of conservative evangelicals in the 1820s and 1830s sought to distance themselves from what they considered to be the liberal thinking of the Bible Society establishment, and accordingly, some transferred their loyalty to the Trinitarian Bible Society.[9]

It was in this context that many rigorist conservatives came to insist, more emphatically than before, on the verbal inspiration of the canonical scriptures, in the definition of which they increasingly used such adjectives as *plenary*, *verbal* or *inerrant*. By the middle of the century, the subject had indeed become a major issue in dispute, and in 1856, the editor of the *Journal of Sacred Literature and Biblical Record* was cautious to avoid committing himself too much to any one position:

> No question more divides the Church at the present time than that of the nature and extent of the divine influence exerted upon the writers of the books of Holy Scripture. Men equally orthodox, zealous, and devout, and equally acknowledging the necessity of inspiration as a quality of the documents of the faith, yet greatly differ as to the measure of that quality. We think we see indications of a tendency to go to an extreme in the assertion of plenary and verbal inspiration, and we are sorry for it, simply because we think the facts or phenomena of the subject do not bear out such a theory.[10]

9.3   SPT's Position on Inspiration

Whatever doubts the editor of the *JSL* may have had on the subject, Tregelles, like his mentor Benjamin Newton, adopted an unequivocal belief in plenary inspiration which he repeatedly affirmed. In 1844, in the introduction to the first of his published books, he made his position very clear:

---

[9] For fuller details of this debate and the divisions that it created among evangelical supporters of the Bible Society, see Stunt, *From Awakening*, 239–46.

[10] *JSL* 3 (April 1856): 203. The Editor was the Rev. Henry Burgess (1808–1886) a dissenting minister who had recently been ordained as an Anglican priest.

I avow my full belief in the absolute, plenary inspiration of Scripture, 2 Tim. 3. 16. I believe the sixty-six books of the Old and New Testaments to be verbally the Word of God, as absolutely as were the Ten Commandments written by the finger of God on the two tables of stone; and *because* I thus fully believe in its verbal inspiration, I judge that it is not labour ill bestowed to endeavour to search into the evidence which is obtainable as to what those words are, and to exhibit the results of such investigation. I trust that this may suffice to hinder charges being brought of want of reverence for the book designed to make wise unto salvation.[11]

A corollary to the affirmation of his belief that the biblical authors were verbally inspired, in their writing, was his comparable intransigence that such inspiration did not extend to the subsequent transmission of their writings. In the same publication, he emphatically denied that the inspiration, of which he was so convinced, could ensure perfection in later transmission:

But just as a copyist might err in transcribing the letters and words of the decalogue which God had thus written, so might he [the copyist] with respect to any other portion of Scripture; and it must not be looked at as want of reverence for the word of God, or want of belief in its verbal inspiration *in the fullest sense*, for this fact to be fully admitted.[12]

Unlike the biblical authors, in SPT's opinion copyists *were* fallible and to establish the original text of the scriptures required a critical evaluation of the copies that had survived. In the introduction to the first volume of his edition of the Greek New Testament (complete with textual apparatus), which was published in 1857, SPT boldly defended his work as a textual critic:

It is not for Christian scholars to fear true criticism or its results: the object of true criticism is not to alter scripture dogmatically on the judgment of any

---

[11] Samuel Prideaux Tregelles, *The Book of Revelation in Greek Edited from Ancient Authorities...* (London: Bagster, 1844) (Tregelles, *Revelation* [1844]), iii.

[12] Ibid., vii. Such a claim may be contrasted with the conviction of Canon Christopher Wordsworth (1807–1885, later Bishop of Lincoln) who in 1856 was by no means alone in affirming 'his belief, that a superintending Providence has ever been watching over the Text of the New Testament, and guiding the Church of Christ, as the Guardian and Keeper of Holy Writ, in the discharge of her duty'. C. Wordsworth, *The New Testament of Our Lord and Saviour Jesus Christ, in the Original Greek: With Notes and Introductions: The Four Gospels* (London: Rivingtons, 1859), xiii.

individual, but it is to use the EVIDENCE which has been transmitted to us, as to what the holy men of God, inspired by the Holy Ghost, actually wrote.[13]

9.4   TREGELLES, HISTORY AND PROPHECY

For a scholar like SPT who was addicted to the study of history, his Christian faith was grounded in the record of the past. To make use of a famous statement, penned some fifty years ago referring to Luther's delight in the historicity of the gospel, it was also the conviction of Tregelles that 'to Christ the centuries lead up, and from Christ the centuries lead out',[14] and his assurance that scripture was the inspired word of God meant that whether it contained a record of past events or whether it was foretelling future developments, it was to be taken seriously because it was totally reliable. In an age when many Christians refrain from any close study of the prophetic passages of scripture, because of the antics of a minority who have become obsessed with the subject, it may be difficult for us to identify with SPT in this aspect of his study, but the prophetic writings (which it should be remembered are a far from insignificant part of the scriptures) remained for the rest of his life a subject that received his devoted attention.[15] In this connection, we should remember that SPT's earliest published work (in 1836) was concerned with the way Old Testament prophecies were used in the last book of the New Testament,[16] and that he later produced two carefully expounded volumes: *Remarks on the Prophetic Visions of the Book of Daniel* (1852) and *The Hope of Christ's Second Coming: How Is It Taught in Scripture? And Why?* (1864).

[13] S.P. Tregelles, *The Greek New Testament: Edited from Ancient Authorities, with Their Various Readings in Full, and the Latin Version of Jerome*, Volume 1 [Matthew—Mark]) (London: Bagster, 1857) 'Introductory Notice,' ii.

[14] R.H. Bainton, *Studies on the Reformation* (London: Hodder and Stoughton 1964), 5.

[15] My use of the words *prophecy* and *prophetic* is in a traditional and popular sense. In current scholarly usage, prophecy often foretells events that are conditional on the hearers' positive or negative responses to moral or religious issues. This is to be distinguished from apocalyptic predictions, which are proclaimed as a fixed future, which is predestined to happen inevitably. Thus, in a more technical analysis, the Book of Daniel and most of the Book of Revelation are typically apocalyptic, as also are some passages in the Gospels, like Matthew xxiv.

[16] [S.P.T], 'Passages in the Book of Revelation Connected with the Old Testament,' *CW* 3 (1836): 58–86, 182–214, 317–59.

This is not the place to enlarge at any length on SPT's understanding of biblical prophecy, but suffice it to say that, like his respected friend and relative, Benjamin Newton, he may be classified as a pre-millennialist, who was a post-tribulational futurist. This means that in the first place, he believed that Christ would return before, as opposed to at the end of, the millennium. He was secondly convinced that most of the prophecies relating to the period before the second coming were as yet unfulfilled, and that in the course of those deteriorating future global developments there would occur the appearance of the Anti-Christ (who was not to be confused with the Papacy[17]) and the great tribulation. A third distinctive point in the eschatology of both Tregelles and Newton was their certainty that, in full view of all humanity, as opposed to secretly, believers would finally be caught up to meet the Saviour at the beginning of His millennial reign.

This scheme of prophecy put Tregelles and Newton at odds with two groups of evangelicals. Their more traditional critics were the post-millennialists, who optimistically believed that the fruitful spread of the Gospel would usher in the millennium in readiness for the return of Christ. It was somewhat ironic, however, that Tregelles and Newton faced perhaps even greater opposition from Christians who shared their belief in the pre-millennial return of the Lord, but insisted on a dispensationalist scheme in which there could occur 'at any moment' the secret rapture of the saints, who would thus avoid the 'great tribulation' of the last days before Christ's return—a position adopted most notably by John Darby and many of the Brethren with whom Tregelles had, for a time been associated.

With his majestic overview in which divine purposes intersect with human history, Tregelles could easily be carried away by his fascination for historic detail. When reading his exposition of prophecy, particularly from the Book of Daniel, the reader can often be distracted from the primary content of the prophet's message, by SPT's exultant grasp of historical detail and his presentation of the sweep of events. It has to be admitted that some of the historical details, included in his exposition, have little

---

[17] In their refusal to identify the Papacy with Anti-Christ, Newton and Tregelles were rejecting a long-held Protestant assumption. In an interesting letter to Canon Christopher Wordsworth, SPT is very emphatic: 'I fear however more from the actings of open infidelity than I do from any workings of Popery, — the real denial of God and of Christ (such as we had a specimen of in the old French Revolution) will I expect be at length fully developed and this will be, I believe *the* Anti-Christ'; SPT, Plymouth 30 January 1850, to C. Wordsworth (London/LPL, Wordsworth Papers MS2144 f.97).

bearing on the prophetic message as such. One is not surprised to find that he understood Daniel's fourth beast to represent the Roman Empire, but SPT's consideration of this part of the prophecy often becomes a pretext for a copious account of ancient history including fascinating details of the Roman occupation of Britain in more than one extended footnote.[18]

His convictions concerning the divine inspiration of scripture naturally led him to reject the suggestion of several German (and other) scholars who maintained that the Book of Daniel was *not* written by Daniel in the sixth century BC, and who claimed instead that it was actually the work of a Jewish writer living at the time of the Maccabees in the second century BC. This was not a new idea and had first been propounded by the Neoplatonic philosopher and critic of early Christianity, Porphyry of Tyre (c. AD 234–305).

The thinking behind this suggestion (which has been adopted by many modern scholars) was that, humanly speaking, it would account for the specific details particularly in the eleventh chapter of the Book of Daniel which, it was claimed, were the work of a writer who must have been acquainted with developments in the Near East following the conquests of Alexander the Great and the subsequent Seleucid Empire. By this explanation, the writer would be familiar with the career of Antiochus Epiphanes, whose infamous conduct towards the Jews, was found, by Porphyry and others, vividly described in Daniel xi.21–45. Refusing to adopt this line of thinking, SPT ultimately treats most of the eleventh chapter as an account of things, which are still in the future.

In any analysis of the Book of Daniel, the expositor has to decide at what point a hiatus has to be identified, dividing the prophecies relating to Babylon and the other ancient empires (Persian, Hellenic and Roman) from the predictions concerning the last times, as yet unfulfilled. Without accepting for a moment, Porphyry's aspersions on the authenticity of Daniel's authorship, SPT nevertheless seriously considered the possibility that the rulers portrayed in these passages were the successors of Alexander the Great, and he shows some sympathy for Jerome's adoption of Porphyry's historical interpretation of this chapter. In the end, however, SPT

---

[18] Tregelles, *Remarks on Daniel*, 61–62n, 65n, 69n, 70–71n. He even tells us twice (in the space of six pages) of the removal of the second Roman legion from Caerleon (not very far from SPT's early workplace in South Wales) to Richborough in Kent. To this reader, the details are endlessly fascinating but they have a minimal bearing on the Book of Daniel!

settled for a major hiatus at the end of verse 4 of Chapter 11 and treated everything after that as relating to the distant future.

This is a critical point in his interpretation and his position is distinctive. Albeit, recognizing the shortage of historical materials for these inter-testamental centuries, SPT the historian could not square Antiochus Epiphanes with the 'vile person' described in these last verses of the chapter, whom instead he identified as the future Anti-Christ. In his *Remarks on Daniel*, SPT allows that Antiochus *may have been* a foreshadowing or 'type' of the 'Man of Sin' described in II Thessalonians ii.3, but he settles decisively for a futurist interpretation of this last section rather than trying to stretch the historical evidence to fit a popular theory.[19]

It is worth mentioning that in this respect he even dissented from his friend and mentor, Benjamin Newton, who reckoned that the last part of Daniel xi *was* concerned with Antiochus Epiphanes. It may be coincidentally significant that SPT drew attention to this disagreement in 1852. Long after Tregelles' death, Newton recalled a time of estrangement between them, which apparently originated in the fact that SPT had visited the Great Exhibition of 1851. In this instance, it seems that Newton's sensitivities were even greater than those of his disciple. Believing that the exhibition was a symptom of Britain's descent into a godless plutocracy, Newton's convictions got the better of him for a time. Looking back almost fifty years later, he recalled:

> It nearly severed Tregelles from me. He went to it [the Exhibition]. And I felt we were walking two paths, my line very distinct and separate from his line.[20]

With increased precision in dogma, disagreements were more liable to emerge and the circle of fellowship was liable to become smaller. Fortunately, the rupture did not last too long. There is a hiatus in SPT's letters

---

[19] In an earlier essay, considering at some length these passages in Daniel, SPT made absolutely no reference to Antiochus Epiphanes; [S.P.T.] 'The Man of Sin,' *The Inquirer* 3 (June 1840): 241–56. Some ten years later he tentatively allowed that Antiochus could be a 'typical' parallel foreshadowing of the Anti-Christ (*Remarks on Daniel*, 182n).

[20] Wyatt MS Book 10 (Manchester/JRUL/CBA 7064), 141. Around the same time (March 1898) Newton was chiding himself for having helped to organize the petition for a supplement to SPTs pension from the Civil List. 'It was very wrong of me', p. 143. It was in 1852 that SPT noted the lone point of disagreement on prophetic subjects in *Remarks on Daniel*, 181.

to Newton from July 1851 until February 1856 by which time their correspondence had resumed.

9.5   THE CHALLENGE OF 'NEOLOGY'

9.5.1   SPT's Rigorist Attitude to Gesenius

In his desire to give no quarter to those with a more flexible approach to biblical inspiration, Tregelles found himself involved in a fair amount of printed controversy. Early on in his biblical studies, in spite of his belief in plenary inspiration, he had recognized the valuable scholarship of the German orientalist, Wilhelm Gesenius (1786–1842) but, as might be expected, was deeply troubled by the German scholar's cavalier attitude to the reliability of the Bible. Anxious to make Gesenius's linguistic expertise available to serious students of scripture, one of SPT's earliest publications was his translation, into English, of the German scholar's massive Hebrew and Chaldee *Lexicon Manuale*. This had been attempted before by an American orientalist, Edward Robinson but, possibly because in his early days when studying at Halle University the translator had lodged in Gesenius's home, Robinson refrained from overtly disagreeing with the older scholar who had effectively become his theological mentor. Instead, he merely omitted or modified passages of which he disapproved in the original.[21] Compromise of that sort was not SPT's way of doing things and his translation of the Lexicon was thorough and faithful—perhaps rather more than faithful!

Energetically rejecting the aspersions that Gesenius had cast on biblical reliability—aspersions, which Tregelles maintained were misguided and unfounded—he took the trouble to insert in square brackets his own corrections of what he considered to be Gesenius's false statements.[22] He was particularly indignant and intervened in no fewer than three places to

---

[21] William Gesenius, *A Hebrew and English Lexicon of the Old Testament, Including the Biblical Chaldee*, translated from the Latin of William Gesenius, by Edward Robinson (Boston: Crocker and Brewster, 1836). For Edward Robinson's friendship with Gesenius, see J.G. Williams, *The Times and Life of Edward Robinson: Connecticut Yankee in King Solomon's Court* (Atlanta, GA: Soc. Biblical Lit., 1999), 138–46. Williams refers to Gesenius as Robinson's 'great German mentor', p. 301.

[22] Tregelles, *Gesenius's Lexicon*. See above Chapter 4, Footnote 32, and Chapter 6, Footnote 48. A typical example of SPT's 'corrections' in square brackets, reaffirming the reliability of scripture, is his curt addition to Gesenius's account of 'Bethel' ['The inspired account is plain enough and contains neither discrepancy nor contradiction'], p. CXVII.

correct the way Gesenius rejected a Christian interpretation of the Messianic prophecies of the servant [*Ebed*] in the Book of Isaiah.[23] Indeed, as if such individual corrections were not enough Tregelles insisted in the introduction to his work:

> It has been a special object with the translator, to note the interpretations of Gesenius, which manifested neologian tendencies, in order that by a remark, or by querying a statement, the reader may be put on his guard. And if any passages should remain unmarked, in which doubt is cast upon Scripture inspiration, or in which the New and Old Testaments are spoken of as discrepant, or in which mistakes and ignorance are charged upon the "holy men of God who wrote as they were moved by the Holy Ghost," — if any perchance remain in which these or any other neologian tendencies be left unnoticed — the translator wishes it distinctly to be understood that it is the effect of inadvertence alone, and not of design.[24]

As we shall see, such thoroughgoing rigorism was bound to bring him into conflict with others, but curiously, in one instance it was misunderstood.

In a lengthy survey of the 'recent' progress of Hebrew studies in England, an 'occasional reviewer' in the *Churchman's Monthly Review* praised the publishers, Samuel Bagster and Sons for the stream of Hebrew Grammars and Lexicons issuing from their presses, designating them (in contrast to the universities of Oxford and Cambridge,) 'the Atlas whose ample shoulders sustain the entire orb of Hebrew literature in England'.[25] He went on to extol the value of SPT's translation of Gesenius, insisting that the German's grammar and Lexicon (translated into English) were far more accurate and useful than the similar productions of Professor Samuel Lee, of Cambridge. To challenge this distinguished linguist was a hazardous undertaking and the querulous professor, who readily engaged in a variety of polemics, didn't take kindly to the favourable rating given to Tregelles for his edition of Gesenius. In the ensuing exchange of correspondence,

---

[23] For fuller detail, see G. Davies, 'The Reception of Gesenius's Dictionary in England,' in S. Schorch, E.-J. Waschke [eds.], *Biblische Exegese und hebräische Lexikographie: Das "Hebräisch-deutsche Handwörterbuch" von Wilhelm Gesenius als Spiegel und Quelle alttestamentlicher und hebräischer Forschung, 200 Jahre nach seiner ersten Auflage* (Berlin and Boston: Walter de Gruyter, 2013), 520.

[24] Tregelles, *Gesenius's Lexicon*, v.

[25] Anonymous, 'Works on Hebrew Literature,' *Churchman's Monthly Review and Chronicle* 5 (February 1847): 136.

Lee foolishly confused the German scholar with his translator and wrongly charged Tregelles with being 'tinctured with Neologian sentiments'. Furiously but curtly SPT responded repeating the part of his preface that we quoted earlier, with the observation: 'These were my sentiments when I translated Gesenius's Lexicon, and every one who has read the Preface might *know* that they were such'.[26]

9.5.2   Horne's 'Introduction'

Many years earlier in 1818, long before Tregelles's evangelical conversion, a learned and pious scholar and bibliographer, Thomas Hartwell Horne, had published *An Introduction To the Critical Study and Knowledge of the Holy Scriptures*, which soon became a standard textbook for divinity students and was reissued and enlarged in a series of new editions during the thirty years between 1818 and 1848. As early as 1828, Horne had made his position on biblical inspiration very clear when he stated categorically:

> It is sufficient to believe, that by the general superintendence of the Holy Spirit, they [the Biblical writers] were directed in the choice of their materials, enlightened to judge of the truth and importance of those accounts from which they borrowed their information, and prevented from recording any material error.[27]

Perhaps, we should note that this was in fact an unacknowledged quotation from George Tomline, successively Bishop of Lincoln and Winchester, whose very popular *Elements of Christian Theology* first appeared in 1799. In this volume, the Bishop had made clear that in affirming the principle of 'superintendence' he was only advocating an overall controlling inspiration that kept the scriptures free from error,[28] and in his *Introduction* Horne likewise avoided proclaiming anything as absolute and categorical as plenary inspiration.

[26] S. Prideaux Tregelles, 20 August 1847, 'To the Editor of the Churchman's Monthly Review,' *Churchman's Monthly Review* (August 1847): 648.

[27] Thomas Hartwell Horne, *An Introduction to the Critical Study and Knowledge of the Holy Scriptures*, 6th ed. (London: T. Cadell, 1828), vol. 1 Appendix No. II 'On Inspiration', 515.

[28] George Tomline [formerly Pretyman], *Elements of Christian Theology: Proofs of the Authenticity and Inspiration of the Holy Scriptures ...*, 2 vols, 9th ed. (London: T Cadell and W. Davies, 1812), 23–24.

After forty years of unquestioned usefulness, this reference book was increasingly in need of revision, but the situation was becoming more complicated as the ranks of biblical scholars had evidently become more divided on the subject of inspiration: conservative scholars like SPT recognized the various advances made in biblical archaeology and linguistic scholarship, but their more precise definition of plenary inspiration was setting them apart from some other scholars. On the other hand, in 1854 Hartwell Horne was in his seventies and felt inadequate for the task of updating the whole of his *Introduction*. With his agreement therefore, the publishing company of Longmans undertook to produce what would effectively be not just a revision of Horne's work but a completely new edition, with parts of it rewritten by younger scholars, incorporating some of the fruits of recent scholarship.

9.5.3   Samuel Davidson

The man whom Longmans approached in the first instance, and asked to revise the Old Testament section of Horne's *Introduction* was Samuel Davidson (1806–1898) an Irish scholar who, a few years earlier, had abandoned his earlier Presbyterian identity in favour of Congregationalism. As a minister, he had been appointed in 1842 to the chair of biblical literature and ecclesiastical history in the Lancashire Independent College at Manchester.[29] In choosing a younger man, in his forties, to revise Horne's work, Longmans were turning to an academic who was personally acquainted with a number of German scholars like the theologian August Tholuck and the orientalist Hermann Hupfeld,[30] and who, in his own publications, had shown himself to be familiar with the work of these scholars.

Davidson's standing had been further enhanced in 1848 when the University of Halle awarded him an honorary doctorate in theology. For reasons that will soon become apparent, we must note that Tregelles was similarly full of admiration for Davidson's work. In a semi-anonymous review in the *Journal of Sacred Literature* for 1849, he applauded the second volume of

[29] This and any other unreferenced details concerning Davidson are taken from Anne Jane Davidson [ed.], *The Autobiography and Diary of Samuel Davidson: With a Selection of Letters from English and German Divines, and an Account [by James Allanson Picton] of the Davidson Controversy of 1857* (Edinburgh: T. & T. Clark, 1899) [Davidson, *Autobiography*].

[30] Both F. August G. Tholuck (1799–1877) and Hermann Hupfeld (1796–1866) were professors in the theological faculty at Halle University.

Davidson's *Introduction to the New Testament*,[31] treating the author as a valued ally in the cause of biblical truth:

> As inquiries with regard to Scripture have been so widely taken up by men of learning and research, who are really opposed to Scripture and to all revelation, and as these inquiries *are* more and more made known, it is in a manner incumbent on the friends of Scripture and Revelation to know *what* those inquiries are — to meet the cavils which might injure the uninstructed, and to obtain such a fundamental knowledge of the whole subject as shall (through God's blessing) be a safeguard against the inroads of cavillers. Of one thing we may be sure, self-satisfied blindness is no safeguard for ourselves or for others in such cases ...
>
> [But] Dr. Davidson tells us what the arguments are by which Scripture is assailed; he instructs how such arguments are met and refuted; he introduces [us] to those points of investigation by which a really accurate knowledge of the Scripture may be attained. Most sincerely do we trust that his labours will be amply appreciated, and that a more extensive acquaintance with the whole range of biblical inquiry may again be found in this country.[32]

That Tregelles at this stage had a high opinion of Davidson is further demonstrated in a lengthy paper that he contributed to the *Journal of Sacred Literature* strongly supporting Davidson's suggestion that Matthew's Gospel was originally written in Hebrew.[33]

We cannot be sure of the extent to which Davidson valued SPT's approval, but it may have been a contributing factor in the recommendation that he made in 1854 that Dr. Tregelles was suitably qualified to undertake the rewriting of the fourth volume of Horne's *Introduction* which was devoted to the New Testament. Longman's publishing house followed Davidson's recommendation, and in his acceptance of their proposition, Tregelles committed himself to the production of a massively detailed piece

[31] S. Davidson, *Introduction to the New Testament, Containing an Examination of the Most Important Questions Relating to the Authority, Interpretation, and Integrity of the Canonical Books, with Reference to the Latest Inquiries*, Vol. ii. *The Acts of the Apostles to the Second Epistle to the Thessalonians* (London: Samuel Bagster and Sons, 1849).

[32] 'Davidson's Introduction to the New Testament', *JSL* 4 (October 1849): 344–45. The review was only semi-anonymous because although it was unsigned, SPT was identified, in the index, as the author (p. 423.)

[33] Tregelles, *Original Language*. SPT later complicated his hypothesis by relating it to his belief in the superiority of the Nitrian or Curetonian version of the Syriac New Testament over the Peshitto.

of work. His *Account of the Printed Text of the Greek New Testament*[34] had just been published by Bagsters and now the new edition of Horne's *Introduction* provided an excellent opportunity to provide a comprehensive survey of the mass of MS material—much of it only recently publicized—and of the questions that were currently engaging New Testament textual critics.

The first 400 pages therefore were to be a completely new work dealing with the textual criticism of the Greek New Testament, which of course, was SPT's speciality, while the remaining 350 pages would be a rewriting and updating of Horne's original work on this part of the Bible. It was a task that would occupy many hours of SPT's life during the next two years, necessarily competing with his text (and apparatus) of the New Testament to which this Introduction would be a valuable supplement. However, there was a problem that proved to be rather more than just a fly in the ointment.

As is not unusual with scholars in their mid-forties, some of Davidson's convictions were changing, and his studies were leading him to modify some of his previously held positions. On his own admission, as indeed had been the case with Tregelles, there had been some changes in his ecclesiastical attitudes. Effectively, Davidson had abandoned some of his earlier Congregationalism, having decided that the scriptures do not provide an ecclesiastical blueprint for later times, but rather 'that Church government is a matter of expediency'.[35]

Such a change would hardly, in itself, have caused much of a problem, as his teaching and published work were not concerned with such issues.

More serious, however, was his growing sympathy for some of the beliefs of scholars (often German) who had serious doubts about the Mosaic origins of the Pentateuch and who questioned the traditional dating of some Old Testament literature as well as the Davidic authorship of some of the Psalms. A shift in Davidson's own position on such questions, particularly that of the documentary hypothesis for the origins of the Pentateuch was now becoming apparent, and perhaps, it was most evident in the volume

[34] Tregelles, *Account* (1854).
[35] Davidson, *Autobiography*, 24.

that he contributed to the new edition of Horne's *Introduction*, and which was published in October 1856.[36]

9.5.4   Controversy

Less than a week after the *Introduction's* publication, Tregelles wrote the following letter to the evangelical newspaper, *The Record*:

> Sir, — As the new edition of *Horne's Introduction* bears, in conjunction with the names of the Rev. T. H. Horne and Dr Samuel Davidson, *my own*, as one of the editors, perhaps you will allow me to state that Mr. Horne and myself are only responsible for the sentiments expressed in those portions which we respectively undertook to edit.
>
> In writing on the subject of Holy Scripture, I trust that I have ever sought to uphold its plenary authority as inspired by the Holy Ghost; and thus it has been with sorrow, as well as surprise, that I have observed that Dr Davidson has used this work as the occasion for avowing and bringing into notice many sentiments and theories with regard to Scripture which his former works would not have intimated that he held, and his adoption of which was *wholly unknown* to Mr. Horne and myself. We find ourselves thus in an unexpected position, being in danger of being supposed to be, in some measure, responsible for opinions which we earnestly repudiate. Indeed, I may say that I am grieved that what I have written with a different object, and on different principles, should appear as part of the same work as that against which I feel bound to protest. *Plymouth*, 29 October 1856. S. Prideaux Tregelles.

This[37] and similar letters from Horne and himself appeared in several reviews causing consternation among some of Davidson's colleagues on the governing Committee of the Lancashire Independent College, with

---

[36] *An Introduction to the Critical Study and Knowledge of the Holy Scriptures.* The Tenth Edition, revised, corrected, and brought down to the present time. Edited by the Rev. T. Hartwell Horne, B. D. (the Author;) the Rev. S. Davidson, D. D., of the University of Halle, and LL. D.; and S. P. Tregelles, LL. D., 4 vols. (London: Longman, 1856).

[37] The text given here is taken from the reprinting of SPT's letter in Thomas Nicholas, *Dr. Davidson's Removal from the Professorship of Biblical Literature in the Lancashire Independent College, Manchester, on Account of Alleged Error in Doctrine: A Statement of Facts, with Documents; Together with Remarks and Criticisms* (London and Edinburgh: Williams and Norgate, 1860), 12. A slightly different text appeared in the *Quarterly Journal of Prophecy* 9 (January 1857): 66–67.

the ultimate result that the pressure of their criticism forced him to resign his position in the college. The episode deeply embittered Davidson, as is apparent from his recollection that he and his family were 'turned out of house and home, with a name tainted and maligned ... My enemies succeeded in blasting my name and blighting my prospect of public usefulness among Congregationalists'.[38] For the rest of his life, he despised the pious convictions of Tregelles, dismissing them as 'partisan zeal' and 'dogmatic prepossessions'.[39] To be fair, there were some grounds for his resentment.

In the controversy, to which SPT's letter gave rise, Davidson pointed out that it had been he who had recommended Tregelles as a co-editor in the first place, but he also claimed that the agreement had been that each of the editors would be solely responsible for the text of his own work. 'Both [Horne and Tregelles] had as much to do with me in regard to authority and prerogative as I had to do with them; that is, *nothing whatever*. All that was stipulated in the legal contract was that each should look over and revise the proof-sheets of the whole work, so that there might be no "accidental discrepancies"'.[40]

In a lengthy letter to the editor of the *Journal of Sacred Literature*, Tregelles recalled the contract somewhat differently.[41] He recognized that Davidson had been 'fully empowered ... to re-write all that he might consider to be desirable', but Tregelles reckoned that this was 'subject to one proviso', that all such alterations 'should pass under the eye of the Rev. T.H. Horne himself, in order that there might be no collision as to the facts or general principles expressed in the work'. In SPT's opinion,

[38] Davidson, *Autobiography*, 34. His account of the episode is so minimal that in preparing his Autobiography for publication, his daughter had to include a chapter by one of Davidson's former students, James Allanson Picton, to cover the controversy.

[39] Both phrases occur in Davidson's unsigned review of SPT's edition of the *Canon Muratorianus* (Oxford, 1867) in *The Athenaeum* (16 May 1868) quoted in Earl Hilgert, 'Two Unpublished Letters Regarding Tregelles' *Canon Muratorianus*,' *Andrews University Seminary Studies* 5 (July 1967): 124.

[40] It was many years ago that I was able to consult Samuel Davidson's, *Facts, Statements and Explanations, Connected with the Publication of the Second Volume of the Tenth Edition of Horne's Introduction to the Study of the Holy Scriptures,* etc. (London: Longmans, 1857) and currently I have no access to it but this passage from page 45 is cited in 'Correspondence' in *JSL* 6 (January 1858): 384.

[41] S.P. Tregelles, 'Dr S. Davidson and Horne's Introduction,' *JSL* 4 (January 1857): 424–25. This is the source for all the quotations in the next two paragraphs.

this proviso was made not as though it would be needful to correct any such points, — *for their introduction was not contemplated* — but rather as giving to Mr. Horne a proper power as to the execution of the new edition of a work which has so long borne his name: but though the need of such a stipulation had not been contemplated, it was provided that if such necessity should arise, whatever statements were deemed improper should be extruded at Mr. Horne's desire.

The result of this arrangement, according to Tregelles, was that 'when statements were introduced to which Mr. Horne objected as not being in accordance with his sentiments, he pointed such things out to Dr. Davidson, expressing his feeling and judgement in the matter, with which it was Dr. Davidson's place of course to comply'. Unfortunately, the outcome proved to have been different because Davidson appeared to have ignored Horne's objections.

From Davidson's point of view, Tregelles's protest to the public that he had been surprised by Davidson's 'avowing and bringing into notice many sentiments and theories … his adoption of which was *wholly unknown* to Mr. Horne and myself', was disingenuous, to say the least, as both Horne and Tregelles had seen the proofs. Indeed, Davidson quoted a letter in which Tregelles had said to Davidson, referring to his work on the Pentateuch where he seemed to have favoured Hermann Hupfeld's theories: 'I did not expect to find a reference to Elohim documents and other theories of that school'.[42]

Tregelles self-justification would have presumably been that when the contract was made, they had been ignorant of Davidson's views, and they were surprised because Davidson had ignored their objections.

There was, on the other hand, something similarly disingenuous in the claim of J. A. Picton (whose account of the controversy was included in Davidson's *Autobiography*) when he claimed that 'while proofs were constantly interchanged between Mr. Horne, Dr. Tregelles, and himself [Davidson], no hint was given that either of his colleagues had any apprehension that his work would create alarm'.[43]

---

[42] *Facts, Statements and Explanations, Connected with the Publication of the Second Volume of the Tenth Edition of Horne's Introduction to the Study of the Holy Scriptures,* etc. (London: Longmans, 1857) cited in 'Correspondence,' *JSL* 6 (January 1858): 393.

[43] Davidson, *Autobiography*, 41.

It was an unpleasant controversy and neither side emerged with much credit. For Tregelles it was something of a watershed as he found that the new editors of such a respected periodical as the *Journal of Sacred Literature* were clearly now on a rather different wavelength from himself over inspiration. While noting Davidson's 'surliness' and 'almost supercilious disdain' for Horne and Tregelles, the editor of the *Journal* nevertheless reckoned, that a person holding Davidson's views could still be 'a firm believer in Divine Revelation or in the Scriptures as given by inspiration of God'. Going further he protested 'against biblical science being thrown back three centuries by a sort of papal intolerance', and he condemned the 'barbarous' way in which *The Record* (which had carried SPT's letter) was 'treating all who cannot indorse its ignorant and bigoted views'.[44] For Tregelles this must have been the writing on the wall suggesting that he was now seriously isolated from a significant part of the world of biblical scholarship, and something of a lone voice in the pages of a journal which had previously often been a vehicle for his articles, reviews and letters.

9.6   OPPOSITION FROM CONSERVATIVES

When Tregelles felt there was a principle at stake, his valour was sometimes liable to get the better of his charity, and this was not confined to his loyal advocacy of plenary inspiration. We observed in another context his chagrin with the Spanish Protestants when he felt they had let their benefactors down. We have also noted his impatience with the British and Foreign Bible Society on account of their failure to provide faithful versions of the Bible for use in Roman Catholic-dominated countries. Likewise in his disagreements with others over the need for textual investigation or accurate translation, his argumentation could be not just relentless but also dry and a bit sarcastic—particularly if he felt his opponents were ignorant or illogical.

One such antagonist was a restless character, Jacob Tomlin (1793–1880) who after graduating from St John's College, Cambridge had tried his hand as a pioneering and far from settled evangelist in the Far East from 1826 to 1836, before returning to England where in due course he was ordained and became something of an ecclesiastical rolling stone with six one year curacies during twenty years, before 'settling down' in his seventies

[44] *JSL* 4 (January 1857): 484.

as a Northamptonshire vicar.[45] He appears to have been a gifted (albeit somewhat *dilettante*) linguist and produced *A comparative vocabulary of forty-eight languages* (in which he claimed that a quarter of the words of the Saxon tongue have a close affinity to Hebrew) as well as becoming involved in the controversy about how the name of God should be translated into Chinese.

Like many conservative evangelicals, Tomlin clung to the *textus receptus* which had been the basis for the authorized version, and he was appalled at the suggestion that there could be any doubt as to the authenticity of the longer ending of Mark's Gospel or the *pericope adulterae* in the earlier verses of John Chapter 8. As one of the many self-appointed teachers who gave their opinions on any number of textual and interpretative questions in the *Christian Annotator*, Tomlin protested 'strenuously', at the latest edition of Tischendorf's Greek New Testament for its omission of the eunuch's baptismal confession in Acts viii.37, one of many scriptures that he claimed had been 'universally received by the Church for many centuries as genuine portions of the Word of God'. He roundly concluded: 'The subject is of great importance, and demands the serious attention of Christians and divines'.[46]

True to his convictions, SPT could not stand idly by! In response, he wrote: 'It will be, I hope, permissible for me to set the Rev. J. Tomlin right as to two facts relative to Acts viii.37'. Going on to establish that the verse is missing in *all* the ancient MSS and almost all the ancient versions, SPT insisted: 'The ancient text is that to which we must adhere, and common use can no more make this sentence part of the word of God, than Romish tradition can make her dogmas to be the truth of God … in all these things we must inquire, what did the authors of Scripture write, as determined by evidence, and not by mere usage or tradition of later times?'[47] Effectively he was repeating what he had been saying for years and would have to reiterate for the rest of his life: 'Critics are not necessarily void of reverence for Holy Scripture; and such charges might be just as well brought against Protestants for not receiving the Apocrypha'.[48]

[45] For Tomlin, see *Al Cantab.* 6: 204 and John Roxborogh at http://roxborogh.com/Biographies/tomlin2.htm [accessed 3 June 2019].

[46] *Christian Annotator* i. (23 December 1854): 356.

[47] Ibid., 2 (20 January 1855): 21.

[48] Ibid., 1 (8 July 1854): 181.

Needless to say, Tomlin didn't abandon the fight! Ten years later he was taking up the issue in the *Record* newspaper but Tregelles was losing enthusiasm for what had become a tedious contest, as he observed in a letter to Newton:

> Mr. Jacob Tomlin is I believe a clergyman, and I think that he must be an old man: he has long been rather conspicuous for his opposition to all textual criticism. He used to write a good deal on the subject in the Christian Annotator, until the editor took him up a little for his false quotations, and uncharitable accusations. He assumes that if a MS. omits anything, found in the common text, it is an intentional 'cancelling', 'a glaring suppression of God's word', a 'rejection of the revelation of the Holy Ghost', etc. He was diligent years ago in warning every one against me and my Greek Test: but I thought that he had become quiet as I have heard nothing of him for a long time.[49]

About a year later Tomlin, now in his seventies, collected a number of letters he had written for *The Constitution* newspaper and published them as *Critical remarks on Dr Tregelles' Greek Text of the Revelation and his two English versions compared with the Received Text and Authorised translation*[50] but when SPT saw it advertised he reckoned 'it will however, be hardly worth my while to look at his book'.[51]

SPT found it hard to suffer fools gladly. On one occasion, when a journalist at one of the Barnet Conferences, sarcastically suggested that 'when their Lord returns ... some would be learnedly discussing the value of MSS', it was understandable that SPT took the criticism personally. When some of the conference participants exhibited what SPT called 'dreamy sentimentalism... [and] asked if I had ever considered that it is very unspiritual and quite *unscriptural* to be occupied with textual criticism: I took the liberty

---

[49] SPT (Plymouth, 21 January 1864) to B.W. Newton (Manchester/JRUL/CBA 7181 [61]).

[50] J. Tomlin, *Critical remarks on Dr Tregelles' Greek Text of the Revelation and His Two English Versions Compared with the Received Text and Authorised Translation Showing the Great Superiority of the Latter, by a Close and Candid Examination of His Various Readings, Tested by the Context, Parallel Places, and General Analogy of Scripture* (Liverpool: Arthur Newling, 1865).

[51] SPT (Plymouth, 27 July 1865) to B.W. Newton (Manchester/JRUL/CBA 7181 [84]).

of asking them if they had not thought how unscriptural it is to use printed books at all'.[52]

9.7   The Gentler Side of Disagreement

Although controversy often had a polemical dimension, disagreement was not always a cause for hostility. In such conflicts, SPT was concerned with issues and principles, and rarely descended to *argumenta ad homines*. While maintaining his concern for truth and accuracy, Tregelles could readily respond to the charm and kindliness of scholars with whom he disagreed. In his dispute with Davidson he made very clear that he would not for a moment entertain the possibility of a non-Mosaic origin for the Pentateuch,[53] but more than once SPT acknowledged in print his appreciative friendship with Wilhelm de Wette who was another proponent of the very documentary hypothesis of which Tregelles was so critical. As we noticed earlier the German scholar from Basel made a great impression on SPT: 'I am under great obligations to [him], and I would that his theological views were such that I could speak as highly of them as I can of his personal kindness and urbanity, and also of his laboriousness in the department of Biblical learning'.[54]

It is in fact, quite possible that de Wette's graciousness prompted SPT to think more carefully about the issue of inspiration. It was during his stay in Basel in 1846 when he first met de Wette that Tregelles also spent some time with Dr William Marriott, a former teacher of English Literature in the University and Pädagogium and a founding member of the Evangelical

---

[52] SPT (Plymouth, 9 December 1863) to B.W. Newton (Manchester/JRUL/CBA 7181 [59]). In July 1863, SPT had attended the seventh (and last) Barnet conference hosted by Rev. William Pennefather.

[53] The strength of his feelings on this issue was all the more evident in 1862 when Bishop John Colenso (1814–83) questioned the veracity of the Pentateuch. Colenso had been a pupil of SPT's friend Henry Addington Greaves, the Vicar of Charles Church, Plymouth, who shared with SPT his distress at 'Colenso's infidel statements ... [and] the falsehood of his teaching and the mischief of his course'. SPT (Westbrook [Plymouth], 17 October 1862) to B.W. Newton (Manchester/JRUL/CBA 7181 [31]).

[54] S.P. Tregelles, *The Book of Revelation Translated from the Ancient Greek Text. With an Historical Sketch of the Printed Text of the Greek New Testament*, etc. A new edition, with a notice of a Palimpsest MS. hitherto unused. (London: S. Bagster & Sons, 1859 [1849]), 63. (Cf. Tregelles, *Prospectus of a Critical Edition* ..., 17).

Alliance.[55] Marriott's evangelical credentials were not in doubt but his respect for those with a different approach to scripture made a considerable impression on SPT who recalled it after another visit to Basel:

> Dr Marriott told me eleven years ago that there was more honesty and more real principle amongst not a few who were called rationalistic, than amongst the mass of the so-called orthodox and evangelical Christians in those parts.[56]

It was a judgement that tallied with SPT's generous tribute to de Wette, with whom he strongly disagreed on matters of biblical interpretation. In fact, his words of affectionate respect date from 1849 shortly before De Wette's death, and before Tregelles had seen De Wette's exposition of the Book of Revelation. In this, his last work, the German scholar appeared in a rather different light. In the face of the revolutionary turmoil in Europe (1848–49) De Wette seemed to have recovered some of his earlier orthodoxy—a development to which, in a footnote to a later edition of his own translation of the Revelation, SPT was glad to draw his readers' attention. Clearly, he was greatly reassured that this good friend had finally been able to affirm: 'this only I know, that in no other name is there salvation but in the name of Jesus Christ the crucified …' There is a charmingly affectionate element in SPT's concluding words about his friend: 'With my stay at Basle in 1846 De Wette was closely associated: his grave in the cemetery of St. Elizabeth, had a melancholy interest to me in visiting that city in 1857'.[57]

In recalling this human aspect of SPT's principled loyalty to his understanding of scripture, we may close this chapter with the generous judgement of an American Unitarian scholar, Ezra Abbot (1819–1884):

> Dr. Tregelles was a man of great simplicity of character and deep religious feeling; a devout believer in the plenary verbal inspiration of the Scriptures and in the doctrines usually denominated evangelical. For any form of 'rationalism' or any deviation from the doctrines, which he regarded as fundamental,

---

[55] For an excellent account of the work of William Marriott (1808–64), see Nicholas M. Railton, *No North Sea: The Anglo-German Evangelical Network in the Middle of the Nineteenth Century* [Studies in Christian Mission, xxiv] (Leiden: Brill, 1999), 130–33.

[56] SPT (Geneva, 29 July 1857) to B.W. Newton (Manchester/JRUL/CBA 7181[12]).

[57] Tregelles, *Revelation* (1859), 63–64n. Perhaps, it should be added that his biographer has argued that de Wette's final position was more complex than the words, quoted by Tregelles, may suggest and warns against taking this affirmation out of its wider context, Rogerson, *de Wette*, 256.

he had no toleration ... Whether or not his zeal was always enlightened need not be discussed. It was honest, and not prompted by malevolence; his denunciations were uttered more in sorrow than in anger ... Rare indeed are the examples of such patient, unwearied, self-sacrificing devotion to a noble object as his life presents, and ever honored be his memory![58]

[58] Ezra Abbot, 'The Late Dr. Tregelles' (*The Independent*, 1 July 1875) reprinted in *The Authorship of the Fourth Gospel, and Other Critical Essays* (Boston: G. H. Ellis, 1888), 182–83.

CHAPTER 10

Tregelles and Tischendorf

10.1 Two Single-Minded Scholars

It was in September 1850 that Tregelles arrived in Leipzig and had his first meeting with Constantine Tischendorf[1] The parallels and contrasts in their careers are striking. The German scholar was two years younger and as a youth had enjoyed a comfortable bourgeois lifestyle. In the case of SPT, the bankruptcy and death of his father had brought the boy's formal education to an abrupt end when he was barely fifteen years old; in contrast, Tischendorf was already an undergraduate at Leipzig University when he lost both his parents. The story of the Cornish autodidact, denied a university education, employed in a Welsh iron foundry, and snatching time to study ancient languages is patently different from the doctorate awarded to the comfortably successful university student at Leipzig.

For a time, Tischendorf's finances had been a bit uncertain but with support from members of the theological faculty, he obtained a government subsidy for two successive years and soon his prolific record of publication became a source of income supplemented by the liberality of his older brother, together with private and royal sponsorship. In contrast, Tregelles

---

[1] An adequate, albeit somewhat over-admiring, recent account of Tischendorf is S.E. Porter's *Constantine Tischendorf: The Life and Work of a 19th Century Bible Hunter* (London: Bloomsbury, 2015).

© The Author(s) 2020   143
T. C. F. Stunt, *The Life and Times of Samuel Prideaux Tregelles*,
Christianities in the Trans-Atlantic World,
https://doi.org/10.1007/978-3-030-32266-3_10

had no academic affiliation and his finances were always somewhat precarious, as his wife had only a modest inheritance and he was reluctant to take the generosity of Benjamin Newton for granted. It was only in June 1863 that he was awarded a pension of £100 from the British government's Civil List.

In 1844, a little more than a year before Tregelles set out for Rome, Tischendorf undertook a much more ambitious project, having been subsidized by the Saxon government, to visit monasteries in Egypt, Palestine, Patmos and Constantinople. Originally, Mount Athos had also been part of the programme but even without visiting the monastic peninsula, Tischendorf brought back from his travels a variety of Greek, Coptic, Armenian and Syriac MSS with which he had persuaded the monks to part.

10.2   A Tradition of Acquisition

The West European traveller in the Near East is a familiar feature of early nineteenth-century memoirs, and Tischendorf was not the first to wonder whether Greek orthodox monasteries might possess unknown manuscripts of interest. Earlier pioneers had made their intrepid way and, like Edward Daniel Clarke [1769–1822], had shared with their readers the low opinion they had of the orthodox monks' attitude to scholarship. Visiting the monastery of St John on the island of Patmos in 1802, Clarke had been appalled at the chaos:

> At the extremity of this chamber, which is opposite to the window, a considerable number of old volumes of parchment, some with covers and some without, were heaped upon the floor in the utmost disorder; and there were evident proofs that these had been cast aside, and condemned to answer any purpose for which the parchment might be required. When we asked the Superior what they were? he replied, turning up his nose with an expression of indifference and contempt, Χειρόγραφα! [Manuscripts]. It was indeed a moment in which a literary traveller might be supposed to doubt the evidence of his senses, for the whole of this contemned heap consisted entirely of Greek manuscripts, and some of them were of the highest antiquity.

In fact, Clarke was primarily interested in coins and mineralogy, but soon discovered an exquisite copy of Plato's *Dialogues*. Anxious not 'to betray any extraordinary desire to get possession of these treasures [which] would inevitably prevent all possibility of obtaining any of them', Clarke casually separated what he wanted 'from a quantity of theological writings, detached fragments, worm-eaten wooden covers (that had belonged to books once literally bound in boards), scraps of parchment, Lives of Hermits, and other litter …'.[2]

Travellers often described experiences of this sort with decided disdain for the 'knavish' Greek monks who were usually characterized by English visitors as woefully ignorant. This was very much the case in the future Lord Curzon's *Visits to Monasteries in the Levant*—a singularly entertaining volume. The account of his visit to the monastery of Caracalla on Mount Athos is deservedly well-known:

> The library I found to be a dark closet near the entrance of the church; it had been locked up for many years, but the *agoumenos* [abbot] made no difficulty in breaking the old- fashioned padlock by which the door was fastened. I found upon the ground and upon some broken-down shelves about four or five hundred volumes, chiefly printed books; but amongst them, every now and then, I stumbled upon a manuscript: of these there were about thirty on vellum and fifty or sixty on paper. I picked up a single loose leaf of very ancient uncial Greek characters, part of the Gospel of St. Matthew, written in small square letters and of small quarto size. I searched in vain for the volume to which this leaf belonged … however, I made bold to ask for this single leaf as a thing of small value. "Certainly"! said the *agoumenos*, "what do you want it for"? My servant suggested that, perhaps, it might be useful to cover some jam pots or vases of preserves, which I had at home. "Oh"! said the *agoumenos*. "Take some more"; and without more ado, he seized upon an unfortunate thick quarto manuscript of the Acts and Epistles, and drawing out a knife cut out an inch thickness of leaves at the end before I could stop him. It proved to be the Apocalypse, which concluded the volume, but which is rarely found in early Greek manuscripts of the Acts: it was of the eleventh century. I ought, perhaps, to have slain the *tomecide* [book killer] for his dreadful act of profanation, but his generosity reconciled me to his guilt, so I pocketed the Apocalypse, and asked him if he would sell me any of the other books, as he did not appear to set any particular value upon them. "Malista [most], certainly," he replied; "how many will you have? They are of no use to me, and as I am in want of money to complete my buildings I shall be very glad to turn them to some account."[3]

---

[2] E.D. Clarke, *Travels in Various Countries of Europe, Asia and Africa. Part the Second: Greece, Egypt and the Holy Land: Section the Second* (London: Cadell and Davies, 1814), 345–6, 348, 349.

[3] R. Curzon, *Visits to Monasteries in the Levant* (London: Humphrey Milford, 1916 [1849]), 365–66. The twelfth-century MS of the Apocalypse is now in the British Museum

10.3   Tischendorf's Secret Discovery

When Tischendorf set out in 1844, he was doubtless aware of such accounts recorded by his predecessors but he would also have been familiar with the report given by another textual scholar of the Greek New Testament, Johann Martin Augustin Scholz, who had published some details of his travels in 1821. Scholz, who had corresponded with Tregelles in the 1840s, made it his business to share with other scholars the details of a number of valuable manuscripts, which he had discovered in a variety of libraries,[4] but his verdict on the monasteries of Egypt was not encouraging:

> Very few monks in Upper Egypt understand Coptic well, and the patriarch said he had known but one who spoke it. I do not believe that there are any ancient MSS. in the convents, or that the inscriptions in their churches are at all interesting, either to history or paleography… nor [do] the two Greek convent libraries (those of the Patriarch and of Mount Sinai) contain any MSS. interesting in a literary view, because they have been always the most exposed to pillage.[5]

In fact, as the world would learn, at a much later stage, Tischendorf's discoveries surpassed his wildest expectations and were far from fruitless. In his very much later account [in 1860] of his first visit in May 1844 to the Convent of St Catherine on Mount Sinai, he described how he had been examining old hand-written books and had unexpectedly come across a

---

(Codex 95 = #2040). It is described by SPT as '95 Codex Parham, "17." Of the twelfth or thirteenth century brought by the Hon. R. Curzon, in 1837, from Mount Athos, now [1872] forming a special treasure in the Parham Library where it has been collated by Mr. Scrivener. This MS. breaks off at chapter xx. 11 of the Apocalypse' (Tregelles, *Greek New Testament* Part VI: Introductory Notice). Scrivener improved on the story somewhat by attributing to the *agoumenos* rather than to Curzon's servant, the suggestion that the MS might have a particular domestic usefulness! F.H. Scrivener, *Six Lectures on the Text of the New Testament and the Ancient Manuscripts Which Contain It* … (Cambridge: Deighton, Bell and Company, 1875), 83.

[4] While rejecting his views on textual criticism, SPT insisted that Scholz was 'entitled to the respect due to a laborious scholar, devoted for years to one object: he has rendered no small service in pointing out where MSS. are preserved; and those who come after him may find from his list some documents worthy of their attention which were previously unnoticed' (Tregelles, *Account*, 94–5). Cf. above Chapter 6, Footnote 65.

[5] John Martin Augustus Scholz, *Travels in the Countries Between Alexandria and Parætonium, The Lybian Desert, Siwa, Egypt, Palestine, and Syria, in 1821* (London: Phillips & Co., 1822), 46, 49.

basket in which had been thrown the remains of various torn and abandoned parchments of which very many of a similar sort had been consigned
to the fire. He noticed, among these remnants, some very old fragments of
the Septuagint [the Old Testament in Greek] but his excitement made the
monks suspicious, and he was only allowed to take possession of forty-three
of the sheets.[6] On his return, Tischendorf presented to the King of Saxony,
all the manuscripts collected on his travels, and the sheets extracted from
the basket on Sinai were placed in the University Library of Leipzig and
named in honour of his patron, as the Codex Friderico-Augustanus, under
which name Tischendorf published them two years later. We should note
at this point that in those days, libraries and museums didn't pose awk-
ward questions about the provenance of 'discovered' antiquities, and *at no
point, for some fifteen years, did Tischendorf reveal from where he had obtained
the fragments of the Codex*. From the account of his visit to the Convent
on Mount Sinai published in 1846, no one would have had an inkling of
what Tischendorf had found there.[7] It seems however that Tregelles may
have guessed the provenance of the royally named Codex, as the following
episode suggests.

We do not know how Benjamin Newton became acquainted with Major
Charles Kerr Macdonald (1806–67) but soon after his retirement from the
army in 1847, this learned military man was employed by the East India
Company to do some surveying in the Sinai region.[8] With a keen interest

[6] Tischendorf's story has been told, repeated, translated and embellished many times.
Reflecting my subject's faith in the value of the oldest MSS, my brief account of the discovery is strictly based on Tischendorf's earliest published version, which reads as follows:
'Quum enim mense Maio anni 1844 in monasterio S. Catharinae ad montem Sinaiticum
veteres libros scriptos investigando incidissem in sportam, in quam conjectae erant vario-
rum codicum lacerorum perditorumque reliquiae, cuiusmodi plures iam furnus acceperat,
detexi illa antiquissimi LXX interpretum codicis fragmenta'. A.F.C. Tischendorf, *Notitia editionis codicis Bibliorum Sinaitici auspiciis imperatoris Alexandri II. susceptae...* (Lipsiae: F.A.
Brockhaus, 1860), 5. His expanded account was published in his *Wann wurden unsere Evangelien verfasst?* (Leipzig: Hinrichs, 1865) which was translated into English and French, the
following year. It is reproduced in full in Porter's biography.

[7] 'I shall merely mention that I found in a modern Greek manuscript, treatises upon astrol-
ogy, natural history, medicine, and other similar studies, treated of in a peculiar manner'.
Constantin Tischendorf, *Reise in den Orient* (Leipzig: Tauchnitz, 1846) translated as *Travels
in the East* (London: Longman, 1847), 107.

[8] For the next century, Major Macdonald remained a very shadowy figure, but he is now
recognized for his pioneer work in Egyptology; see J.D. Cooney, 'Major Macdonald, A Victorian Romantic,' *Journal of Egyptian Archæology* 58 (August 1972): 280–85; P.J. Dyke,

in antiquities, he was later responsible for some valuable Egyptological excavations, but in 1849 he reported to Newton that he had visited the Convent of St Catherine on Mount Sinai and had seen an ancient Greek MS of the bible.

Newton immediately wrote to Tregelles encouraging him to look into the matter but possibly for reasons of health SPT was reluctant to take the matter any further.[9] It was, after all, in 1849 that he had been stricken with cholera when working in Paris.

Nevertheless, SPT wrote to Tischendorf, asking him what he thought of the MS seen by Macdonald in the monastery on Mount Sinai, and similarly when visiting Leipzig in 1850, he showed Tischendorf Newton's letters and asked again whether Macdonald's report was worth acting upon. Each time, the German scholar's reply was categorical and he assured Tregelles 'in the strongest manner both in writing' and in conversation, that there could be no such manuscript.[10] With what we now know, we can see that there was no way that Tischendorf was going to let the British scholar, who was already beginning to appear as a rival, to pick up the scent that might lead him to the Convent of St Catherine![11]

10.4   THE BEGINNINGS OF RIVALRY

Leaving the Sinai trail on one side for the moment, we should bear in mind that SPT's ambitions in the field of biblical scholarship were very different from those of his German contemporary. He was neither seeking career advancement nor pecuniary advantage: his was first and foremost

---

E.P. Uphill, 'Major Charles Kerr Macdonald 1806–67,' *Journal of Egyptian Archæology* 69 (1983): 165–66.

[9] For Newton's recollection of this episode, see Wyatt MSS 4 (Manchester/JRUL/CBA 7059), 83, 119, 122.

[10] SPT recalled Tischendorf's assurances twelve years later in a letter written from Leipzig in June 1862 (see Stunt, 'Some unpublished letters,' 19, 25).

[11] Years later Tischendorf liked to tell a very implausible story: 'A learned Englishman, one of my friends, had been sent into the East by his Government to discover and purchase old Greek manuscripts, and spared no cost in obtaining them ... but I heard that he ... had not even gone as far as Sinai "for" as he said in his official report "after the visit of such an antiquarian and critic as Dr. Tischendorf, I could not expect any success"' (Porter, *Tischendorf*, 125). We have yet to learn of a British government-sponsored scholar with a comparable commission in the 1840s and 1850s! It sounds like a garbled account of SPT conflated with Major Macdonald, suitably embellished for the telling.

a project of piety. From the start when he published his books, he was sharing his textual collations with the wider world and, as he expressed his intentions in 1856, he hoped that the details in his *Introduction to the New Testament* and his earlier *Account of the Printed Text* (with its 94 supplementary pages of variant editorial readings)[12] 'may suffice for the present [until his final Greek Text would be complete] for communicating to others the results of my own studies'.[13] His declared aim, as expressed in the introduction to his edition of the Codex Zacynthius, was that his collations would be 'freely used by Christian scholars: I desire to labour for the common benefit of all who feel the importance of such studies'.[14] As will become apparent, Tischendorf's ambitions were rather different and very much more concerned with recognition, fame and profit; where the work of Tregelles may well be described as a vocation, it is not unfair to suggest that such labours were part of a professional career, for Tischendorf.

But at this point, if we are to understand the rift that began to develop between the two scholars, we need to clarify and distinguish between two separate aspects of the work of a textual critic. The first is the somewhat mechanical and tedious process of collating MSS and establishing what is written in them. For example, if we ask whether in Romans v.1 the Codex Vaticanus reads ἔχομεν [we have] or ἔχωμεν [let us have], we find that the original text reads ἔχωμεν but a later hand changed this to ἔχομεν. We may be sure that in the short periods of time that SPT was allowed to examine the Vatican Codex, this would have been one of the verses he looked at carefully, but even when that is established, in this first part of the textual critical process, all the other MSS have to be collated as well, to establish their readings. Only when this has been done can the second part of the task be undertaken—the evaluation of all the readings and a decision as to which is more likely to have been the original text.

In this second part of the process, when he gave greater weight to the older MSS rather than the traditional *textus receptus*, SPT's approach was similar to that of Tischendorf. It was in the earlier part of the task that the rivalry between them emerged.

---

[12] Tregelles, *Account*, separately paginated after p. 274.

[13] Tregelles, *Introduction*, ix.

[14] Samuel Prideaux Tregelles [ed.], *Codex Zacynthius* Ξ : *Greek Palimpsest Fragments of the Gospel of Saint Luke, Obtained in the Island of Zante, by the late General Colin Macaulay and Now in the Library of the British and Foreign Bible Society* (London: Bagster, 1861), xix.

Tischendorf was something of a workaholic. He was increasingly in a hurry to finish the task and get on with the next job. The scholarly world was astonished at the sheer quantity of his work: published texts of MSS, a series of editions of the Greek Text of the New Testament, revised in the light of new discoveries, the decipherment of palimpsests like the fifth-century Codex *Ephraemi Rescriptus* in Paris, not to mention his travels to remote monasteries in the deserts of Egypt and Palestine. In contrast, Tregelles was more painstaking and systematic—and slower. Referring to his first meeting with Tischendorf, he publicly acknowledged the German scholar's 'vigour and energy, as if no amount of literary work came amiss with him; as if his head, hands, and eyes knew but little of the weariness which often oppresses mine'.[15] Tregelles was a slower but more thorough worker. He too toiled over quasi-illegible MSS but in reporting on the progress of his work he presented it with fewer flourishes and as less of a star-performance. Indeed, it could be argued that he was a little less possessive of his achievements in the field.

In an editorial footnote to SPT's very complimentary review of Tischendorf's 1849 edition of the New Testament, in the *Journal of Sacred Literature*, John Kitto drew attention to Tischendorf's recognition of his obligations to Tregelles—something to which out of modesty Tregelles had made no reference but which, as editor, Kitto thought should be mentioned:

> In the latter part of [Tischendorf's] Prolegomena [Tregelles's] name occurs in almost every page. To ourselves, this kind of intercourse and acknowledgment, between the scholars of our own country and of the Continent, is a source of the highest gratification, in which we doubt not that most of our readers will partake.[16]

At that stage therefore, cooperation seemed to be the *modus operandi*, and therefore, when visiting Tischendorf in 1850, Tregelles suggested that they compare some of their collations with a view to finding where they differed

---

[15] Tregelles, 'Letters from the Continent,' 454.

[16] Tregelles, 'Tischendorf's Greek Testament', 216. John Kitto was the editor of the *JSL* until July 1853. His successors, Henry Burgess (1853–1861) and B. Harris Cowper (1861–1868), were less positive in their attitude to SPT.

and thus establishing which readings were correct.[17] On the face of things, the scholars were on friendly terms. SPT was accompanied by his wife, and Tischendorf presented her with a card on which he had mounted an olive leaf from Gethsemane, an oak leaf from Mount Tabor and a pomegranate blossom from Mount Sinai—all souvenirs of his travels in 1844.[18] Unbeknown to Tregelles however, the situation was becoming somewhat precarious because Tischendorf appears to have begun to resent SPT's corrections, treating them as a challenge to his competence, but for the moment, it seems that he gave no indication to his rival, as to how he felt.

10.5   Entrepreneurial Projects

In 1853, with the Convent on Mount Sinai very much in his sights, Tischendorf went on another Near Eastern expedition. He did not locate the rest of the Codex Friderico-Augustanus (as he had hoped to) but nor did he return empty-handed. His activity in the next few years was remarkable, and his biographer demonstrates that his productivity was as great as ever,[19] but Dr Porter seems unaware of another side to Tischendorf's *wanderlust*.

Back in Leipzig in August, writing to SPT he gave details of some MSS he had acquired and now wanted to sell, and Tregelles suggested that he might well do so in England. Not only was Tregelles happy to write to Sir Frederick Madden, the keeper of MSS at the British Museum, listing the

---

[17] SPT's collation of the Florentine Codex Amiatinus with Tischendorf's annotations in red was acquired by James Rendel Harris and was housed in the Museum of the Woodbrooke Study Centre, Birmingham, see A. Falcetta, *The Daily Discoveries of a Bible Scholar and Manuscript Hunter: A Biography of James Rendel Harris (1852–1941)* (Edinburgh: T & T Clark, 2018), 432–3.

[18] The card with its mountings was also preserved in the Woodbrooke Museum, ibid., 432.

[19] Porter, *Tischendorf*, 35–40. With predictable adulation, Porter credits Tischendorf with the discovery in Cambridge in 1855 of 'a manuscript by the Italian humanist Aonio Paleario', which he translated and published in German (p.35, n.84). In fact, the text in question was a *copy* of the original *printed* edition (Venice, 1543) of *Il Beneficio di Cristo* (now usually attributed to Benedetto da Mantova), which had been recently [1843] found in the Library of St John's College, Cambridge (*with no help from Tischendorf*), by Churchill Babington who edited it for publication in 1855. Tischendorf's German translation appeared in 1856. For the extraordinary history of this sixteenth-century book and the controversy it has aroused, see Philip McNair, 'Benedetto da Mantova, Marcantonio Flaminio, and the *Beneficio di Cristo*: A Developing Twentieth Century Debate Reviewed,' *The Modern Language Review* 82 (July 1987): 614–24.

documents that Tischendorf had acquired, and recommending the necessary expenditure as worthwhile,[20] but he indicated in a further letter that
he had invited Tischendorf to bring his wife (and the MSS!) on a visit to
England.[21] From another letter, it is apparent that with the uncertainty following the political unrest of 1848–1849 'in Saxony they have no public
money to spare for MSS' and Tischendorf had 'the permission of his own
government to offer the MSS which he has brought from the East, to the
British Museum'.[22]

As the negotiations developed, Tregelles now found himself in a position
of some delicacy:

> … as I first suggested to Tischendorf that he should offer them them [sic]
> to the Brit. Mus. (and indeed wrote to stop him from otherwise disposing of
> them without making the offer), and as he is a friend of mine, it might seem
> to the trustees of the Museum as if I were interested in getting him well paid
> for them: on the other [hand] it might appear to Tischendorf as if I wished
> to get them bought for the Library as cheap as possible…
>
> 'As a friend of Tischendorf I wish him to have a fair price for what his enter-
> prize has procured, as an Englishman I wish the Brit. Mus. to be enriched
> with valuable MSS at a fair but not extravagant outlay'.[23]

In fact, nothing was settled for another year or two and even then
the result was a confused compromise. The British Museum appears to
have declined to purchase Tischendorf's collection of seventeen MSS in
its entirety, at the price for which he was asking[24] with the result that he
then approached the Bodleian Library in Oxford, offering the MSS for sale
individually.[25] Perhaps out of duty, having made the original suggestion,
Tregelles offered to buy one of the MSS for himself but later found that
Tischendorf had withdrawn the offer and that that particular MS *had* been

---

[20] S. Prideaux Tregelles (Plymouth, 10 August 1853) to Sir Frederick Madden (Lon-
don/BL, Egerton MSS 2845 ff 263–4).

[21] SPT to F. Madden, 18 August 1853 (London/BL, Egerton MSS 2845 ff 266–7).

[22] SPT to F. Madden, 27 August 1853 (Ibid., Egerton MSS 2845 ff 268).

[23] SPT to F. Madden, 21 October. 1853 (Ibid., Egerton MSS 2845 ff 291–2).

[24] SPT to F. Madden, 7 May 1855 (Ibid., Egerton MSS 2846 f.31).

[25] In a letter to the Bodleian library (6 May 1855) Tischendorf listed the individual prices,
coming to a total of £800 (Oxford/Bod, Library Records b. 43, fol.297).

bought by the British Museum,[26] while the Bodleian had agreed to purchase three Greek, ninth-/tenth-century MSS for a total of £373.[27] In this particular deal Tischendorf's pecuniary motivation emerges very clearly as one of the MSS that he sold to the Bodleian was taken from a ninth-century Septuagint, another part of which he sold to the British Museum. He later acquired other parts of the MS and presented (?sold) them to the Imperial Library of St Petersburg.[28] For Tischendorf to have thus contributed to the permanent dismemberment of a ninth-century MS may be indicative of his entrepreneurial flair but today would be considered irresponsible.

10.6   THE STORM

Tregelles had felt free, when writing to Sir Frederick Madden, to describe Tischendorf as 'a friend of mine' and himself as a 'friend of Tischendorf'. Whether the German scholar reciprocated the sentiment was less evident. In the Prolegomena to the seventh edition of his Greek New Testament in 1859, Tischendorf gave way to his pent-up resentment. Forgetting SPT's readiness to help him in his financial transactions, he now heaped some ten pages of abusive criticism (albeit in Latin) upon the hapless Tregelles including the devastating judgment:

> I cannot help saying here how badly I take it that [Tregelles] should seem to labour under such envy and malevolence; ... excluding all true piety and good faith, and indulging a lust for invention and vituperation.[29]

---

[26] SPT to F. Madden, 7 May 1855 (London/BL, Eg MSS 2846 ff 31). SPT refers to the document as 'the MS of the Acts of the Apostles' which in his first letter (10 August 1853) he described as 'A MS of the Acts of the Apostles, written in 1054'. Clearly, this is what is now listed as BL Add MS 20003 (see F.G. Kenyon, *Handbook to the Textual Criticism of the New Testament*, 2nd ed. (London: Macmillan, 1926), 134. It had reached the British Museum by December 1855; see Tregelles, 'Nitrian Palimpsest,' 452.

[27] Falconer Madan [ed.], *A Summary Catalogue of Western Manuscripts in the Bodleian Library at Oxford, Vol. V, Collections Received During the Second Half of the 19th Century and Miscellaneous MSS Acquired Between 1695 and 1890* (Oxford: Clarendon Press, 1905), 483–85.

[28] H.B. Swete, *An Introduction to the Old Testament in Greek* (Cambridge: University Press, 1902), 134–35. The Bodleian reference is MS. Auct. T. inf. 2. 1; the BL reference is Add MS 20002.

[29] 'Non possum quin hoc loco dicum, quam aegre feram recenti memoria tanta illum videri invidia ac malevolentia laborare; ... quod vero pietate omni ac fide exuta illis non satis habet,

We need not go into his complaints in detail but suffice it to say that not only did he accuse Tregelles of having repeatedly questioned Tischendorf's readings of Greek MSS, but also of criticizing the way Tischendorf had edited the Syriac Codex Nitriensis, without producing something better himself.[30] Likewise, SPT had (in Tischendorf's opinion) claimed credit for correcting Tischendorf's reading of the Codex Claromontanus for the examination of which the German scholar had travelled to Paris on no fewer than four occasions. The reaction of other textual critics is unlikely to have mollified Tischendorf's bitterness. In a substantial review, the Cambridge scholar Fenton Hort compared at length the Greek text of the gospels as edited by both scholars, and invariably found SPT's collations to be more detailed and accurate than those of Tischendorf, concluding in no uncertain terms:

> But Tischendorf is becoming less careful than he used to be. We must add that the merits of his labours would be at least equally appreciated by duly qualified judges, if he were less given to proclaiming them himself ... His old ungenerousness to every other editor is worse than ever: such an absurd effusion of wounded vanity and spite against his friend Dr Tregelles ... will do him no good in the eyes of candid men.[31]

Needless to say, this was all deeply distressing to SPT whose capacity for modest self-criticism and readiness to reconsider earlier judgments are repeatedly manifest in his writings. The last thing he wanted was to be in competition with his German contemporary. At Christmas time in 1860, composing the preface to his edition of the Codex Zacynthius, he sought to pour oil on the troubled waters and affirmed very emphatically:

> My obligations to Tischendorf are very great: I trust that he may see that no one wishes to detract in the slightest degree from his deserts, by mentioning what he has himself done, or what at any time he intended to do.

---

sed fingendi calumniandique, indulget libidini'. Tischendorf, *Novum Testamentum* (1859): cxvii.

[30] For SPT's account of the episode, see Tregelles, 'Nitrian Palimpsest,' 451–52.

[31] F.J.A.H[ort], 'Notices of New Books,' *Journal of Classical and Sacred Philology* 4 (1858): 211.

In a footnote he spoke even more directly:

> I hope that he [Tischendorf] may himself see that he has charged me ground-lessly … His letters are in my hands; and I wish so far to value them as the expressions of kindly feeling, and the acknowledgement that I did render some service to him by communicating my collations (as indeed he has stated in print), as to overlook the remarks which he has since put forth, and which I hope that he may wish unsaid.

The actual publication of Tregelles's edition of Codex Zacynthius was delayed by a 'severe illness', which rendered him 'incapable for several months of doing anything, which requires mental or bodily exertion'. In a later postscript to his preface, he was therefore able with some satisfaction to state that his earlier hope that 'Professor Tischendorf might see that he had acted under misapprehension in the charges, which he made against me, has been realized: he now writes to me in a wholly different tone'.[32] In fact, the friction between the scholars had been overtaken by other developments.

10.7   Earth-Shaking News from Sinai

Tischendorf always had an eye for an influential sponsor, and when he set out for the third time to visit the Convent of St Catherine at the beginning of 1859, he was travelling under the patronage of Tsar Alexander II of Russia who was also the Patron and Protector of the Orthodox churches and therefore of the monastery on Mount Sinai. For the sequence of events that led to his discovery of the rest of the fourth-century MS (parts of which he had brought to Leipzig fifteen years earlier), we are largely dependent on Tischendorf's account of how in late January, the monastic steward had shown him the Sinaitic Codex (no longer in a rubbish basket!) and how he then persuaded the monks to let it be taken to Cairo for him to copy it.

He broke the news of his sensational find in a letter (dated 15 March 1859 from Cairo) addressed to the Saxon Minister von Falkenstein and published in the *Leipziger Zeitung* on 17 April. From this, one of the editors of the *Journal of Sacred Literature* was able to provide the readers of the July issue of the magazine with an English translation of the substance

---

[32] Tregelles, *Codex Zacynthius*, xix; xxvi.

of Tischendorf's letter.[33] In the circles of biblical scholarship, the excitement was immense, as Tischendorf was writing about an almost complete Greek MS of the entire Bible, in age and scope comparable to the Vatican and Alexandrinian codices—a discovery that would add a completely new dimension to the evidence requiring the attention of biblical textual critics.

On a less exalted level, the find may also have helped to transform the personal dynamics that we have been considering between Tischendorf and Tregelles. A momentous development of this sort could provide Tischendorf with the distinction and recognition that he craved and perhaps in the blaze of the accompanying renown he would be able to let go some of his resentment arising from complaints about the inaccuracies in his work and with it some of the unfair accusations with which he had charged his rival. Clearly, the German scholar now had a totally new focus for his work.

Without going into the intricate negotiations (some of the details of which are still in dispute a century and a half later[34]), we know that Tischendorf persuaded the monks on Mount Sinai to let him take their Codex to St Petersburg in September, for its accurate publication in facsimile. As the Codex was only on loan from the monks and was not Tischendorf's property, in all probability he was abusing the trust of the monks when in November he presented the Codex to the Tsar. However, the emperor agreed to pay for its publication and stipulated that this should be in 1862 to coincide with the Russian celebration of the thousand-year anniversary of the accession of Rurik, the first prince of Novgorod. This was a demanding schedule, and Tischendorf threw himself into the project with all his characteristic energy. His family had connections with the paper industry,

[33] B.H. Cowper, 'Extraordinary Discovery of a Biblical MS by Dr Tischendorf,' *JSL* 9 (July 1859): 392–94.

[34] This is not the place to delve into the dispute as to whether Tischendorf acted honourably in the acquisition of Codex Sinaiticus or to what the monks of St Catherine actually agreed. The case in favour of Tischendorf was strongly argued by Erhard Lauch, 'Nichts gegen Tischendorf' in E.H. Amberg, U. Kühn [eds.], *Bekenntnis zur Kirche: Festgabe für Ernst Sommerlath zum 70. Geburtstag* (Berlin, 1960), 15–24. Subsequently, the late Harvard Professor, Ihor Ševčenko, cast serious doubts on Tischendorf's claims in 'New Documents on Constantine Tischendorf and the Codex Sinaiticus,' *Scriptorium* 18 (1964): 55–80. The subject has recently been revisited by C. Böttrich's 'Constantin von Tischendorf und der Transfer des *Codex Sinaiticus* nach St Petersburg' in A. Gössner [ed.], *Die Theologische Fakultät der Universität Leipzig* (Leipzig, 2005), 253–75 and in a cautious restatement of the question by M.D. Peterson, 'Tischendorf and the *Codex Sinaiticus*: The Saga Continues,' *Greek Orthodox Theological Review* 53:1–4 (2008): 125–39. See most recently D.C. Parker, *Codex Sinaiticus: The Story of the World's Oldest Bible* (London: British Library, 2010).

and therefore, he insisted on the four-volume royal jubilee edition being printed at Leipzig where he could control the facsimile fonts and the quality of the paper, though its publication was in St Petersburg, as the title *Codex Sinaiticus Petropolitanus*, made clear.

10.8   TREGELLES AND *SINAITICUS*[35]

Needless to say, Tregelles was anxious to see the newly discovered Codex and began making plans in early 1860 to travel to Russia to collate the MS, but understandably he was apprehensive of possible opposition from Tischendorf who had recently criticized him so fiercely in print. We don't know how he approached his sponsors, but in March 1860 more than twenty-five distinguished biblical scholars[36] rallied round and wrote testimonials in support of SPT's plan giving assurances that his collation of the newly discovered text would in no way compete with Tischendorf's proposed printed edition. The plan was that Tregelles would apply through Lord Shaftesbury, as an intermediary for the government's support in the person of the British minister plenipotentiary at the Imperial Court in St Petersburg, Sir John Crampton[37] to whom the several scholars addressed their commendations. Newton's recollection of the episode, many years after the event, is somewhat confused but it seems that Lord Shaftesbury let matters slip and the project never materialized.[38]

[35] Much of the material in this section is covered in fuller detail in Stunt, 'Some Unpublished Letters'. When that was written the letters were in private hands, but now most of them are in the CBA in Manchester.

[36] The list included such leading biblical and textual scholars as Henry Alford, William Cureton, Fenton J.A. Hort, J.B. Lightfoot, James Henthorn Todd, B.F. Westcott and Christopher Wordsworth. The high regard in which SPT was held at Trinity College Cambridge is reflected in the significant number of sponsors who were fellows of that college.

[37] Sir John Fiennes Twisleton Crampton [1805–1886].

[38] Presumably, some months later, when nothing had been done, all the papers were returned by Shaftesbury's secretary to Newton which explains why SPT's letter to Shaftesbury, dated 3 March 1860, was among Newton's papers which are now in the Christian Brethren Archive (Manchester/JRUL/CBA 7181 [19]). Some fifty years ago, all the commendatory letters were also in the Fry Collection and I was able to make Xerox copies of them, but since 1982 they appear to have been in the British Library (Add. MS. 61835); see R.A.H. Smith, 'Department of Manuscripts: Acquisitions January-December 1980,' *British Library Journal* (1982): 222.

It was a great disappointment but SPT treated it as something to be received 'as coming to me in the Providence of God'. Looking at it positively, he hoped that he could revive the project in the following year when 'I trust that I shall be in a fitter state for collating *such* a document for my eyes more need rest than work of a minute kind, my left eye especially is now very dim and confused'.[39] In fact, as we observed in a previous chapter, SPT and his wife travelled south-west to Spain that summer rather than north-east to Russia, after which, as we also noted above, he had to cope with a further setback in the first part of 1861 when he was severely challenged by a condition of paralysis which left him effectively incapable of textual work, for some months.

In consequence, it was only in 1862, by which time Tischendorf had persuaded the imperial authorities to let him take the Codex to Leipzig for the facsimile printing process, that Tregelles was able to travel to Germany to examine the MS. He had corresponded with Tischendorf and seems to have satisfied the German scholar as to his honourable conduct in connection with both his intentions regarding the Nitrian Syriac palimpsest and in the editing of the Codex Claromontanus. At this stage, he seems to have been unaware that an anonymous contributor had translated and published at length in the *Journal of Sacred Literature* for July 1862, Tischendorf's criticisms as made three years earlier in 1859. Writing after the event, Tregelles expressed his surprise 'to see charges reproduced against me which Tischendorf would not now make; and that not in the obscurity of a learned language, but translated into English'. At the same time, he could state publicly:

> It has been at his [Tischendorf's] desire that I have been examining the Codex Sinaiticus; of which he gave me the free use prior to its publication; and of which I availed myself for several days at Leipsic.[40]

But from his private correspondence it is clear that the two men were temperamentally ill-suited to work together. Knowing that there would

---

[39] SPT (Plymouth, May 5 1860) to B.W. Newton (Manchester/JRUL/CBA 7181 [20]).

[40] The translated passages, from Tischendorf's 7th edition of his Greek NT (1859), appeared as 'New Testament Critics: Tischendorf versus Tregelles,' *JSL* (July 1862): 369–76. For SPT's reply, see his letter to the editor, *JSL* (October 1862): 178–79. It is apparent from Tischendorf's letter (Leipzig, 2 April 1861) to Samuel Davidson (Glasgow/UGL, GB 247 MS Gen 527/1) that the anonymous translator was Davidson himself, SPT's old antagonist. Tischendorf refers to Tregelles as 'unseren gemeinsamen Gegner' ['our common enemy'].

soon be a printed edition, Tregelles didn't attempt the mammoth task of a complete collation, which would have been impossible in the space of only a few days. Instead, he paid attention to the characteristics of the MS and how Tischendorf was going to render, in his printed edition, such things as the MS's later corrections. As he still had reservations about the precision of Tischendorf's work, 'I examined many things, so as to test his accuracy in copying and printing'.

In a revealing passage, we begin to appreciate the challenges faced by this quiet, systematic worker:

> In order to judge the MS more closely I have begun a collation of the Catholic Epistles. Tischendorf gave me leave to do this and I *hope* that he will be gracious enough to allow me to finish it …
>
> Tischendorf's arrogant behaviour to me has been most strange; I should not have borne it, were it not for the importance of doing something in connection with the MS. Today I am letting my head and eyes *rest* (which is quite needful) & tomorrow I hope to continue my collation. I go again one of the early days of next week and this I suppose will be *all* Tischendorf will allow me to do.
>
> Indeed even in this, he interrupts me constantly, so that it is difficult for me to do carefully what I want. I found it an indescribable relief to get from Tischendorf to Wilhelm Dindorf who is at least both a gentleman & a scholar and who behaves as a person ought to do.[41]

Not all the irritation, however, was on one side. Tischendorf's estimate of SPT was probably not helped by his own friendship with Samuel Davidson whose controversy with SPT we considered in an earlier chapter. In his correspondence with Davidson, Tischendorf sometimes writes as if the Codex Sinaiticus were his own private possession and expresses his indignation at Tregelles having dared to disagree with him on such questions as whether the last verse of John's Gospel had been part of the original

---

[41] The full text of this copy of SPT's letter (Leipzig, June 20, 1862) is in Stunt, 'Some Unpublished Letters' 19. It is also now accessible at https://www.brethrenarchive.org/manuscripts/letters-of-sp-tregelles/extract-of-letter-from-dr-tregelles. He wrote a similar but more restrained letter to the Cambridge scholar F.J.A. Hort which was published in *The Guardian* (13 August 1862) and is reproduced in J.K. Elliott, *Codex Sinaiticus and the Simonides Affair* (Thessaloniki, 1982), 23–24. In fairness to both parties, we should note that in a more guarded letter to B.F. Westcott, SPT observed: 'I ought to say that in parting, Tischendorf was as amiable as possible' (SPT, Leipzig 25 June 1862 to B.F. Westcott, Cambridge/CUL, Westcott Papers, Add.8317/1/215).

Sinaitic text. In the German scholar's opinion, as he expressed it to David-son, SPT's questioning of Tischendorf's opinion in the matter was not just 'naïve and malicious' but so 'laughable' that 'it will come down about his head, as he deserves'.[42] He went on to complain that Tregelles had only spent 'four or five days in my house' and 'every single correction [made to Tischendorf's text] is nothing more than a sin of haste on his part'.

For anyone familiar with the devout sincerity that characterized SPT's careful approach, there is something not a little incongruous in Tischen-dorf's self-satisfied declaration:

> What cut off in the strongest way my Plymouth rival's justification for com-peting with me are the extraordinary enrichments of textual knowledge, which the Lord imparted to Christian scholarship through me.

There is no record of Davidson's side of the correspondence but know-ing his similar hostility to Tregelles we may well conclude that it fur-ther enflamed the antipathy displayed by Tischendorf in whose opinion Tregelles was a humbug, 'always acting so piously, always bandying talk of "God" and "God's word" around, without scorning to use the most spiteful weapons of this world'.[43]

There is a delicious irony in the fact that although Tischendorf regret-ted having allowed Tregelles to see the Sinaitic Codex in Leipzig in 1862, his having done so enabled the English scholar to give his wholehearted support to Tischendorf in his controversy with the mischievous but gifted calligrapher Constantine Simonides who claimed that as a young man in a monastery on Mount Athos, it had been he who had written the Codex Sinaiticus.[44] There was a potentially comic element in this part of the story,

---

[42] Tischendorf's reading of the MS on this point was only partially vindicated seventy years later, when examination under ultraviolet light confirmed that the text had originally stopped at verse 24. It also established that it was the original scribe (and not as Tischendorf claimed, a later corrector,) who added verse 25; H.J.M. Milne, T.C. Skeat, *Scribes and Correctors of the Codex Sinaiticus* (London, 1938), 12f. This finding and the agreement of several other scholars with Tregelles, at the time, suggest that his differing opinion was not entirely unrea-sonable.

[43] C. Tischendorf (Paris, 1 December 1864) to S. Davidson (Glasgow/UGL, GB247 MS Gen 527/7). The quoted extracts are from the translation by Dr James Bentley in his *Secrets of Mount Sinai: The Story of the Codex Sinaiticus* (London: Orbis, 1985), 124–25, 88.

[44] The raw materials for an account of the extraordinary career of Simonides may be found in J.K. Elliott's analysis in *Codex Sinaiticus and the Simonides Affair* (Thessaloniki: Patriarchal

as Tischendorf had earlier played an important part in exposing Simonides as a very skilful forger of ancient documents, and the German scholar's indignation was now aggravated by his belief that a desire for revenge was Simonides's deliberate motive for casting doubt on Tischendorf's credentials. For Tregelles, it was a sacred duty to testify to the authenticity of the Sinai Codex against the spurious claims of Simonides. On the other hand, it was a bit galling for Tischendorf to welcome SPT's support for the cause of truth.[45]

As one might expect from his previous financial dealings, when it came to the publication of the Codex, Tischendorf secured for himself a number of copies, which he hoped to sell for £37.10. 0. Tregelles, who had already ordered his copy, at the advertised market price, was somewhat taken aback to find Tischendorf offering him a copy, '*as a personal favour* if I will pay him £25.0.0. ... I am to consider it, I believe, as a *present*, from the Emperor'. SPT chose to wait for the copy he had ordered from Williams and Norgate,[46] 'so that when they get copies, I shall have one from them at £25.0.0', adding a final and typically wry comment: 'I understand what buying things means: but I do not like to *purchase presents*'.[47]

It is unlikely that Tregelles ever thought of himself as a public figure and his only real ambition was probably his desire to complete his edition of the Greek New Testament—a project that would never be particularly

Institute for Patristic Studies, 1982), *passim*. For a more chronological account, see 'Greek Forgery: Constantine Simonides' in J.A. Farrer, *Literary Forgeries* (London: Longman, Green and Co, 1907), 39–66. See also, most recently P.M Pinto, 'Simonides in England: A Forger's Progress', in A.E. Müller, L. Diamantopoulou, et al. [eds.], *Die getäuschte Wissenschaft: Ein Genie betrügt Europa – Konstantinos Simonides* (Vienna, UP, 2017), 109–126.

[45] For most of SPT's letters on the Simonides affair, see Stunt, 'Some unpublished letters' 23–25. SPT's profound disapproval of Simonides' behaviour was still apparent in an indignant letter that he wrote some years later, 'Codex Mayerianus and Simonides', *Notes and Queries* 4th series 3 [24 April 1869] 369. Having examined the original codex when visiting Tischendorf in Leipzig, Tregelles was able to confirm 'as an eyewitness' certain statements about the codex made by another scholar, F.H.A. Scrivener in a lecture given in Plymouth in October 1863. SPT disagreed with Scrivener on many matters but probably attended the lecture to give his support in person to Scrivener's rejection of the claims of Simonides. F.H. Scrivener, *A Full Collation of the Codex Sinaiticus, with the Received Text of the New Testament, to Which is Prefixed a Critical Introduction* (Cambridge: Deighton, Bell and Co, 1864), xxxi, n.6.

[46] Williams and Norgate were publishers and book importers with offices in London and Edinburgh.

[47] SPT (Plymouth, 29 December 1862) to B.W. Newton (Manchester/JRUL/CBA 7181 [36]).

spectacular. The goal for which he strove was demanding, and any appreciation of his work was confined to a very limited number of spectators. Particularly ironic was the fact that many, who shared something of his devout piety and his faith in the plenary inspiration of scripture, had little time for textual criticism—an activity, which they were inclined to dismiss as unspiritual and intellectual. To have incurred the enmity of a scholar, who lived for the applause of approval, made the predicament of a modest and retiring scholar all the more undeserved.

Dr. James Bentley whose account of the finding of the Codex Sinaiticus gives full recognition to the remarkable achievement and scholarship of Tischendorf, nevertheless observes that 'even at the height of his fame, [Tischendorf] displayed a quite extraordinary viciousness towards any scholar whose reputation might diminish his own standing in the eyes of the world … *anyone* who studied in Tischendorf's field was liable to come under the German's lash'. It was Tregelles's misfortune to find himself working in that particular field and 'Tischendorf responded to his views on the Codex Sinaiticus with an astonishing viciousness'.[48] In contrast, we may conclude this chapter with Tregelles published *eirenicon* when, in 1861, he reckoned that he had reassured Tischendorf of his honourable intentions:

All may make mistakes; but such mistakes need not be supposed to spring from any wrong motives: those who charge others may perhaps be themselves in the wrong; but let us always be ready to receive candid explanations so as if possible to remove causes of dissension, and maintain that Christian spirit which should be connected with Christian studies.[49]

[48] Bentley, *Secrets*, 88, 125, 123.
[49] Tregelles, *Codex Zacynthius*, xxvi.

CHAPTER 11

Recognition, Controversy and Crisis (1850–1861)

11.1   A Changing World

Having considered several aspects of SPT's thinking, and some of the ways in which he reacted to people whose opinions he could not share, we must now revert to a more chronological account of his life to see the context in which he adopted these attitudes. In passing, we should also bear in mind that the subject of our enquiry was living through a time of enormous change.

Because of the decidedly non-political posture, which was taken by the Plymouth Brethren—an attitude that was shared by both Tregelles and his friend Benjamin Newton—we find minimal references in his correspondence to the political developments of the day, but innovations like railway travel and the penny postage (to mention but two!) clearly had a huge impact on SPT's daily life. By the 1860s, he was taking full advantage of a postal service that enabled him to exchange thoughts with Newton in London, sometimes writing as many as five letters to him in the course of a month. On the other hand, unless he was very enterprising it is unlikely that he used one of the early fountain pens, and this meant that he always had to travel with some nibs and a reasonable supply of ink. However, travel itself was becoming easier and SPT's long-drawn-out journey to Rome in 1845 soon became a thing of the past so that less than twenty years later in 1862, we find him making a critical comparison of 'the rapidity and

© The Author(s) 2020   163
T. C. F. Stunt, *The Life and Times of Samuel Prideaux Tregelles*,
Christianities in the Trans-Atlantic World,
https://doi.org/10.1007/978-3-030-32266-3_11

vibration of our English Express train' with the European transport of his recent continental travel.[1]

Perhaps the most important invention that came too late for SPT was the advent of the electric light. With his challenged eyesight, he was always glad to be able to work at home, upstairs at the top of the house where there was more daylight, and a cloudless sky was always a cause for thankfulness.[2] The use of gaslight was too great a risk in libraries which, in consequence, almost invariably presented him with a challenge. To be allowed to use a rare MS outside a dimly lit library, as he was allowed to do in Basel thanks to the good offices of Professor de Wette,[3] was always a bonus, and it was an indication of the high esteem in which Tregelles was held, that the Town Council of Leicester authorized him in 1852, to collate the fourteenth-century cursive Codex Leicestrensis in his own home in Plymouth.[4] The journeys required for such consultation, both in the UK and on the continent, were extensive, but in the course of fifteen years, the improvements in travel facilities made movement from one municipal library to another significantly simpler for Tregelles. In contrast to the boundless energy of Tischendorf, who was ready to undertake wearisome journeys to such remote locations as Sinai, the physique of SPT was less robust, and he confined himself to European destinations being thankful to profit from the convenience of the steam locomotive.

When we say that Tregelles was less energetic than Tischendorf, we are touching on a vital factor in the development of his career. In 1850, our scholar was not yet forty years old, but there would soon be signs of physical debility. A contemporary recalled the familiar sight of SPT taking 'the regular "constitutional" which his sedentary occupation made so necessary, the small spectacled figure, starting off briskly with his stick over his shoulder',[5] but by the mid-1850s, several of his letters refer to the need for him to 'recruit his strength' and rest his head which was easily wearied

---

[1] SPT (Plymouth, 29 August 1862) to B W Newton (Manchester/JRUL/CBA 7181 [27]).

[2] The crucial importance of sunlight is well illustrated in a letter from SPT to Joseph Lightfoot referring to some faint letters in the Muratorian Fragment in Milan from where 'Dr [Antonio] Ceriani of the Ambrosian Library wrote to me a few weeks ago that even while he was writing, a cloud covering the sun had caused these letters to become wholly indiscernible'. SPT (Plymouth 25 June 1859) to J.B. Lightfoot (Durham/Cathedral, CJBL/B/1859/3.16).

[3] Tregelles, *Account*, 150.

[4] Tregelles, *Account*, 156.

[5] Tregelles, 'Life of a Scholar,' *FQE* (1897): 454.

by concentrating on the textual *minutiae* with which he was invariably concerned. Physically, he was already in decline.

11.2 RECOGNITION AND REPUTATION

One of the finest theological scholars, with whom Tregelles was closely associated in the 1840s, was the Scottish Hebraist, Henry Craik of Bristol who with his fellow elder George Müller played a key part in the early activities of the Plymouth Brethren when SPT was one of their numbers. We know that in 1849, the University of St Andrews proposed to confer a doctorate of Divinity or of Canon and Civil Law on Henry Craik but that when he learnt of the plan, Craik 'courteously declined this honour, but recommended a Christian gentleman, who had laboured much in biblical literature, for the degree, as it might be of great use to him as an author'.[6] There can be little doubt that it was as a result of Craik's suggestion that in 1850, his *alma mater* awarded their Doctorate of Laws to Tregelles—a significant source of encouragement for an autodidact who had been denied a University career and a recognition that he gratefully acknowledged by dedicating to the Scottish University his *Account of the Printed Text of the Greek New Testament* published in 1854.[7]

Comparable by way of distinction was the invitation by Longmans for Tregelles to take responsibility for the fourth volume of the new edition of Horne's *Introduction to the Holy Scriptures* even though it was an honour, which, as we have seen, brought him into controversial conflict with Samuel Davidson. In the previous year, there had been further evidence of the increasing respect in which SPT was held in the academic world when the possibility of restoring the obliterated older sixth-century uncial writing in the Dublin palimpsest of St Matthew's Gospel came up for discussion. The Provost and members of the Board of Trinity College agreed in October 1853 to allow Tregelles to supervise the chemical restoration process, which made possible his successful decipherment of the entire MS.[8]

---

[6] W. Elfe Tayler, *Passages from the Diary and Letters of Henry Craik of Bristol* (London: J. F. Shaw, [1866]), xvi.

[7] SPT's letter (13 April 1854) requesting permission so as to dedicate his *Account* is preserved in St Andrew's Archives (Senatus Academicus; Misc. Papers, UYUY459, Box B File 4).

[8] For the Codex Dublinensis [Z], see Tregelles, *Introduction* (1856), 4: 181–82.

A few years later, it was a logical sequel to this triumph when in the summer of 1858, Dr Paul de Lagarde of Berlin[9] reported to Tregelles his discovery of a seventh-century palimpsest MS of St Luke's Gospel, in the Library of the British and Foreign Bible Society. In due course, the Society authorized SPT to take the MS (Codex Zacynthius) to his home in Plymouth with a view to his deciphering and editing it for publication.[10]

11.3   A CONTINENTAL BREAK

A year earlier, in the summer of 1857 it had become clear that the worrisome details of proofreading and other complications connected with publication were imposing too great a strain on Tregelles, and the need for close attention to *minutiae* had been particularly demanding on his eyesight, which was already somewhat impaired. In dire need of rest and relaxation, he travelled with his wife to spend some weeks in the vicinity of Geneva.

It seems however that SPT may have had an ulterior motive because towards the end of their holiday, they travelled South to Milan where, with the help of Antonio Ceriani of the Ambrosian Library, he was able to examine the Muratorian Canon. This eighth-century MS contains a list of the writings that were regarded as canonical in the second century, and it is clear from a lecture given by SPT in Plymouth in 1851 that he regarded it as a valuable piece of evidence for the early MS tradition from which he was deriving the text of his Greek New Testament.[11] In his account of his time in Milan, he gives the impression that it was a chance recollection that led him to study the MS, but it is a little strange that when he was ostensibly on holiday, he was able to make from the document 'a facsimile tracing,

---

[9] Paul Anton de Lagarde (1827–1891) was a distinguished German Orientalist but is also notorious for his anti-semitic beliefs and is regarded by some as a precursor of National Socialism.

[10] The MS had been brought back from the island of Zante in 1821 by General Colin Macaulay, an uncle of the historian. It was published as *Codex Zacynthius. Greek Palimpsest Fragments of the Gospel of Saint Luke, obtained in the Island of Zante, by the Late General Colin Macaulay, and now in the Library of the British and Foreign Bible Society*, deciphered, transcribed and edited by Samuel Prideaux Tregelles, LL.D. (London: Bagster, 1861). As part of the BFBS archives, it was deposited in 1984 with Cambridge University Library who purchased the MS in 2014 for £1.1 million.

[11] Tregelles, *Historic Evidence*, 15–17.

materials for which I had happily with me in Milan'.[12] On his way home, SPT briefly visited, in Heidelberg, the scholar-diplomat Baron Christian von Bunsen with whom he had previously discussed the text of the Canon, and together they compared the recent collation made by Tregelles with another transcript.[13] In fact, it was another ten years before SPT's edition of the Canon saw the light of published day, and it would be yet another distraction, which, with the other ancillary engagements mentioned earlier, interfered with the Greek New Testament which was his overall project, but at least that *magnum opus* was underway.

11.4   UNIVERSITY CONTACTS

Although his vacation on the continent had been occasioned by the stress of the final arrangements that accompanied the appearance in June 1857 of the first volume of the Greek New Testament, the production rapidly won the respect it deserved. In the introduction, SPT acknowledged the encouragement he had received from two eminent (but deceased) Oxford scholars, Dr Martin Routh[14] the President of Magdalen and Professor Gaisford, the Dean of Christ Church whose approval of SPT's textual principles 'sufficed to outweigh the well-meaning but unintelligent remarks of many who passed a judgment on a subject that they did not understand'.[15] However, there were other, living, Oxford scholars whose support and approval he also valued like Prebendary Robert Scott, soon to be elected Master of

[12] Tregelles, *Canon Muratorianus*, 8.

[13] Ibid., 7–8. It was during this short stay in Heidelberg that SPT found time to pay his respects at the tomb of Olimpia Morata [1526–1555] the *fanciulla prodigio* of the Italian Reformation. Regrettably, the graceful sonnet that SPT wrote on the fly-leaf of his guide book, while standing beside her grave, as recorded by Augusta Prideaux, has not been preserved; Cambridge, MA/AHTL, Prideaux, MS Life [p. 25].

[14] SPT's appreciation of Routh's encouragement was apparent in a letter to the President of Magdalen, recalling an interview with him in May 1851, SPT (3 September 1851, Plymouth) to M.J. Routh (Oxford/Magdalen, MC: PR30/1/C4/6f.346); cf. above Chapter 8, Footnote 14. From the meticulous accuracy of SPT's work, one could imagine that it had been to him (and not to Dean Burgon) that Routh had offered his much quoted advice to younger scholars 'always to verify your references, Sir!' J.W. Burgon, *Lives of Twelve Good Men*, 2 vols. 3rd ed. (London 1889), 1:73.

[15] 'Introductory Notice to the first part of Dr. Tregelles's Greek New Testament', Plymouth, 23 June 1857, p. viii.

Balliol, and B. W. Newton's old colleague, J.D Macbride, the Principal of Magdalen Hall.[16]

At Cambridge, in contrast, Tregelles's academic contacts were less elderly. It had been in the summer months of 1845, before his time in Rome that, armed with an introduction from the Dean of Trinity,[17] he had collated the Codex Augiensis in the College Library.[18] Trinity College had been the home of the great eighteenth-century textual scholar, Richard Bentley, for whom SPT had immense admiration.[19] Needless to say, the nineteenth-century scholar seized the opportunity to acquaint himself with Bentley's papers of which the library had custody.[20] This was the beginning of a long-standing connection that Tregelles had with Trinity College, more particularly with a younger generation of scholars including the future Bishop of Durham, Joseph Lightfoot, who arranged for him to make a further trawl through the Bentley papers in 1857 made necessary by Tischendorf's discovery of a document that SPT had missed in his earlier searches.[21] That this was not an isolated connection at Trinity is apparent from the fact that in 1860, when SPT was seeking testimonials for his proposed visit to Russia to collate the newly discovered Codex Sinaiticus, no fewer than ten Fellows of Trinity signed one of the letters in support of SPT's project. But perhaps more significant still were the independent commendations from two former Fellows of the College, whom we must now consider in their own right.

In some ways, it could be argued that New Testament Textual Criticism was *the* subject *par excellence* in England during the 1850s. In addition to

[16] See SPT's letter (Plymouth, 7 September 1854) to J.D. Macbride with his opinion concerning the admission of dissenters to Oxford University (Oxford/Bod., MS Eng. lett.d.185).

[17] William Carus (1804–1891), Senior Fellow and Dean of Trinity, was the editor of *The Memoirs of Charles Simeon* [1847] and was a cousin of William Carus-Wilson who was supposedly the original of Charlotte Bronte's 'Mr. Brocklehurst' in *Jane Eyre*.

[18] Tregelles, *Account*, 155.

[19] For Bentley, see *supra*, Chapter 5, n.6ff.

[20] 'I examined all Bentley's collection as well as I could consistently with the rule prohibiting strangers from going into the *classes* [sc. library stacks] and I made lists of the contents of the different volumes in case I should have any further opportunity of making use of them', SPT (29 December 1848, Plymouth) to C. Wordsworth (London/LPL, MS2143f.373v).

[21] This was the Abate Rulotta's revised collation of Codex Vaticanus; see SPT (8 May 1857, Plymouth) to J.B. Lightfoot (Durham/Cathedral, CJBL/B/1857/3.189)

the publication in 1857 of the first volume of SPT's own Greek New Testament (Matthew and Mark) and in 1859 the seventh edition of Tischendorf's text (including its vitriolic criticism of Tregelles), the first volumes of other scholarly editions of the Greek New Testament produced independently by Canon Christopher Wordsworth[22] and Dean Henry Alford[23] also appeared in the same decade. Tregelles was well aware of the work of his contemporaries, and, with the exception of Tischendorf, their communications were amiable even though Tregelles disagreed with some of their textual judgements.

In the same decade, a more crucial development, of which SPT soon became aware, was the collaboration (which would last for twenty-eight years) of two younger Fellows of Trinity College, Brooke Foss Westcott[24] and Fenton J. A. Hort[25]—a project which had its beginning early in 1852.[26] Both of these men had great respect for Tregelles, and, like him, they too were adamant in their rejection of the *textus receptus*. Writing to his mother in October 1855, Hort speaks admiringly of the older scholar:

> Another visitor, who is here still, is Dr. Tregelles of Plymouth, whose life is completely given up to the restoration of the Greek text of the New Testament, and whom I was therefore particularly glad to know personally, though we had exchanged several letters before.[27]

Clearly, there was some potential for rivalry, and as early as April 1857, we find SPT confiding in Newton:

> *Westcott and Hort* have advertized a revision of the Greek Test. now in preparation: *I know them both* – they are good scholars — but I want to issue part of mine before any of theirs appears. They have collated no MSS themselves — but they have paid much attention to the Patristic citations.[28]

---

[22] Christopher Wordsworth (1807–1885) was Bishop of Lincoln (1869–1885).

[23] Henry Alford (1810–1871) was Dean of Canterbury (1857–1871).

[24] Brooke Foss Westcott (1825–1901), later Bishop of Durham (1890–1901).

[25] Fenton John Anthony Hort (1828–1892), Professor of Divinity, Cambridge (1878–92).

[26] A.F. Hort, *Life and Letters of Fenton John Anthony Hort*, 2 vols. (London: Macmillan, 1896), 1: 240.

[27] Ibid., 1:314. [Letter 24 October 1855, Cambridge, to his mother.]

[28] SPT (17 April 1857, Plymouth) to B.W. Newton (Manchester/JRUL/CBA 7181 [10]).

In contrast to the erratic behaviour of Tischendorf, the younger Cambridge scholars remained on amicable terms with Tregelles who was always ready to share his work with others. Indeed, less than a year after his letter indicating the possible element of rivalry, we find SPT in his somewhat isolated existence in Plymouth explaining to Hort his appreciation of their friendship in a soul-baring letter early in 1858:

> My lot is not only to be far from manuscripts and all libraries, but also far from those who know or care anything about Biblical scholarship. On every side I am looked on by those with whom I meet as a kind of dreamer, who have given up my life to a vain pursuit, just as profitless as would be the following of shadows. I am therefore glad to be sometimes in contact with some who at least understand what I intend.[29]

That the appreciation was mutual is apparent in a letter from Hort to his publisher:

> Dr. Tregelles has most kindly promised to let me have the sheets of his *St. Luke*, etc., as they are printed off; this is a very great help. Poor old fellow; he seems sadly lonely down at Plymouth, all his friends and neighbours thinking him only a madman; and then to have to bear a savage attack from Tischendorf.[30]

It was a friendship, as we shall see, that stood the test of time.

In passing, we should perhaps note another aspect of the loneliness to which Hort referred, when a little more than a year later SPT and his wife entertained in their home his distant Fox cousins, who had known him as a boy and who were now visiting Cornwall. The youngest of the sisters, Tabitha Fox [1811–1894], described the 'wonderful evening' in which 'the little "Prid" of old was [able to expatiate] on his own subject'. Her account is a moving commentary on the isolation of the independent scholar:

> How he poured out from the full cistern of his pent-up love. It seemed to be a positive relief [for him] to open the flood-gates and to let the stream float without stint or stay. He showed facsimiles of the precious parchments traced by his own hand, in Rome, in Florence, in Paris, in various cities of

[29] Tregelles to Hort, January 30, 1858 quoted from Hort's Theological Correspondence in G. Patrick, *F.J.A. Hort: Eminent Victorian* (London: Bloomsbury, 2015 [1987]), 107.

[30] Hort, *Life and Letters*, 1: 396. [Letter 3 Febuary 1858, St Ippolyts, to A. Macmillan].

Germany as well as in our own England, and as he hurried almost breathlessly along the deep channels of Christian learning whence flows the broad river of Truth, he would stop for a brief moment on the bank to draw a portrait of some scholar of the old world or some interpreter of the young world and to tell how he looked or spoke or moved.[31]

Clearly, it was something of an event for SPT to have a receptive audience other than his wife who would already have been familiar with the details.

11.5   1859–1860: A CRITICAL YEAR

There can be little doubt that Tischendorf's aggressive behaviour towards Tregelles was a source of deep distress and pain. We do not know if SPT was aware of the friendship between Tischendorf and Samuel Davidson whose ongoing disdain for Tregelles's convictions about biblical inspiration must have made him a ready listener to Tischendorf's sweeping and unsubstantiated charges against his reluctant rival. The replies of SPT to Tischendorf in his 'Additions' to the later edition of Horne's *Introduction* reflect the pain he felt and are almost embarrassingly over-conciliatory in his efforts to heal the breach. Given that earlier, Tregelles had attempted to help Tischendorf in his efforts to sell MSS to the British Museum, and that this was soon followed by the excitement in 1859–1860 arising from the news of Tischendorf's discovery of the Sinai Codex, which seemed to be redrawing the map of textual criticism, one is not surprised to find SPT overwhelmed with mixed emotions at this stage.

1860 was therefore a key year. SPT's 'Introductory Notice' to the second volume of his Greek New Testament containing the Gospels of St Luke and St John is dated the twenty-ninth December. It was the culmination of a highly productive year's work. Not only had he completed his edition of the Codex Zacynthius, but, in addition, he had penned a magisterial (albeit anonymous) assessment of Cardinal Mai's edition of the Codex Vaticanus, for the *Edinburgh Review*,[32] as well as making abortive plans to consult the

---

[31] From a letter dated 30 October 1859 (kindly transcribed for me by the late Brigadier H.A. F. Crewdson in October 1983); for the context, see H.A.F. Crewdson, *George Fox of Tredrea and His Three Daughters: A Century of Family History* (Slindon, Sussex, 1976), 110–111.

[32] [S.P.T.] 'Cardinal Mai's edition of the Vatican Codex,' *Edinburgh Review*, 112:227 (July 1860): 256–65. In the previous year, the same periodical had carried his anonymous review of 'Dr Cureton's *Syriac Gospels*' (*ER* 110 (July 1859), 168–90.

Codex Sinaiticus in St Petersburg. He had replied as tactfully as he could to Tischendorf's unwarranted accusations, but he had also undertaken an altogether different mission. Travelling with his wife in Spain, he had experienced all the excitement of actually seeing cities and palaces with which he was familiar as a historian. Perhaps even more enthralling for a man of piety, he had met in secret, with persecuted Christians whose activities he and his wife had been following for some years. This in turn led to the invitation by the Protestant Alliance in Edinburgh to give a report of what he had seen in Spain, but it was at that point that he was stricken with paralysis.

His sister-in-law, Augusta Prideaux, tells us that it was after visiting some friends as he was travelling back, on his own, from Scotland in January 1861, that his first attack of paralysis occurred. Fortunately, he managed to make his way home, but for some months, his scholarly work had to be put in abeyance and the only reading permitted was for recreation.[33] His own words, six months later in June 1861, give us some idea how critical were his circumstances:

> Severe illness has made me incapable for several months of doing anything which requires mental or bodily exertion … I trust, however, that by the mercy of Almighty God, such measure of health and mental stability may yet be granted to me, that I may after a while continue and *properly complete* this edition of the Text of the New Testament from Ancient Authorities.[34]

Altogether it was a discouraging situation for him in which to begin what was to prove to be the last decade of his active life, but perhaps it gave a greater urgency to his work on the *magnum opus*.

[33] Cambridge MA/AHTL, Prideaux, MS Life [pp. 27–28].

[34] Tregelles, *Codex Zacynthius*, p. xxvi.

CHAPTER 12

The Later Years

12.1   Health Challenges

It is hard to say how soon Tregelles can be said to have fully recovered from his first stroke. The postscript to the Preface of Codex Zacynthius, which indicates progress but not yet complete restoration is dated June 1861, but in November of that year he was a guest of Henry Alford at the Deanery in Canterbury. Alford, who was also a textual scholar, was said by his wife to have 'always found great pleasure' in SPT's company, and this occasion was no exception. Clearly, Tregelles was back to his sociable self as Alford's journal bears witness:

> Nov. 7 [1861] At three Dr. Tregelles came, a most wonderful man for information on all subjects. I took him to see the library and the lions. He kept us amused during his visit … [The following evening several guests] dined at the Deanery. Dr. Tregelles most amusing.[1]

In 1861, SPT was not yet 50 years old and seems to have been making good progress, but as we have noted before, his health always tended to be fragile. There are several indications that for quite some time his eyes, in particular, had been giving him serious trouble, probably aggravated by

---

[1] Henry Alford, *Life, Journals and Letters of Henry Alford*, 3rd ed., edited by his widow (London: Rivingtons, 1874), 339.

© The Author(s) 2020
T. C. F. Stunt, *The Life and Times of Samuel Prideaux Tregelles*,
Christianities in the Trans-Atlantic World,
https://doi.org/10.1007/978-3-030-32266-3_12

'the vapour of the Hydro-sulphate of Ammonia' with the help of which, in October 1853, he had been able successfully to decipher the palimpsest of St Matthew's Gospel preserved in Trinity College, Dublin.[2] Such chemical treatments were of course only a last resort, and usually the reading process was simply a long drawn out test of endurance.

The palimpsest (Codex Nitriensis [R]) acquired by the British Museum in 1842 exemplified the problem at its worst. The Syrian monks in the monastery of St Mary Deipara in the Nitrian desert in Egypt had done their best to scrape away the original (sixth century) Greek uncials of part of St Luke's gospel and had used the recycled vellum on which to record a more recent treatise in Syriac. It was to collate the palimpsest, Tregelles explained to his readers, that he had been 'in London for many weeks in the summer of 1854 and I investigated almost every legible letter of these Palimpsest fragments'.[3] From his account, it is clear that the challenge was daunting:

> The ancient writing is so faint that it requires a clear day, with as much light as the British Museum affords,[4] and also an eye well and long accustomed to read ancient MSS: in parts also a strong lens was almost indispensable; and sometimes it was difficult to trace any of the erased letters, except by holding the leaf to the light and catching the traces of the strokes by which the vellum had been scraped *rather thinner* by the style ... These hindrances were such as to make much patience requisite...[5]

Over the years such demanding work took its toll and at one point, in 1857 SPT notes that 'at present my eyes are so inflamed that I can hardly use them'. A year later in February 1858, he had probably not yet seen the British Museum's magnificent newly opened reading room, with its window-topped dome, inspired by the Pantheon in Rome, and when he mentions his desire to re-examine the Nitrian palimpsest his comment is stoically philosophical:

---

[2] Tregelles, *Account*, 167; Tregelles, *Zacynthius*, xxii. See also Frederick Jarratt [c.1845–?1934, a Devonian who was for many years the Rector of Goodleigh, Barnstaple], 'Dean Alford and Dr Tregelles,' *Notes and Queries* 8 (28 September 1895): 246.

[3] *Tregelles*, 'Nitrian Palimpsest,' 451.

[4] SPT worked on the palimpsest and wrote his account in Horne's *Introduction* some years before the new reading room was completed in 1857.

[5] Tregelles, *Introduction* (1856), 4: 183.

If the days are not clear it will be in vain to try: my eyes especially the right, are often rather dim. Indeed I at times am much discouraged at progressing so slowly, and I fear it must disappoint others: but I cannot hurry, for if I did I should of necessity make mistakes; and to be accurate it takes me five times as long to look at a reference or a passage as it did when my eyes were less worn.[6]

But clearly, the problems with his eyesight were only an aspect of a more general frailty that could afflict him at any time of the year. Late in 1863, he attributes it to winter temperatures:

I doubt much if I can write any thing satisfactory at present: the cold has left me so weak especially in my head that I am very little capable of definite thought or giving expression properly to what I want.[7]

In August two years later, he gives a similar account of the delay in his preparation of the proofs for the third part of his Greek New Testament:

My head has been in such a condition as to make me nearly powerless: however today I am thankful to say it feels much better while in my room at the top of the house than it did yesterday.[8]

Such positive moments were easily qualified by a wider sense of discouragement that often troubled him. In a letter to the Master of Balliol in 1864, his initially upbeat tone soon gives way to something less optimistic:

I am truly thankful for the measure of restored health, which I am permitted to enjoy. I am now able to spend a good part of each day closely occupied in my study; altho' the quantity produced in result is often very little; for I get on with any thing very slowly, as my vigour of brain is far less than my general health.[9]

[6] SPT (Plymouth, 9 February 1857; 10 February 1858) to B.W. Newton (Manchester/JRUL/CBA 7181 [9, 15]).

[7] SPT (Plymouth, 12 December 1863) to B.W. Newton (Xerox copy in the writer's possession from original formerly in the Fry Collection, but now missing from CBA 7181).

[8] SPT (Plymouth, 28 August 1865) to B.W. Newton (Manchester/JRUL/CBA 7181[86]).

[9] SPT (Kingsbridge, 15 July 1864) to R. Scott (Oxford/Pusey, Scott Papers, 1/39/2). At a later stage, his throat too was affected, so much that one obituary writer observed that those

Sometimes, indeed, one is tempted to dismiss such references to his health as a variety of hypochondria, were it not for the evident vexation to which such obstacles gave rise. In one particularly moving letter to his long-time patron and supporter, he puts this sense of frustration in a wider context:

> It has been, as I believe you know, very far from agreeable to me that the work has occupied so much of my life. I did hope that it might have been completed years ago, leaving me with vigour and ability to earn my maintenance in some other way without being in any way burdensome to others; but the Lord has not seen fit to give me the measure of health needed for proceeding as I wished: and now every proof sheet leaves me with my eyes thoroughly dim
> …
> I can assure you that there neither is nor will be a day of needless delay on my part. [For] Life and ability to accomplish this, the one piece of Christian service for which I seem to have been fitted, has long been my daily prayer.[10]

12.2   FAMILY RESPONSIBILITIES

If SPT's state of health was a cause for concern in these last years, there were other similar but more foreseeable difficulties. Both he and his wife had elderly relatives whose health was growing problematical. Back in 1812, when Walter Prideaux, SPT's maternal uncle and future father-in-law had moved to Plymouth, several of his siblings remained in his home town, Kingsbridge, and perhaps it was natural that when the twenty-one-year-old SPT left his Welsh home in Neath in 1834–1835, his widowed mother, Walter's sister would sooner or later return to her birthplace where there were still some of her relatives. So now, in 1861 she was over 70, living in Kingsbridge, with SPT's unmarried sister Anna Rebecca who was not always at home.[11] From time to time, therefore SPT, who was deeply devoted to his mother, would make the journey, with Sarah Anna, to Kingsbridge (twenty miles SE of Plymouth) to spend some time with mother Tregelles and other members of the Prideaux family. Another motive for such a break

---

who only knew him in his later years would perhaps be surprised to learn that earlier 'he was a fluent and distinct speaker', Brooking-Rowe, 'Tregelles,' 388.

[10] SPT (Plymouth, 19 October 1868) to B.W. Newton (Manchester/JRUL/CBA 7181[105]). Elsewhere in this letter, he mentions having been 'laid by with the [W]Hooping Cough'.

[11] For SPT's sister, Anna Rebecca Tregelles (1811–1885), see below pp. 24–25, n.51.

was that it separated SPT from his library for a few days and provided his eyes with some relief. It was therefore a particularly poignant moment when, in 1866, he learnt of his mother's sudden 'almost total loss of sight. On the 23rd of February, she was able to read with her usual ease, but the next morning she could not see a letter.'[12]

More frequent were Sarah Anna's visits to her widowed mother, Sarah Elizabeth Prideaux, who lived a mile or two away in Frankfurt Street, Plymouth, with her unmarried daughters, Augusta and Lucy and her widowed son Charles whose wife Eliza had been the sister of Benjamin Newton's first wife, Hannah. Sarah Anna's mother was four years older than SPT's mother and her health was regularly a cause for concern until her death in December 1866.

12.3   ECCLESIASTICAL ANXIETIES

12.3.1   Uncertainty at Compton Street

Rather different from these domestic anxieties, but in some ways more disturbing were the recurring ecclesiastical worries and responsibilities in Plymouth from which SPT found it very hard to escape. To understand why these were such a burden for him, we need to go back to the congregation of Brethren in Ebrington Street, which had been the first church with which SPT had been associated after his evangelical conversion. Significantly diminished in numbers by the withdrawal of John Darby and his followers, it had relocated in 1848 to a smaller building in Compton Street where it came to be known as an 'Evangelical Protestant Church.'[13] In spite of their being cut off from almost all the people who liked to call themselves

---

[12] SPT (Kingsbridge, 14 April 1866) to BWN [letter formerly in the Fry Collection but now missing from CBA 7181; Xerox copy of F.W. Wyatt's transcription in the author's possession].

[13] In a statement made in 1863, by Prideaux Tregelles and W.G. Haydon (elders of the church,) we learn that the Evangelical Protestant Church in Compton Street was established on 14 December 1847 when many Christians in Plymouth had 'found themselves in peculiar circumstances'. 'From that time we have continued in union professing to hold the doctrines of Evangelical Protestant Christians and the definite principles of stated ministry (without of necessity its being an exclusive ministry) of open communion in the Lord's Supper together with the maintenance of Godly discipline'; Evangelical Protestant Church, Compton Street Chapel, Plymouth, *Confession of Faith and other papers connected with the settlement of the Rev. William Elliott as pastor; addressed to the pastors of Christ's Churches* [hereafter 'Compton Street, *Confession*'] (London: Houlston and Wright, 1863), 19–20.

'Brethren', there can be little doubt that some of the congregation hankered after the earlier unstructured brethren style of 'open meeting', but to which SPT was now strongly opposed. As one of the elders of the church in Compton Street, he pressed the congregation to remain true to what had effectively been the Presbyterian ideal advocated by Benjamin Newton when he had been calling the tune in earlier years. They practised open communion, which required no membership but recognized the need for 'Godly discipline'. Some of their numbers were recognized as teachers but, true to their Brethren roots, they insisted that theirs was not necessarily an exclusive ministry.

Deeply wounded by the behaviour of Darby and his followers, Tregelles and others like him insisted that they were now no longer part of the 'Brethren.' SPT might sometimes do some teaching but he made clear that he was not their minister. For a time that role was taken by John Offord[14] who had joined the Brethren in the early 1840s but his removal to London in 1862 posed a serious problem because SPT and his fellow elders, William Haydon[15] and Dr. J. P. Riach,[16] now had to turn for help from visiting ministers like Henry Bellenden Bulteel[17] and Henry Heywood.[18] Tregelles was now clear in his own mind about the priority of his textual work and was adamant that it was no longer his role to be a principal pillar of this congregation. In fact, he was beginning to think that the days of the assembly in Compton Street were numbered:

[14] John Offord (c.1810–1870). Born in Boston, Lincs, he is described (in 1841 and 1851 Census records) as Minister of the Gospel in Exeter, St Austel and Plymouth. From 1862, Minister of Palace Garden Chapel, Bayswater, London; see *Baptist Handbook* (1870), 198–99.

[15] Captain William G. Haydon (1779–1864), often referred to as Admiral Haydon, was from an old Plymouth family. One of his cousins was the father of Benjamin Robert Haydon (1786–1846) the Plymouth painter who committed suicide.

[16] Dr James Pringle Riach (c.1798–1865) was the son of a Church of Scotland minister and had a colourful career in the Middle East before retiring to Plymouth; see Stunt, *Elusive Quest*, 231n.60. His death in 1865 deeply affected SPT to whom he had been 'for more than twenty years ... so valued and so intimate a friend' (SPT Plymouth, 21 February 1865 to B.W. Newton [letter missing from CBA, Xerox copy of F.W. Wyatt's transcription in author's possession]).

[17] Henry Bellenden Bulteel (1800–1866) was from an old Devonian family and had seceded from the Church of England to be associated for a time with the Brethren; see Stunt, art. *s.n.* in *ODNB*.

[18] Henry Heywood (1823–1891+). Described in the Census records as 'Preacher of the Gospel', Compton Gifford, Plympton St Mary.

The more I see, the more satisfied I am that any attempt to keep on Compton
St as a meeting would only be a protracted weakness, in which souls would
not be *really* blessed ... I am *unable* to take any responsibility in the matter
myself; and if more able, I might plainly say that I have had too many years
the weariness of trying to put to rights what others have put very wrong.[19]

With the elders and deacons looking for a new full-time minister, the
situation became particularly alarming for Tregelles in December 1862
when his fellow elder Captain Haydon supported a candidate named Henry
Hake of whose teaching SPT very decidedly disapproved. Haydon was
quite outspoken in his support for Hake and when he accused Tregelles of
being harshly dogmatic and unreasonable, there were some members of the
congregation who supported him. At this point in some desperation, SPT
appears to have resorted to subterfuge. In a private approach to Benjamin
Newton, he asked him to write to Haydon and Newton did so. Coming
from the much-revered former minister, the intervention seems to have
done the trick:

I am greatly obliged to you for your prompt kindness in writing to Mr Haydon; you have rendered good and effectual service in this matter, and it has
been very successful; Haydon now seems to wonder at what I can only regard
as an infatuation. He is now like a man who is just got out of a mist. I do not
think that he is likely to go wrong again about *this* matter.[20]

For the time, being the church seemed to be at peace and this appeared
to be even more the case early the next year when the church found a
ministerial candidate who enjoyed SPT's full approval.

12.3.2   *A New Pastor*

William Elliott (1829–1904) was an Irish graduate of Trinity College
Dublin who had served for a few years as the pastor of an Evangelical
Protestant chapel in Epsom, Surrey.[21] Both Tregelles and Newton, whose

---

[19] SPT (Plymouth, 31 August 1862) to B.W. Newton (Manchester/JRUL/CBA
7181[28]).

[20] SPT (Plymouth, 21 December 1862) to B.W. Newton (Manchester/JRUL/CBA
7181[34]).

[21] My only source of information about William Elliott's career, other than SPT's letters is
the minimally informative obituary in *The Gospel Magazine* (October 1904): 615–19.

judgement, albeit given at a distance, was still treated with great respect by the older members of the church, were decidedly in favour of the candidate's appointment. Believing that the doctrinal foundations of Elliott's teaching were sound, the sense of relief is clear in SPT's letter to Newton and the strength of his convictions is also evident:

> [the members of the church] knew very well that unless decided ground was taken that [*sic*] I would not stay in Compton St, and thus things have assumed their present form. The letter to Mr Elliott cost me a little thought in drawing up: I was almost surprised that Haydon did not object to a single word; his judgement seemed quite to be led right in the matter which is a great cause for thankfulness. It [sc. Tregelles's letter to Elliott] was read at a meeting (of which notice had been given) and no objection of any kind was made. The terms introduced are those, which I used years ago in registering the chapel in Compton St. so that there was no new designation devised. I trust that Mr Elliott coming here maybe for blessing ...[22]

At last, it seemed that the church at Compton Street was set for consolidation and steady growth, and Tregelles could rest assured that the leadership was in good hands. Attendance numbers began to increase and the stormy days of ecclesiastical conflict seemed to be over. Again the note of satisfaction in SPT's letter to Newton is apparent:

> I am quite surprized at the kind of influence that I am now allowed to have in Compton St; the confusion introduced by Mr Henry Hake has been I think overruled for much good. Things can be done definitely now, which were opposed a while ago ... I have had to deal with strange forms of perversity; this has needed some patience; but I do trust there is fruit to be found at last.[23]

At Elliott's inauguration in Compton Street Chapel on 4 March 1863, it was Tregelles who introduced him and on behalf of the church welcomed him, explaining with typical care and precision the circumstances that had

[22] SPT (Plymouth, 4 February 1863) to B.W. Newton (Manchester/JRUL/CBA 7181[43]).

[23] SPT (Plymouth, 10 February 1863) to B.W. Newton (Manchester/JRUL/CBA 7181[45]).

preceded the appointment.[24] Elliott in turn replied agreeing with all the positions that Tregelles had outlined.

12.3.3   Dissolution

For some three years, the church seems to have prospered but in 1866 it was evident that the new pastor wanted a greater degree of control and found himself in public dispute with the deacons over financial matters. Elliott appears to have been somewhat confrontational in public—a form of behaviour that was unlikely to endear him to SPT who was the epitome of discretion and diplomacy. Many perceived Elliott's conduct as outrageously boastful and we have no reason to doubt the reliability of SPT's account, bearing in mind his continued approval of the content of Elliott's teaching:

> To me it is a very sorrowful thing that a person of Mr Elliott's ability and who has so generally correct an apprehension of Scripture truth, should mar everything by his entire want of self control and his extraordinary doings. There are many things, which I should have said to him, had it not been that his habit of making public use of private communications (misapprehending them or misrepresenting them) has effectually prevented me.

When Elliott publicly criticized the deacons, identifying some of them individually by name, hardly surprisingly they submitted their resignation as a group, which was probably what Elliott had hoped for, but on the wider front reactions were not concerted and seem to have been unplanned as SPT's sadly pathetic comment indicates:

> As far as I know there has hardly been any conference even, among those who have separated themselves from Mr Elliott: it has rather been, as Dr Hingston said to me as to his own course & that of his family, that various persons (without planning any course for the future) alike felt that they must 'cease to do evil' ... We and most of our friends are now scattered and all the future I leave in the Lord's hands ...[25]

---

[24] Compton Street, *Confession*; SPT's address on this occasion is given in full, 19–29. Cf. above Footnote 13.

[25] SPT (Plymouth, 4 April 1866) to B.W. Newton (Manchester/JRUL/CBA 7181[96]). Dr Charles Hingston (1805–1872) who is quoted in the letter, had, like SPT, Quaker origins but his wife had been attached to the Brethren. See Stunt, *Elusive Quest*, 37

A week later, he was considering the alternative places of worship in which his fellow members might find solace:

> Mr [Frederick] Courtney[26] at Charles Chapel is attractive to some; others feel more confidence in Mr Greaves[27] at Charles Church; Mr [Joseph] Wood at the Presbyterian Chapel, Eldad, would get most of my consideration, if he were not so excitable in his manner in the pulpit. He is most gentle in private, but his voice and manners in preaching make me nervous almost.[28] Some I suppose will quietly settle at the Baptist Chapel in George St.[29]

We cannot be sure, but in all probability those who had abandoned Compton Street and (in SPT's words) were 'now *afloat*' were predominantly the older members of the congregation, and at one point, SPT refers to some fifty of them gathering for prayer and discussing the possibility of a communion service, but on that occasion, SPT made clear his objections to reviving anything like the old Brethren identity of Compton Street and took the opportunity 'to tell them most distinctly my views in the matter; and that I could not be a party to anything which is intended to be in any sense "an open meeting".'[30]

It was a resolution that he maintained, because a year later we find him writing to Newton: 'I hope that I may be able to keep clear at Plymouth of all ecclesiastical matters; I cannot attend to them and do other things also; and I have my own work.'[31] So in the last years of his life, prior to his final

---

[26] The son and successor of Rev. Septimus Courtney, for whom see Stunt, *From Awakening*, 289n.29, 369.

[27] Henry Addington Greaves (c.1802–c.1880), *Al Cant.* 3: 123; vide supra Chapter 9, Footnote 53.

[28] Joseph Wood (c.1827–1911) was of Irish origin and had previously served in Warrington before coming to Plymouth where he retired in 1897; see R. Buick Knox 'The Irish Contribution to English Presbyterianism,' *JURCHS* 4:1 (October 1987): 33.

[29] SPT (Plymouth, 11 April 1866) to B.W. Newton (Manchester/JRUL/CBA 7181 [98]). It would have been through his friends at this Baptist chapel where the minister was Thomas C. Page [1823–1882] that Tregelles learnt of the arrival in Plymouth of a dying American missionary in September 1866. John Sydney Beecher (1819–1866) had served as a Baptist missionary in Burma and he now 'enjoyed calls from the pious and learned Dr. Tregelles and a few other friends', C.H. Carpenter, *Self-Support, Illustrated in the History of the Bassein Karen Mission from 1840 to 1880* (Boston: Rand, Avery, 1883), 319.

[30] SPT (Plymouth, 25 April 1866) to B.W. Newton (Manchester/JRUL/CBA 7181 [99]).

[31] SPT (Plas Newydd, Neath, 26 July 1867) to B.W. Newton (Manchester/JRUL/CBA 7181 [102]).

paralysis, he worshipped either with the Presbyterians (in spite of Joseph Wood's unpredictable style of preaching) or with the Anglicans at Charles Church under the ministry of his old friend Henry Addington Greaves.[32] In describing this as his ultimate ecclesiastical attachment, we hesitate to treat it as SPT's final considered ideal. Rather was it a question of what was available.[33]

12.3.4 The 'Brethren Nemesis'

In any reading of Tregelles's letters, one cannot fail to notice, the prevalent recurrence of ecclesiastical issues—particularly those relating to his rejection of what he disparagingly referred to (after 1852) as 'Brethrenite' teaching. Even though the little church at Compton Street could no longer be regarded as a Brethren assembly, Tregelles was still obsessed with what he regarded as the errors of 'Brethrenism'—indeed such matters often distracted him from his efforts to focus on his great textual project. It could even be argued that Brethrenism became his nemesis. As an evangelical in the Reformed tradition, SPT's commitment to the doctrine of the imputed righteousness of Christ hardly comes as a surprise, but as time went on it became a major doctrinal bone of contention between him and the Brethren. This is not the place for a lengthy discussion of evangelical soteriology, but to understand the way the subject at times seemed to consume Tregelles we need to look again at the early Brethren among whom SPT had for a time been numbered.

Although they rejected the traditional credal statements as 'man- made' formulations, the early Brethren were only too ready and indeed delighted to investigate at great length and in close detail some of the doctrinal mysteries, which the apostle once described as unsearchable and 'past finding out' (Ro.xi.33). Lacking the balance of the creeds, which they rejected, they were particularly prone to stress certain aspects of doctrine at the expense of others. If we forget for a moment the rivalry and clashes of

---

[32] This was the testimony of the Plymouthian, Joshua Brooking-Rowe (1837–1908) in an obituary notice in *The Journal of the Plymouth Institution* 5 (1876): 388.

[33] After SPT's death, Henry Scrivener maintained that SPT had begged him to keep in mind that 'his last years were more happily spent as a humble lay member of the Church of England' and that he had assured Dr A. Earle that his reason for this was 'the results of his study of the Greek N.T.' Scrivener, *Plain Introduction* 2: 241n. My familiarity with SPT's correspondence during his later years leads me to treat Scrivener's claim with some scepticism.

personality that nurtured the division of the late 1840s, we have to recognize that it was in the course of his exposition of the humanity of Christ, that Benjamin Newton gave expression to unguarded opinions concerning the Lord's mortality that, on reconsideration, he withdrew but which his opponents never allowed him to forget.

Holding in balance such mysteries as the humanity and deity of Jesus has been an ongoing challenge to the Christian church, and—not to put too fine a point on it—when it came to the need for judicious balance, the Brethren were somewhat lacking in equilibrium as well as charity.[34] Being a historian, Tregelles was well versed in the early creeds as well as in the Reformed confessions and was deeply troubled by the growing popularity, among other evangelicals, of what he considered to be the unbalanced teaching of the Brethren:

> If a turbid stream is confined to its own channel, it may excite but little notice; but if it overflows its banks, causing devastation, and depositing its unfruitful sediment where once there had been fertile soil; and if many are induced to desert clear and healthful springs, in order to drink the muddy and deleterious water, it is high time to shew the difference between what is wholesome and what is poisonous.[35]

Early in January 1863, SPT learnt that John Darby had produced a pamphlet[36] in Toronto dismissing the doctrine of Imputed Righteousness as 'Newtonianism'. For some months Tregelles pondered as to how best Darby should be answered, but in late August and early September he and his wife spent some time away from home and took lodgings in North Malvern from where he addressed five letters to the Editor of the *Record* under the general heading: 'On Recent denials of our Lord's vicarious life.' From the very first essay ('On the Denial that Christ is our Law-fulfiller'), Tregelles made clear that he regarded Darby and the Brethren as a source

---

[34] For what is probably the most judicious and eminently balanced account of the Christology of the early Brethren and the difficulties they encountered when expounding the Lord's humanity, see F.F. Bruce. 'The Humanity of Jesus Christ.' *Journal of the Christian Brethren Research Fellowship* 24 (1973): 5–15, available online at https://biblicalstudies.org.uk/pdf/ffb/humanity_bruce.pdf [accessed 6 June 2019].

[35] Tregelles, *Five Letters*, 5.

[36] SPT (Plymouth, 7 January 1863) to B.W. Newton (Manchester/JRUL/CBA 7181 [37]). The pamphlet was soon published in William Kelly's *Bible Treasury* (1862) and subsequently as 'The Righteousness of God' in Darby's *Collected Writings* 7 (Doctrinal 2): 302–48.

of false teaching. Put quite simply, Brethren writers were so concerned to emphasize the atoning death of Christ that they had effectively devalued 'The vicariousness of our Lord's Life' which was the title of SPT's second letter. In a later letter, he makes it still clearer that in his opinion the Brethren's rejection of the Lord's vicarious life was in fact a logical consequence of their reluctance to recognize the full humanity and mortality of the Saviour.[37]

Tregelles can hardly have been surprised when his letters provoked some published replies but one in particular irritated him considerably. At the time of the division in the 1840s, Captain Catesby Paget had sided with the Open Brethren but he had been involved with the Brethren for some years previously.[38] In a badly argued reply to SPT's *Five Letters*, Paget began by recalling the pamphlet *The Blood of the Lamb and the Union of Saints* that Tregelles had written more than twenty years earlier—a work full of SPT's earlier enthusiasm for the Brethren but which he now preferred to forget. With fulsome approval Paget praised the work of SPT's earlier years: 'No tract,' he claimed, 'has had greater influence in leading Christians away from the traditions of men to hearken to and obey the word of God than this tract of yours'; but then he went on to accuse SPT of now setting the writings of the Reformers 'above the Scriptures'.[39] The situation was not without some irony and SPT's comment was characteristically sardonic:

> He [Paget] tries to convict me of inconsistency because 'the blood of the Lamb and the union of Saints' does not treat of imputed righteousness. To this it would be enough to answer that this was not the subject of the tract, and that twenty-four years ago [sc. 1839] I should not have imagined

---

[37] 'Letter IV: The Brethren's Pathway of error in Doctrine', Tregelles, *Five Letters* 18–24. The same point was at issue as late as 1866 when SPT wrote to defend the Rev. Nassau Cathcart [c.1828–1911+], Vicar of Holy Trinity, Guernsey who was in dispute with the Brethren for their espousal of the doctrine of Christ's 'heavenly humanity'; SPT (Plymouth, 16 March 1866) to B.W. Newton (Manchester/JRUL/CBA 7181 [95]).

[38] Catesby Paget (1809–1878) was a nephew of the first Marquess of Anglesey and had been a Captain in the 7th Royal Fusiliers. His first wife was Florinda Frances Mason and the marriage was celebrated at Powerscourt Lodge in August 1839.

[39] Catesby Paget, *A Letter to Dr Tregelles on Vicarious Law fulfilling* (London: Yapp, 1863), 3–4.

[that] anyone professing orthodox evangelical truth would have denied the doctrine.[40]

We have no reason to pursue SPT any further in this particular aspect of his quest for doctrinal balance, except to observe that this exchange with Paget fittingly exemplifies my earlier suggestion that the Brethren sometimes seemed to be his nemesis. As we saw earlier, just at the point of his separation from the movement, they had captured his interest in Italy where he defended them—eventually to the point of distraction. In England, the situation was similar. Truly, he had difficulty shaking off the skin of his earlier involvement.

12.3.5   Evangelical Isolation

In fact both SPT and Benjamin Newton were becoming increasingly isolated in their refusal to compromise on such issues as plenary inspiration and doctrinal orthodoxy. Their scheme of futurist prophecy was similarly another field of disputed biblical interpretation in which they refused to make any concessions. They were adopting such intransigent positions just when many evangelicals were taking refuge in a more flexible and tolerant approach to disputed truth. In the wider evangelical world, rigorous, hard-line orthodoxy was yielding to a more kindly posture emphasizing experience rather than dogma.

In 1863, when Tregelles attended the seventh of William Pennefather's annual Barnet Conferences (which were the predecessors of the larger Mildmay Conferences in North London[41]), one of his aims in his conversations had been 'to counter false teaching' but he noticed that 'the definite stand for the word of God' taken by a clergyman[42] who shared his desire for doctrinal clarity 'was by no means pleasing to those who advocate dreamy sentimentalism'. A few days later, SPT went a step further referring to

[40] SPT (Plymouth, 6 November 1863) to B.W. Newton (Manchester/JRUL/CBA 7181 [57]).

[41] For details of the evolution of these conferences see R. Braithwaite [ed.], *The Life and Letters of Rev. William Pennefather, B.A.* ['Cheap edition'] (London: John F Shaw, 1878), 297–490 *passim*.

[42] Rev. Charles Dallas Marston (1824–1876) Vicar of St Mary's, Bryanston Square, London.

William Pennefather's 'false spirituality, which might more fittingly be spoken of as ethereality'.[43] That his use of words like *dreamy sentimentalism* and *ethereality* was perceptive and well founded is apparent from an extract from the report of a later Mildmay Conference, which could have been written—albeit disapprovingly—by SPT himself:

> The object of the addresses [in the conferences] has never been theological teaching or clear doctrinal statement, but spiritual lifting and advancement in the Christian life. Worship and practical holiness a step nearer to GOD, and nearer to one another have been the desired attainments.[44]

Such subjectivity would never be acceptable to a man like Tregelles whose long-standing convictions were very well established and therefore not a matter for mere friendly or casual discussion.

12.4   The *Magnum Opus* and Its Distractions

It will have become evident that the cares we have been describing must have been a hindrance impeding SPT's focus on his Greek New Testament text. His own health and that of his family, the needs of the Compton Street Church and his published defence of the doctrine of 'Imputed Righteousness' were all bound to divert his attention from the *magnum opus*—distractions, which could only interfere with the completion of the last parts of his planned project. But in treating these cares merely as distractions, we fail to recognize that SPT was honouring what he saw as moral priorities. Family responsibilities, pastoral obligations to an ecclesiastical body with which he had been associated almost since its inception thirty years earlier, and, on a wider front, the vigorous exposition of truths both doctrinal and prophetic, which he believed God had entrusted to him for the nurture of his soul and those of others—these were sacred duties that he was loath to neglect.

---

[43] SPT (Plymouth, 9 December 1863) to B.W. Newton (Manchester/JRUL/CBA 7181 [59]; and SPT (Plymouth, 12 December 1863) to B.W. Newton (Xerox copy in the author's possession [original missing from CBA 7181]).

[44] *The Mildmay Conference, 1894: Reports of the Addresses, Corrected by the Speakers* (London: Shaw, 1894), viii. For SPT's published dislike of what he called 'dreamy ethereality' and 'sentimental religion' see Tregelles, *The Hope*, 87–95.

12.4.1   Continental Collations

Nevertheless, in spite of such legitimate diversions, the greater project slowly wound its way to completion. As soon as he had fully recuperated from the effects of his stroke, his wife and sister joined forces to take SPT to the continent where their first principal stop, in the summer of 1862, was Leipzig—the home of Tischendorf and a place, which SPT inevitably approached with mixed feelings. Needless to say he was hugely excited to examine the newly discovered Codex Sinaiticus and to make a collation of the Catholic Epistles from it, but he could not forget the unjust accusations with which a few years earlier Tischendorf had publicly blackened his reputation, and even if that matter was now closed, Tischendorf's behaviour, as we noted in an earlier chapter, was far from agreeable. Even in a letter to Hort's collaborator, Brooke Foss Westcott, with whom he was far less well-acquainted, SPT did not mince his words:

> I have had much to put up with on Tischendorf's part since I came here: it has been only for the sake of the MS that I have submitted to his extraordinary conduct: but he is now the same to every one: I wish to value his services & not to dwell unduly on other matters.[45]

It was probably at the insistence of his female companions that they then took a break with friends in Halle and visited some places like Wittenberg and the Wartburg, associated with the life of Martin Luther, before travelling by train to Vienna.[46] From there, they took a steamboat up the Danube to Nuremburg, but it is clear from several of SPT's letters that the motivation for this last part of the holiday was his own, as Nuremberg was in easy reach of Erlangen, the home of Professor Franz Delitzsch.

Here finally, SPT was able to examine the long lost but newly discovered Codex Reuchlini of the Revelation, which Erasmus had used for the last

---

[45] SPT (Leipsic, 25 June 1862) to B.F. Westcott (Cambridge/CUL, Westcott Papers, Add.8317/1/215).

[46] It was probably the ladies' choice to visit the sites of Lutheran significance as SPT had been in Wittenberg twelve years earlier in 1850 when he shared some of his thoughts about Luther's life with readers of the *JSL* (see Tregelles, 'Letters from the Continent,' 455). For the journey to Vienna, see my transcript below of SPT's 'lost' letter from Vienna included in the 'Appendix of Unpublished letters' (Letter 6).

part of the text of his New Testament.[47] This must have been an emotional moment for SPT reminding him of the time in the early 1840s when, working on the text of the Apocalypse, he had become increasingly aware of the need for a reliable Greek text of the New Testament as a matter of first priority. The MS used by Erasmus lacked the last six verses of the Apocalypse, so that the Dutch scholar had to translate the text of these verses from the Latin Vulgate, into his own Greek, using some words that occur in no known existing MS, but which can still be found in the *textus receptus* so highly valued by the advocates of the King James translation.[48]

For SPT, it was a moment of vindication to see the inadequacies of this text, which Erasmus had trusted but which in the 1840s Tregelles had recognized as incomplete. He had been sure that Erasmus must have had difficulty using the MS and now, as he read part of it by candlelight, as Erasmus would have been obliged to do when working hurriedly in January 1516, SPT found that the red markings were very much harder to distinguish than the black ones.[49] The closure that collating this long-lost MS gave to our punctilious textual scholar is evident in his letter to Newton:

It is a satisfaction to be able to say *positively* that some of the false readings in the Apocalypse are *not* in any MS; and that it was by mere blunder that they were introduced into the text.[50]

[47] See above Chapter 5, Footnotes 5 and 6. Delitzsch was working on the MS in his home and he allowed Tregelles to take it to his rooms at the Whale hotel, in Erlangen. The MS is now in Augsburg University Library.

[48] For one example of Erasmus's textual creativity, which has survived in the *textus receptus*, we may refer to Rev xxii.18 where the Codex Reuchlini came to an end. Here he translated the Latin Vulgate *Contestor ego* back into a literal (classical) Greek Συμμαρτυροῦμαι—a word which occurs nowhere else in the New Testament—where all the extant Greek MSS (to which unfortunately Erasmus did not have access) read μαρτυρῶ ἐγώ. A similar dependence on the Vulgate occurs in the next verse where the *textus receptus*, following Erasmus, notoriously replaces *the tree of life* with *the book of life*. See above Chapter 5 Footnote 6.

[49] Tregelles, 'A Few Notes,' 2.

[50] SPT (Trèves, 11 August 1862) to B.W. Newton (Manchester/JRUL/CBA 7181 [26]). For the 'lively recollection of the enthusiasm' of SPT and Franz Delitzsch 'over this unexpected discovery' as described by the Aberdeen Professor of Theology, Stewart D.F. Salmond who was in their company at the time, see his account of 'Franz Delitzsch,' *The Expositor, series* 3, vol. 3 (1886): 467.

12.4.2   *Diversion in Brittany*

It was in one of his letters written during this continental journey that SPT referred in passing to his sister 'whom we have found a most efficient travelling companion'.[51] Anna Rebecca Tregelles (1811–1885) was two years older than SPT, and we don't know much about her. At one stage, she took an active philanthropic and evangelistic interest in the welfare of the labourers or navigators ('navvies') building the railways and gave an anonymous account of her work which she said was a response to the 'eloquent appeal' of Catherine Marsh 'on behalf of that peculiar race of men, the Railroad Excavators' whom polite society often treated as subhuman.[52] We cannot tell to what extent SPT approved of his sister's philanthropy, which had typically Quaker overtones, and we have little reason to think that they previously had a particularly close sibling relationship.

However, it does seem that on this continental holiday SPT may have bonded with his sister in a new way, because, less than three years later, during one of his visits to his mother in Kingsbridge, Anna Rebecca proposed that the two of them should take a month's holiday in Brittany in the early summer, and, with SPT's concurrence (and the encouragement of his physician), they immediately made arrangements.[53] It proved to be a great opportunity for SPT to rediscover his earlier interest in Celtic history and literature. In a charming little book, he provided an account of the places and monuments visited on their trip but, being the man he was, he provided more than just history. In a fascinating note on the similarities of Welsh to Breton (and sometimes Cornish!) vocabulary, he emphasizes the impossibility of this leading to anything more than a minimal form of conversation and then (as one would expect from SPT), he raises the

---

[51] SPT [Vienna, 17 July '62] to BWN (letter formerly in the Fry Collection but now missing from CBA 7181) see below 'Appendix of Unpublished Letters' (Letter 6) for my transcription made in 1962.

[52] [A.R.Tregelles], *The Ways of the Line, a Monograph on Excavators* (Edinburgh: Oliphant; London: Hamilton Adams, 1858), 5. For the work of Catherine Marsh [1818–1912] see *ODNB* art by G.C. Boase, rev. T.C.F. Stunt, 'William Marsh'; see also C. Marsh, *English Hearts and English Hands or The Railway and the Trenches* (London: Nisbet 1857) Cf A. Mallery, *Crossing the Line: Women and the Railway Mission* (Sheffield, 2018) 192–3. Of Anna Rebecca's later life we know little except that after the death of her mother and brother she went to live in Falmouth, the town of her birth (G.C. Boase, W.P. Courtney, *Bibliotheca Cornubiensis: A Catalogue of the Writings, Both Manuscript and Printed, of Cornishmen, and of Works Relating to the County of Cornwall, with Biographical Memoranda and Copious Literary References* (London: Longmans, 1878), 2: 752.

[53] SPT (Plymouth, 31 May 1865) to B.W. Newton (Manchester/JRUL/CBA 7181 [83]).

whole question of what was required for evangelism in Brittany to be truly effective.[54]

For both SPT and his sister, it must have been a refreshing experience, though by the end of it Anna Rebecca may have had enough of her brother's phenomenal ability to remember the Celtic details of who was who and what was what in mediaeval and early modern times. For him, it may have been yet one more distraction from the great work in which he was engaged, but one suspects that he returned to the *minutiae* of his textual work, invigorated by the broader brushstrokes of wider historical issues and their significance.

12.4.3   An Oxford Break

By the mid-1860s, much less of SPT's textual work was focused on collation and instead he was of necessity devoting most of his energies to preparing and proof-reading his text and apparatus for publication, the third part of which (the Acts and the Catholic Epistles) appeared in print in 1865. However, for the Pauline Epistles (most of which would be published as the fourth part in January 1869), SPT reckoned in October 1865 that one further collation was needed. Described by Griesbach in 1793 and pre-served in the Bodleian, there was an eleventh-century cursive MS of which the text 'appeared [to Tregelles] to be worthy of particular attention'.[55] There was possibly, however, an ulterior motive in SPT's interest in the MS as it gave him an excuse to visit Oxford where he had several trusted friends who appreciated his scholarship—the sort of academics of whose company he was bereft in Plymouth—and who would also be able to boost the number of subscribers to his work.

For some reason, his intimate friend Benjamin Newton had always avoided returning to his *alma mater* and whenever Tregelles visited Oxford, he always made a point of passing on to Newton the latest 'news' as he picked it up from the few remaining dons who had known Newton back

---

[54] S.P. Tregelles, *Notes of a Tour in Brittany* (Edinburgh: Johnstone, Hunter [1865]) see, for example, pp. 52–54, 100–12, 148–52.

[55] The MS is usually listed as cursive 47: Roe 16; see J.J. Griesbach, *Symbolae Criticae ad supplendas et corrigendas variarum N.T. Lectionum collections* ... (Halle, 1793), 2: 155–58. For SPT's interest in the MS, see his *Greek New Testament* Part IV (1869) Introductory Notice, p. ii where the first volume of Griesbach's *Symbolae* is wrongly cited in place of the second volume.

in the 1820s and 1830s, and this made SPT's visits all the more purposeful. J. D. Macbride [1778–1868],[56] the Principal of Magdalen Hall, and Benjamin Symons [1785–1878], the Warden of Wadham, were conservative evangelicals with whom SPT was thankful to share some of his anxieties concerning current theological scholarship, and he had other friends like John Prideaux Lightfoot,[57] [1803–1887] the Rector of Exeter and Robert Scott [1811–1887] the philologist who had been elected as Master of Balliol by a single vote over the liberal and heterodox Benjamin Jowett—most surely to SPT's relief![58] Dons like these appreciated a visit from the genial and knowledgeable scholar from Plymouth and gave him a warm welcome. Contrary to what one might have expected, SPT was far from being a dry and dusty 'stick-in-the-mud' and as we noted earlier could be a very entertaining dinner-guest.

12.4.4   *The Canon Muratorianus: An Exercise in Apologetics*

It was during this visit to Oxford that Tregelles resurrected his earlier plan to publish a facsimile edition of the Canon Muratorianus, the text of which he had traced in 1857 when he was in Milan.[59] Subsequent communications with the Ambrosian Librarian Dr. Antonio Ceriani had been hampered in 1859 by the war between France and Austria, which accompanied the beginnings of Italian Unification, and after this the project was halted—seemingly indefinitely—by SPT's paralysis in 1861. He later explained that during his time in Oxford in 1865 'Dr Scott and others urged me to get my notes into form and completeness',[60] and once again a rival project seems

---

[56] SPT had kept Macbride informed of his work since 1854, see SPT (Plymouth, 7 September 1854) to J.D. Macbride (Oxford/Bod., MS Eng. lett. d.185).

[57] Not to be confused with the Cambridge scholar John Barber Lightfoot. Tregelles appreciated the Rector's donnish humour when, in a reference to their shared second name, Lightfoot 'amusingly introduced me to people as his "cousin"'. SPT (Roebuck Hotel, Oxford, 28 October 1865), to B.W. Newton (Manchester/JRUL/CBA 7181 [88]).

[58] The name of Robert Scott [1811–1887] is forever linked with his fellow Greek lexicographer Henry Liddell [1811–1898], the Dean of Christ Church and the father of the eponymous 'Alice in Wonderland'.

[59] See above Chapter 11, pp. 4–5, Footnotes 11–12.

[60] SPT (Plymouth, 13 March 1868) to B.W. Newton (Manchester/JRUL/CBA 7181 [103]).

to have distracted SPT's focus on the *magnum opus*. Of course the Greek
Text of the New Testament was not completely abandoned but although
the fourth volume (published in January 1869) was devoted to the *corpus paulinum*, it did not include the Pastoral Epistles or the letter to the
Hebrews, which were only published after his second stroke, and the Muratorian project may well have preoccupied him.

Once again we can observe our subject's conflicted sense of duty. His
Greek New Testament was always the project of prime importance, but as a
devout Christian he was loath to shirk other responsibilities like his efforts
on behalf of the Compton Street chapel and his devotion to the cause of
defending the faith against what he considered to be false doctrine. The
same sense of obligation came into play with the Muratorian Canon. For
thirty years, SPT had felt that Christian Apologetics was a field in which he
had a part to play, and now he perceived his duties to be unchanged.

In 1851, he had delivered a much-quoted lecture to the Plymouth
YMCA on the *Historic Evidence of ... the New Testament*[61] and in it he had
made repeated use of the list of canonical books contained in the eighth-
century fragment found by Ludovico Muratori [1672–1750] in the Biblioteca Ambrosiana. In the judgement of Tregelles, the text of this Milanese
fragment that he had carefully traced in 1857 was a valuable witness to the
validity of the documentary transmission of the New Testament. In 1865,
a critical edition of the Muratori fragment might be a distraction from his
magnum opus but it was a logical counterpart to the earlier defence he
had made of the authenticity of the New Testament and its message. His
motive is encapsulated in the motto that SPT included on the title page
of his edition of the *Canon Muratorianus*. Here, we are reminded of Per-
icles' insistence (as recorded by Thucydides) that having understanding is
in effect useless if one cannot explain it to others.[62] SPT's convictions as to
the authenticity of the New Testament documents were not in question,
but it was part of his Christian testimony to explain them.[63] Such work may

---

[61] Tregelles, *Historic Evidence*, 15–19, 22, 43, 52, 56, 61.

[62] 'ὅ τε γὰρ γνοὺς καὶ μὴ σαφῶς διδάξας ἐν ἴσῳ καὶ εἰ μὴ ἐνεθυμήθη.' Thucydides, *History
of the Peloponnesian War*, 2: 60.

[63] As an example of his editorial convictions and the reasoning behind his work, the following may serve: 'But if we do not claim intuitive and unerring knowledge as to things spiritual,
it is for us to make Scripture the rule of our faith, and not some subjective feeling of our own
the test of what we ought to receive as Scripture.'

have been a distraction from the greater project, but clearly SPT considered it to be a duty.[64]

'Whoever casts doubt on this Gospel, seeks to render uncertain now that on which there was no doubt in the second century, and that on the part of those who had all the facts before them. One testimony such as that of the Muratorian Fragment shews the futility of all the surmises that could be brought together'. Tregelles, *Canon Muratorianus*. 80–81.

[64] For some reactions to SPT's edition of the Muratori fragment, see E. Hilgert, 'Two unpublished letters regarding Tregelles' Canon Muratorianus', *Andrews University Seminary Studies* 5 (July 1967): 122–30. Hilgert included several citations *verbatim* from SPT's letters to Newton which, I shared with him fifty years ago, before they became part of the Christian Brethren Archive in Manchester.

CHAPTER 13

A Muted Finale

13.1   A Long-Standing Friendship

One of the key characters in the life of Tregelles and the progress of his Greek New Testament was William Chalk, [1814–1878] a proof-reader whom Tregelles regularly acknowledged as a person to whose faithful services over some thirty-five years he was greatly indebted, but details of whose life are hard to establish. It seems that his earliest association with SPT arose from their shared involvement in the production of George Wigram's Concordances in the late 1830s. From the single obituary notice that has survived for Chalk, we learn that it was because he recognized the value of Wigram's Concordances that he 'made himself sufficiently acquainted with the Hebrew and Greek characters to enable him to render great assistance in correcting the proof sheets of these valuable works as they passed through the press'.[1]

A year younger than his colleague, Chalk was, like SPT, a man of piety and an autodidact. As young married men in their twenties, they had both lived in Islington and Chalk soon won the full confidence of Tregelles. It was apparently in 1838 that SPT first mooted the possibility of producing his own edition of the Greek New Testament, and in the Introductory Note

---

[1] *The Bookseller* (3 April 1878): 296. In Wigram's appreciative words, it was 'W. Chalk, with whom the correction of the press has chiefly rested'. *The Englishman's Hebrew and Chaldee Concordance of the Old Testament ...*, 3rd ed. (London: Bagster, 1866), vii.

© The Author(s) 2020
T. C. F. Stunt, *The Life and Times of Samuel Prideaux Tregelles*,
Christianities in the Trans-Atlantic World,
https://doi.org/10.1007/978-3-030-32266-3_13

to Part II (dated December 1860), we find him, 'after more than twenty years' recalling that 'when I first planned the preparation of a Greek New Testament, Mr. Chalk proposed to undertake the reading of the proof-sheets'.[2] In the intervening years, the mutual trust and friendship survived SPT's move to Plymouth, and many of his letters contain appreciative references to Chalk's dependability and expertise in the ever-shifting demands of the publishing world with which the proof-reader was fully conversant.[3]

13.2   APPREHENSIONS

It was therefore a cause for no little alarm when Tregelles learnt, some time in 1869, soon after the publication of the fourth part of his Greek New Testament that the eyesight of his old friend was seriously deteriorating. They were both only in their fifties and for Chalk's sight (as well as his own) to be threatened was very troubling for Tregelles, who was well aware that his own general health was unmistakably fragile. In addition to anxieties prompted by memories of his earlier paralysis, SPT was now beginning to be afflicted with 'pain and discomfort' in the chest, and understandably, he must have feared the worst.

Possibly on the recommendation of his Baptist medical practitioner, Dr. William Square, Tregelles took the train up to London and, after spending some time with his trusted friend Newton, went for a consultation with Dr. Joseph Kidd, a renowned physician of Irish Quaker origins.[4] SPT may have been unaware of Kidd's sympathy for the Plymouth Brethren, but he came away in a positive frame of mind ready to give 'a fair trial to [Kidd's] mode of treatment in which there is much more of ablutions than of medicine'. Before he returned home, however, he was further encouraged with some more good news:

---

[2] S.P. Tregelles, *Greek New Testament Part II: Luke and John* (London: Bagster, 1860), iv.

[3] In the census returns, William Chalk is variously identified as a 'press corrector' (1841), a 'merchant's Book Keeper' (1851) with Walton and Maberley and finally as a 'bookseller'.

[4] W. Kidd, *Joseph Kidd 1824–1918: Limerick, London, Blackheath: A Memoir* (priv. printed 1920). For Kidd's Brethren sympathies see 'Septima' [Grace Guinness], *Peculiar People* (London: Heath Cranton, 1935), 53. SPT's Plymouth physician, Dr. Square, was an alumnus of Regents Park Baptist College.

Mr Chalk came to see me at the Gr[eat] Western Hotel[5]; he seems to have fallen into the hands of a good oculist; and not only does all mischief to the other eye seem to be arrested, but by using glasses his right eye does him some service: he has been able to read many pages for me of the Pastoral Epistles, and he quite hopes to be able to render the same aid to the end of the N. Test.[6]

This must have provided real relief at a time when he was well aware not only of the precarious state of his own health but also, troubled by the consequent uncertainty of his being able to complete the *magnum opus*. In his letter he continues:

These two things, Mr Chalk's eyes and my health, have been very trying to me; for it [sc. they] seemed like unexpected hindrances in my way when in sight, as it were, of the shore. However I do hope that by God's blessing there will only be a slight delay: life and ability to finish is now almost all that I have to ask for in this world.

13.3 STRICKEN WITH PEN IN HAND

However, the respite was only brief as his unstated premonitions were not unfounded, and early in 1870, his fragile body succumbed. In the words of his sister-in-law:

When literally engaged in his library, on the last chapters of the Revelation, with pen in hand, he was seized with another attack of paralysis, much more severe and disabling than the former one; from this he never rallied sufficiently to walk again![7]

There is an undeniably tragic element characterizing the last years of this indefatigable scholar. Recognizing the harsh realities of the situation, it was decided that the concluding part of his work would be issued in two parts. In August 1870, therefore, the remainder of the Greek New Testament [Part V], excluding the Revelation, was issued together with an

---

[5] What is now the Hilton London Paddington Hotel was built in the early 1850s to serve travellers on the Great Western Railway, like SPT coming from Plymouth.

[6] SPT, (Plymouth, 26 July 1869), to B.W. Newton (Manchester/JRUL/CBA 7181 [108]).

[7] Cambridge MA/AHTL, Prideaux, MS Life [p. 35].

'advertisement' explaining that although SPT's 'intellect mercifully remains unaffected, his strength is not sufficient to render it safe for him to under-take even the direction of the publication of the completed portion of his work'.

Augusta Prideaux's account reminds us that SPT bravely accepted his disability as part of the permissive will of God, and he is said to have been heard on at least one occasion, exclaiming with Job, 'Though he slay me yet will I trust in Him', but it is nevertheless a melancholy picture that she paints:

> during the first three years of his confinement to the house he was able to enjoy reading and would notify what book he wished from his library telling the exact place where it would be found: the mornings were spent in bed and those who visited him cannot forget the picture nor the feelings excited on seeing the fine countenance still full of intellect; there he lay surrounded by books, yet prostrate from weakness; he was at first fully alive and entered with interest into all that was going on in the world and the family circle, only too keenly sympathizing with those in sickness or sorrow.[8]

When in March 1872 the Revelation was issued under the direction of Benjamin Newton, it contained a brief message dictated by Tregelles himself:

> It is with exceeding satisfaction and thankfulness that I am able to put the last part of my Greek Testament into the hands of the Subscribers, thereby finishing my responsibility in connection with so much of God's word, a work which has only deepened my apprehension of its Divine authority. I am thankful to say that this is shared on the part of those who have kindly undertaken any assistance in the completion of it.

During these last years of paralysis, SPT was invited to be a member of the Committee entrusted with the preparation of the Revised Version of the Bible for which Convocation had voted in 1870. Of necessity, he was prevented from attending the meetings in the Jerusalem chamber at Westminster, but from time to time, he received for his perusal papers with details of the committee's deliberations in which he took great interest.

In 1873, however, there was a marked increase in the extent of the paralysis, probably aggravated by the fact that his powers of speech were

---

[8] Ibid. [p. 35].

almost gone with the result that he was unable to give expression to his sorrow on learning of the death of his eighty-three-year-old mother. It was on the 24 April 1875 that he too breathed his last.

His funeral was a typically unostentatious occasion conducted by Joseph Wood, the Presbyterian minister, but, true to the man whom they were burying, it was attended by ministers and members of other denominations. Tregelles had never been a 'party' man and ecclesiastical labels had rarely counted for much in his experience: his funeral was a similarly non-denominational event.

13.4 CONCLUSION

To compose the epitaph of a modest man lays the writer open to the charge of disloyalty to his subject, as fame and distinction are not sought by people of such character. While he wished for credit where he felt it was due, SPT shunned public attention. The fact that Tischendorf and Tregelles were born within two years of each other and their deaths were separated by only a few months, led to several writers venturing, at the time, to draw a comparison between them. The German critic Oscar von Gebhardt noted how, one after another, 'the swiftly ripened fruits of Tischendorf's restless activity', had come continuously into the public eye, and he contrasted this with the way in which SPT's 'one great aim' could only be appreciated with its final completion.[9] In making such a comparison, it was perhaps a little too easy to exaggerate the different motivation of the scholars, but in reality, it was appropriate. Professor William Milligan of Aberdeen University was not overstating the situation when he wrote of Tregelles that he

> struggled with difficulties to the last, had little encouragement, either in money or applause, from the Church, which he served so well, and pursued his labours supported only by the consciousness of the good cause that he had chosen, and by the hope that he would be successful in advancing it.[10]

---

[9] O. von Gebhardt, 'Bibeltext des N.T' in Herzog, *Real-Enzyklopädie* ... 1896; cited by Philip Schaff, *A Companion to the Greek Testament and the English Version,* 3rd ed. (New York: Harper & Bros, 1889), 265.

[10] W. Milligan, 'Tischendorf and Tregelles as Editors of the Greek New Testament,' *British and Foreign Evangelical Review* 25 (January 1876): 120.

Indeed the Professor justly concluded that the modest English scholar embodied 'unwearied, self-sacrificing devotion to the cause of divine truth' and was

> a man who had laboured his whole life long, not in the public eye, and surrounded with the applause of religious meetings, but in his own quiet closet, for the most part before the eye and seeking the approbation of God alone ...[11]

It is perhaps this single-minded focus that is most impressive. Repeatedly a separate inquiry or obligation would occupy his energies and threaten to eclipse or overshadow his primary objective, but in due course, he resumed the greater project. As early as 1855, an admiring (anonymous, but probably American) scholar could exclaim:

> Dr. Tregelles is emphatically a man who has lived for an idea. For more than a quarter of a century he has been engaged, with most unwearied industry, in the investigation of the Greek Text of the New Testament. He has ransacked almost every library of Europe where there is a fragment of a Greek MS.; he has read, and studied, and copied enough to wear out the hundred eyes of Argus; he has conversed and corresponded with all the best critical scholars of the present generation, Scholz, De Wette, Lachmann, Tischendorf, among the number; with feeble health he has exhibited an iron diligence; he pursues his labour in a truly Christian spirit; his patience and enthusiasm never seem to fail; and we wonder how he finds time or means to prosecute, as he does, so laborious and so costly a work, and one which can never yield him anything like an adequate pecuniary reward for so much toil and expense.[12]

Some twenty years later, when the travails of eyesight and paralysis had taken a greater toll than ever, he retained his focus to the end, even dictating, when prostrate and confined to his bed, some of the final details for the last instalment of his *magnum opus*.

Particularly striking is the huge respect for Tregelles expressed by one of his most vocal critics and a staunch defender of the *textus receptus*. J. W. Burgon, the Dean of Chichester, was a relentless opponent of SPT and of his approach to textual criticism, but, having given vent at length to his

[11] Ibid., 132.

[12] 'Tregelles on the Printed Text of the Greek New Testament,' *Bibliotheca Sacra and American Biblical Repository* 12 (July 1855): 645.

disapproval, he had to admit his grudging admiration for what his *bête noir* had achieved. It is an impressive testimony:

> Of the scrupulous accuracy, the indefatigable industry, the pious zeal of that estimable and devoted scholar, we speak not. All honour to his memory! As a specimen of conscientious labour, his edition of the N. T. (1857-72) passes praise, and will *never* lose its value.[13]

With plaudits such as these, we take our leave of the memory of Samuel Prideaux Tregelles, historian, linguist, biblical scholar, textual critic, Christian apologist and witness to the truth as he found it in Holy scripture.

---

[13] J.W. Burgon, *The Revision Revised. Three Articles reprinted from the 'Quarterly Review'* ... *to which is added a Reply to Bishop Ellicott's Pamphlet in defence of the Revisers and their Greek Text of the New Testament* ... (London: Murray, 1881), 22.

EPILOGUE

Some years before his death it was clear that Tregelles would be unable to supervise the completion of his life's work. His text and footnoted apparatus of Revelation for Volume VI was well on the way to completion and its final preparation for publication in 1872 was largely the work of Samuel J. B. Bloxsidge, a first-class graduate of Exeter College, assisted by SPT's faithful friend and print-setter, William Chalk, under the overall supervision of Benjamin Newton.

An important part in the final completion of the *magnum opus* was played by another loyal friend, whom we encountered earlier. Somewhat younger than SPT was the Cambridge scholar, Fenton Hort who greatly respected and valued SPT's independent judgment.[1] Hort was by no means in full agreement with SPT in matters textual, but, as will become apparent, he shared with SPT a common starting point and an overall objective. Together with his colleague Brooke Foss Westcott, he had the highest opinion of the accuracy of Tregelles's work, much of which SPT had made available for them in the preparation of their Greek text which was later published in 1881.

Such was Hort's appreciation of SPT's scholarship and integrity that he took great pains to assist the widowed Sarah Anna in her final efforts to complete her husband's project with the preparation of a list of *addenda*

---

[1] See above Chapter 11, Footnotes 27–30.

© The Editor(s) (if applicable) and The Author(s),
under exclusive license to Springer Nature Switzerland AG 2020
T. C. F. Stunt, *The Life and Times of Samuel Prideaux Tregelles*,
Christianities in the Trans-Atlantic World,
https://doi.org/10.1007/978-3-030-32266-3

and *corrigenda* incorporating relevant readings—more particularly those from the Codices Vaticanus and Sinaiticus, which had only recently become available after the earlier volumes of SPT's text had appeared. Together with these additions and corrections, Hort made a selection from earlier publications of Tregelles to provide a *Prolegomenon* composed of his *ipsissima verba*. Hort was most emphatic that he had

> been careful not to allow any critical views of my own to exercise influence over the handling of the materials before me. It was a clear duty to aim at making this concluding Part as exclusively representative of Dr. Tregelles's own purposes and views as its predecessors, whether I agreed with them in all respects or not. On the other hand, the task would have been embarrassing, and perhaps unbecoming, had we differed fundamentally about the comparative merits of the various authorities for the text of the New Testament.[2]

Dr. Peter Head has made a close study of the correspondence between Hort and the widowed Sarah Anna and has established that, at the request of SPT and his widow, all his notes and collations were passed on after her death, by her sister Augusta, to Hort[3]—a circumstance that underlines the similarity of the positions that they occupied.

In fact however, Hort and Westcott had developed a distinctive hypothesis of their own relating to the transmission of the New Testament text in which they elaborated considerably on the earlier ideas of critics like Bengel and Griesbach, categorizing MSS into *families*. It was a theory on which Tregelles had no occasion to express an opinion but it took them in a direction that was similar to his. In their analysis, Hort and Westcott identified a family of MSS (which they labeled as *neutral*). Reckoning that these were the nearest to the original text, they also recognized an Egyptian or *Alexandrian* family of MSS containing modest and scholarly changes to the *neutral* text of the originals. Two other groups, which they named *Western* and *Syrian*, were characterized by more significant changes. In Hort's analysis, the first of these later families included textual variants known to the early fathers like Irenæus and Tertullian while the text of the last family (*Syrian*, supposedly originating in the region of Antioch but

---

[2] Tregelles, *Greek New Testament*, Part VII (1879), xxxi.

[3] At the time of writing, the results of Dr. Head's findings in this matter are confined to his contributions on line in his 'Evangelical Textual Criticism' blog; see, for example, Peter M. Head, 'Reading in the Wren Library' (7 September 2015) at http://evangelicaltextualcriticism.blogspot.com/2015/09/reading-in-wren-library.html.

now more commonly known as *Byzantine*) was only found in MSS written in the time of Chrysostom or later.

In fact, of course, their analysis was much more complicated than this, but it left Westcott and Hort taking a position which they shared with Tregelles, with a profound disdain for the last *Syrian* family of MSS, which they identified as the source of the *textus receptus*. Instead they gave priority to the *neutral* family as exemplified in the Vatican Codex. While SPT sat lightly to the idea of MS families, he too scorned the later *textus receptus* as a gross corruption of the original, in the quest for which his aims were similarly aligned with those of Westcott and Hort.

Although the Cambridge scholars avoided SPTs dogmatic insistence on the inerrancy of biblical inspiration, they were nevertheless unambiguous in their desire to get as near to the original text of the scriptures as possible. Although Westcott would soon be the Bishop of Durham, he and Hort were not 'high-churchmen' nor were they prepared to countenance the variations of the *textus receptus* as corrections with which a Divine Providence had allowed the Church in her Wisdom to improve on the primitive teaching of scripture. Churchmen like J. W. Burgon, the Dean of Chichester and Christopher Wordsworth,[4] the Bishop of Lincoln might argue thus, but in this respect Westcott and Hort were co-belligerents with SPT, with the somewhat ironic result that their hypothetical account of textual transmission eclipsed SPT's more basic and eclectic text. Contributing to their success was the decisive part played by Westcott and Hort in the choice of text used in 1881 by the scholars responsible for the Revised Version of the Bible—a distinction that further overshadowed the importance of SPT's work.

In one way or another, the 'Westcott and Hort' hypothesis held sway in the field of New Testament textual studies for most of the following century, but in the last forty years 'W & H' have lost their pre-eminence for a number of reasons. In addition to the unyielding protests of a vociferous and doctrinaire old guard (so well known to SPT!), whose advocates insist on treating the *textus receptus* and more particularly the authorized or King James Version as the sacred ark of the fundamentalist covenant, preserved for a later age by Divine Providence, there has also emerged, somewhat

---

[4] See above Chapter 9, Footnote 12.

unexpectedly, a scholarly and articulate defence of the authenticity of the Byzantine text.[5]

More significantly several representatives of a new generation of textual critics have adopted a very different perspective in their objectives. Downplaying the earlier quest for the original text which they are inclined to dismiss as myopic or chimerical and therefore pointless, these critics have chosen to focus their attention on how in the first centuries of the church, early Christian beliefs evolved—a process for which, it is suggested, the developing textual variations provide usefully precise evidence.[6] Without openly espousing a clerical ecclesiology, where the Church is the authoritative interpreter of scripture, such revisionists have perhaps further diminished the esteem in which scripture has been held and have thus widened the gulf between themselves and evangelical conservatives. Hardly surprisingly the already somewhat isolated insistence of Tregelles on the inerrancy of the original text has become even more of a casualty than the hypothesis of Westcott and Hort.

The fact remains, however, that SPT's edition is still used, partly because his apparatus conveniently marshals, in a beautifully large print the conflicting evidence from the principal ancient MSS, and partly because his judgement is eminently dispassionate in its eclecticism. It is noteworthy that in 2011, Professor Michael W. Holmes used Tregelles's Greek Text as one of the four editions on which he based the Greek New Testament published by the Society of Biblical Literature, maintaining that 'Tregelles offers a

[5] M.A. Robinson, W.G. Pierpont, *The New Testament in the original Greek: Byzantine Textform* (Southborough, MA, 2005). Such a work was not envisaged in 1926 when Sir Frederick Kenyon wrote that what Hort called the Syrian text 'is now abandoned by all but a few scholars, though it is enshrined in the affections of the English people through its incorporation in our Authorised Version' (F.G. Kenyon, *Handbook to the Textual Criticism of the New Testament*, 2nd ed. [London: Macmillan, 1926], 362).

[6] This radically different approach to textual criticism is well exemplified in Bart D. Ehrman and Michael W. Holmes [eds.], *The Text of the New Testament in Contemporary Research: Essays on the Status Quaestionis*, 2nd ed. [New Testament Tools, Studies and Documents 42] (Leiden: Brill, 2013). Particularly helpful are the editorial essays by M.W. Holmes, 'From "Original Text" to "Initial Text": The Traditional Goal of New Testament Textual Criticism in Contemporary Discussion,' 637–686 and by B.D. Ehrman, 'The Text as Window: New Testament Manuscripts and the Social History of Early Christianity,' 803–30.

discerning alternative perspective alongside Westcott and Hort'.[7] A similar respect for, and use of SPT's text as a starting point, are acknowledged by Dirk Jongkind and Peter Williams in their recent edition of the Tyndale House Greek New Testament.[8]

With the recent partial publication by the Institute for New Testament Textual Research in Münster of the latest all-inclusive *Editio Critica Maior* [*ECM*] of the Greek New Testament, one of today's most distinguished textual critics, Professor David Parker, ventured to compare the *ECM's* text of the Epistle of James with the various nineteenth-century editions from Lachmann to Westcott and Hort. Finding how well Tregelles emerged from this exercise in comparative analysis, Parker concluded that perhaps 'we need to reconsider the usual view of nineteenth century textual criticism as a linear development culminating in *The New Testament in the Original Greek* [of Westcott and Hort]. It may be that we have overlooked the significance and standard of Tregelles' achievement. For thoroughness of citation, the *Editio Critica Maior* may be the new Tischendorf, but so far as its text goes it deserves to be called the new Tregelles'.[9] Perhaps the nineteenth-century scholar has finally found the recognition that he deserves.

[7] M.W. Holmes [ed.], *The Greek New Testament: SBL edition* (Atlanta, GA: Society of Biblical Literature, 2010), x.

[8] D. Jongkind, P. Williams [eds.], *Tyndale House Greek New Testament* (Cambridge, 2018).

[9] David C. Parker, 'The Development of the Critical Text of the Epistle of James: From Lachmann to the *Editio Critica Maior*,' in *Manuscripts, Texts, Theology: Collected Papers 1977–2007* (Berlin: W. de Gruyter, 2009), 215.

Appendix of Unpublished Letters

The following letters, written by SPT from abroad, are included here, in chronological order, as they provide valuable source materials, which would otherwise have been inaccessible. Four of them were previously in the Fry Collection where I transcribed them in 1962 but were 'lost' before Mr Fry donated the collection to the Christian Brethren Archive in Manchester. Three of these have recently been acquired by Mr Tom Chantry who has included them with the text of my transcriptions on his website. The whereabouts of the fourth is unknown though I have my transcription of the original. I have included two other letters, which were published either wholly or partly in Welsh. Mrs Wonnacott's translation renders the content usefully accessible.

LETTER 1
MS Letter from SPT to Lord Congleton
January 18th 1846, Rome
Transcribed [1962] and annotated by T.C.F. Stunt.
Formerly in the Fry Collection. The original is now accessible on line at Mr Tom Chantry's website
https://www.brethrenarchive.org/manuscripts/letters-of-sp-tregelles/four-page-letter-to-lord-congleton/

© The Editor(s) (if applicable) and The Author(s),   209
under exclusive license to Springer Nature Switzerland AG 2020
T. C. F. Stunt, *The Life and Times of Samuel Prideaux Tregelles*,
Christianities in the Trans-Atlantic World,
https://doi.org/10.1007/978-3-030-32266-3

Rome Jan 1846

Dear Lord Congleton,

I was very glad to receive the few lines from you, for here anything of intercourse with Christians is particularly felt as cheering one on the way. The £30 which you kindly mentioned as sent through your bankers came to me by the same post in the form of an order upon Torlonia and Co.[10] I gave the enclosure to Mrs Galton as directed by you; in consequence she gave Mrs Tregelles £2 which you will have the kindness to put down as so much money paid to me. I am much obliged to you for all the pieces of information which you gave me about Plymouth; there is indeed much to call for prayer on behalf of many there; I have felt things which I have heard exceedingly; I do earnestly desire that all this may lead to much carefulness in walking in individual conscious responsibility before God, and that we may all feel that we have to bring disunion and every thing of the kind among our brethren before the Lord as calling for confession and humiliation on <u>our</u> part; the sin of those with whom we are one. It may be that several have practically forgotten in some measure their oneness with the whole body of Christ; — this will never do; if the body of Christ at large is in weakness we <u>must</u> sympathize with it; not to do so will prove a kind of callousness almost inconsistent with the existence of life; if this has been at all forgotten we must surely expect that our God and Father will in his own graciousness make us feel these things, by finding the same condition in our own circumstances which exists in the church at large. I am glad to hear all that I can about those at Plymouth, tho' every thing almost has been trying: — there has been I believe individual blessing to some from true exercise of soul before God; I also fear that to others there has been just the <u>contrary</u>. I suppose the latter part of Acts xx describes what we must

p.2

expect in the church until the Lord Jesus comes; but as there was then "God and the word of His grace" whereunto to commend the saints so is there still, and this alone can give the spirit of the believer any sort of calmness in looking at the evil and desolation brought about by grievous

---

[10] The Torlonia bank in Rome was established by Giovanni Torlonia (1755–1829), created duke of Bracciano in return for his successful management of the Vatican finances; see Henri Ponchon, *L'Incroyable Saga des Torlonia: des monts du Forez aux palais romains* (Olliergues: Les Éditions de la Montmarie, 2005); Daniela Felisini, *Alessandro Torlonia: the Pope's Banker* (Cham, Switzerland: Palgrave Macmillan, 2016), 2.

wolves that enter in, or ~~from~~ by those within who speak perverse things. Of one thing I feel very sure, that we should receive this as a chastening from the Lord, and then if it exercise us aright it will afterward yield the peaceable fruits of righteousness.

We have had much kind sympathy about things from Mrs Galton; her coming is quite a comfort to us: – she and her maid break bread with us in our room in this pension where we are lodged, each Lord's day; — today they have been hindered by the violent weather and Mrs Galton having a bad cold and swelled face.

We have not found out many Christians here yet; — I was taken ill and the doctor whom I had (Dr Trayer[11]) is a nice Christian person; he lives while here with an Irish clergyman and his wife, Mr and Mrs Laurenson, both Christians of a very nice spirit; Mr L.[12] has a scripture exposition at his house every Wednesday morning; I was there twice, and it was quite refreshing; I am generally at the library of the Augustines at the time, so that I cannot be there; Mrs Tregelles generally goes. We have been introduced to a family named Gell, Christian friends of Mrs Galton's, a father and son both evangelical clergymen,[13] Mrs Gell and some of the daughters ~~both~~ also appear to be Christians: we have spent one evg with them very happily. These, and Lord and Lady Gainsborough are I think about all the Christians with whom we have had much or any thing in the way of intercourse here: — Lady G.[14] is reading my tracts on Daniel, but I have only the two first; I find that she is much interested in prophetic truth; — this may be used as leading on to almost any other portion of what God has revealed. I fear on account of some of the Christians here, lest Mr Erskine has not too

[11] Probably Dr. James John Trayer [1815–1877] later Medical Officer of the Bagenalstown dispensary, county Carlow.

[12] Probably Rev. William Robert Lawrenson, [c.1802–1877] also sometimes spelt Laurenson. He matriculated from Oriel College, 12 February 1819 aged 17; BA 1824 (*Al Oxon. 1715–1886*, iii. 825). He was Prebendary of Howth from 1852–1874.

[13] Probably Rev. Philip Gell, [1783–1870], Minister of St John's, Derby and his wife, Elizabeth. Their son Frederick (1820–1902) Fellow of Christ's College Cambridge, was later (1861–1898) Bishop of Madras who subscribed to receive two copies of SPT's Greek New Testament; see J.A. Peile [ed.], *Biographical Register of Christ's College, 1505–1905...*, 2 vols (Cambridge: Cambridge University Press, 1913), ii. 467–68.

[14] The Countess of Gainsborough was recorded as having become a Roman Catholic in 1851; see W. Gordon Gorman, *Converts to Rome: A List of About Four Thousand Protestants Who Have Recently Become Roman Catholics*, 2nd ed. (London: W Swan Sonnenschein and Co, 1885), 48.

great a hold on their minds, and lest they should become unsettled as to the elementary truths, which ought never to be questioned.

There is in this pension a young Irish gentleman named Robert Monsarrat,[15] in very poor health in whom I am

p.3

much interested; — I have had a good deal of intercourse with him, and after some time he consented to my reading scripture daily with him; I pray the Lord to bless this. In consequence of his being so ill, a younger brother of his named Henry[16] has come from Ireland to take care of him; I am thankful for this because he needed a caretaker, and especially glad am I to find that he is an established Christian, one whose intercourse will prove, I hope, profitable to his sick brother.

For two months I have been taking almost daily trouble about getting access to the Vatican MS, so as to be able to collate it. Cardinal Acton[17] has really been very kind and has taken a great deal of trouble for me; - he got the prefect of the Vatican Monsignor Laureani[18] to promise to let me have what access his regulations permitted; this amounted to only seeing the MS in his hands: for anything farther leave must be obtained from those in higher authority. Card. Acton then promised to apply to Card. Lambruschini[19] the Secy of State to the Pope; this was hindered first by

---

[15] Robert Law Monsarrat (1820–1847) was a son of Mark John Monsarrat (1770–1834) a Dublin merchant of Huguenot origins, importing French luxury goods. Robert died the following year; see https://www.ancestry.com/genealogy/records/mark-john-monsarrat_148566237 [accessed 7 June 2019].

[16] Robert's younger brother, Henry John Monsarrat (1822–1901) graduated BA from Trinity College, Dublin in 1855 and was ordained the following year. He served for many years as the Vicar of St Thomas's, Kendal; see Crockford's Clerical Directory for 1870, http://www.hallowesgenealogy.co.uk/halgen02.htm [accessed 7 June 2019].

[17] Cardinal Charles Januarius Edward Acton (1803–1847), an uncle of the historian Lord Acton, had been a respected Papal diplomat despite his youth. By 1845 when he gave so much help to Tregelles he was already a dying man. See Charles S. Isaacson, *The Story of the English Cardinals* (London: Elliot Stock, 1907), 238–41.

[18] For Gabriele Laureani (1788–1849), see Philippe Boutry, *Souverain et Pontife: recherches prosopographiques sur la curie romaine à l'âge de la restauration: 1814–1846* (Rome: École française de Rome 2002), 712–13.

[19] Cardinal Luigi Lambruschini (1776–1854) who was a strong candidate, later, in 1846, to be the successor to Pope Gregory XVI but eventually lost out to Mastai Ferretti, Pius IX. This very conservative prelate should not be confused with his nephew, the liberal minded

the visit of the Emperor Nicholas,[20] then by Christmas, and then by Card. Acton having been very unwell; the application was made last Monday, but from Card. Acton being too much engaged, I was not able to see him till Friday: — after speaking to Card. Lambruschini about it, he said that it must be mentioned to the Pope and this Card. Acton has engaged to do, not exactly as making an application from me but making it his own request. He was to see the Pope this morning, and tomorrow I expect to know the result; — I shall thus see how or whether the Lord has seen fit to prosper me in this undertaking or whether I must return without accomplishing the object for which I came hither: — in this case tho' deeply disappointed, I must look on it as the Lord's ordering, and therefore right, even if it were only to teach me submission to His will. While waiting on I have been busy in the library of the Augustines collating an ancient MS containing the Acts and the Epistles: access to this was refused me at first but a letter from Cardinal Acton removed all difficulties; and from that time on each day when the library has been open I have been always there by 8 o'clock in the morning; there are often plenty of monks and priests there — a strange sort of sight to meet. [January] 19th [1846]. This morning I saw Cardinal Acton, and he gave me the Pope's answer: no objection is made, and the formal permission to collate the MS will be sent: I am indeed thankful to the Lord for this: - I suppose that I shall have to wait for

p.4

Abbott Raffaello Lambruschini (1828–1873) of San Cerbone in Tuscany who was on notoriously good terms with numerous Protestants; see Veronica Gabbrielli [ed.], *Gino Capponi – Raffaello Lambruschini, Carteggio (1828–1873)* (Florence: Spadolini-Le Monnier, 1996), 91–92, n.2.

[20] Czar Nicholas I of Russia. Cardinal Acton acted as interpreter between the Tsar and the Pope; see [Nicholas Patrick] Cardinal Wiseman, *Recollections of the Last Four Popes and of Rome in their Times* (London: Hurst and Blackett, 1858), 479–80.

the formal permission for a few days as they are very busy making three new cardinals, but I hope before this reaches you I shall be at work on the Vatican MS. I may perhaps finish at the Augustines first, as I have not many more days work there. I should like John Howard[21] & B W Newton to know of the answer from the Pope; will you kindly inform them; perhaps you would forward this letter to Plymouth: I do not know that I have touched on anything to render it undesirable. I wish Newton & others to know how I have got on thus far. Mrs Tregelles unites with me in sending her love to you and Lady Congleton; I remain your affectionate brother in the Lord

S. Prideaux Tregelles

[posted and postmark] Roma 20 Gen [Jan]. 1846, and 1 Feb 1846 [also] 30 Jan 'St Louis', Autriche.
[Addressed to] Lord Congleton

1 Osnaburgh Street, Regent's Park, London

---

[21] John Eliot Howard (1807–1884) another former Quaker, like SPT, associated with Brethren.

LETTER 2
Letter from SPT to Eben Fardd
March 1846, Rome
Welsh original in *Y Traethodydd* 9 (July 1853) 367-371.
Translated by Mrs Olwen Wonnacott.
Annotations by T.C.F. Stunt.

[p.367]
Dear Friend and Brother in the Lord,
            Here I am in this great city amongst all kinds of things. Everything is to be seen and heard here, except the gospel of Jesus Christ. I am afraid that you have been expecting to hear from me before this, and indeed the only reason which has prevented me from writing to you earlier is the bondage of duties and tiredness. I am most indebted to you for your kindness in sending me your ode [*awdl*] when I was on the point of leaving England.[22] I looked over it when I received it, but to tell you the truth, I did not have leisure to read it until the following Tuesday [21st October], as I journeyed over the plains of *Picardy* with the forests of *Cressy*[23] on my left and the little port of *St. Valerie*,[24] quite out of sight a little way on my right; the port William the Conqueror sailed from for England.

We stayed the space of three days [Oct 22nd to 24th] in *Paris* where we met some Christian friends; then we went on the *Diligence* to *Obélons*,[25] on the River *Saone*, which we reached early the following Sunday morning [25th Oct]. We spent the day there and found a few poor Protestants there. The following day [26th Oct] we went down the beautiful *Saone* river on a steamship. Caesar and other Romans call this river the *Arar* and it is said that they called it so because of its slowness and tranquility.[26] It is obvious that that this is the same word as *araf*.[27] In the afternoon we reached *Lyons*,

---

[22] Monday 20 October 1845.

[23] Usually spelt Crécy, the scene of the English victory in 1346, early in the Hundred Years War.

[24] St Valéry-sur-Somme, where William the Conqueror assembled his fleet in 1066 for the invasion of England; not to be confused with St Valéry-en-Caux, some miles SW on the coast, also in Normandy.

[25] A misreading of Châlons [-sur-Saone].

[26] Caesar, *De Bello Gallico* i. cap 12 "incredibili lenitate".

[27] *Araf* is the Welsh word for 'slow.'

the second city of France, which stands between the *Saone* and the *Rhone*, which join a little further downstream.

The following morning [Monday 27th Oct], we took a ship on the *Rhone* expecting to reach *Avignon* in the afternoon. We went past many very beautiful sights and many interesting places – *Vienne* where Pilate was banished and where he died[28]; *Valence* where Pope Pius VI was taken prisoner by the French and where he died in captivity.[29] During the course of the afternoon it became pretty obvious that we could not get to *Avignon* before nightfall and since it is difficult to sail on the river, because it is shallow, we saw that we should be obliged to spend the night on the river; this was not very comfortable, since there were many passengers on board, and nowhere convenient to sleep. Amongst others we had several nuns and an abbess who were going to a convent in Egypt. There are very many bridges over the *Saone* and the *Rhone*; and there is one of great note over the latter, which has twenty arches; it is one of the longest bridges in the world.[30] We spent the night on the river, in a place called *Roquemaur*[31] where Hannibal crossed the *Rhone*, and went on to *Avignon* the next morning [Tuesday 28th Oct]. There we stayed five days [Tuesday 28th to Saturday 1st Nov] since I was quite ill and we both, my wife and I, needed rest. This is a most interesting place and in a very interesting situation; it was the residence of the Popes for something over 70 years, and their palace still stands in the town centre on a high rock. From *Avignon* we went down the *Rhone* to *Arles*, a city, which has a wide amphitheatre, together with
[p.368]

---

[28] Eusebius, *Historia Ecclesiae* ii.7 omits this detail, which comes from the apocryphal *Acta Pilati*.

[29] Pope Pius VI refused to co-operate with the French revolutionaries in 1798 and died as a prisoner in Valence in 1799.

[30] The bridge at Pont-St-Ésprit was famed for its twenty arches extending nearly 1000 yards across the Rhône. SPT's fellow N.T. textual critic, Henry Alford, described it in his journal (September 1855) as the 'longest stone bridge in the world'. F.O. Alford [ed.], *Life, Journals and Letters of Henry Alford, D. D. Late Dean of Canterbury, edited by his Widow*, 3rd ed. (London: Rivingtons, 1874), 257.

[31] Known in modern times as Roquemaure. Tregelles's familiarity with the accounts of Hannibal in Livy's *History of Rome*, xxi and Polybius *Histories*, Book iii is apparent, but, in identifying Roquemaure, he was *au courant* with the recent researches of J.A. De Luc, *Histoire du passage des Alpes par Annibal: dans laquelle on détermine d'une manière précise la route de ce général, depuis Carthagène jusqu'au Tésin, d'après la narration de Polybe, comparée aux recherches faites sur les lieux...* (Geneva: Paschoud, 1818), ix, 49.

other Roman remains. From there we went overland to *Marseilles* where we had our first sight of the Mediterranean Sea; we left this port in a steamship on Wednesday 5 Nov, but we encountered such stormy weather that we had to put into *Toulon*, where we remained till mid-day Sunday [9th November]. Monday morning [10th Nov] we reached *Genoa*, the capital of the old *Liguria* from which country the *Lloegrwys* [the English] came to Britain, leaving their name en route on the *Loire* in France.[32] We landed at *Genoa* for the afternoon. It is a fine city, full of palaces, and it has a good anchorage; the *Appennines*, or rather the coastal *Alps*, rise up near it, behind. The next morning [Tuesday 11th] we disembarked at Leghorn; then we went by train[33] to the ancient and interesting capital city of *Pisa*, where the clocktower of the cathedral leans so far from the vertical. I had some people to visit in *Pisa*; then we returned to *Leghorn* and went aboard ship again [Wednesday 12th November]. Since the weather was still stormy we could not reach *Civita Vecchia* until the following afternoon. The next day (the 13th) we came from *Civita Vecchia* to Rome. Much of the road had been destroyed by the overflowing of the rivers from the mountains; and we could not but see our God's gracious and providential care preventing us from reaching our journey's end as quickly as we would have done, except for the storm, for on the day when we expected to be travelling to Rome, the roads were covered with water to such an extent that many of the travellers were placed in great danger and some of the *postilions* were drowned.

It is hopeless for me to think of describing Rome on a sheet of paper. I should have much too much to say; for in truth, this is the strangest place I have ever seen or shall see on this earth. The modern city stands almost completely to the north of the ancient one, from the time of the *Republic*.

---

[32] The connection between Liguria, the Loire and the Lloegrwys [the Welsh name for the inhabitants of England] was suggested by W. Owen Pughe, *A Dictionary of the Welsh Language Explained in English with Numerous Illustrations, from the Literary Remains and from the Living Speech of the Cymmry*, 2nd ed. (Denbigh: Thomas Gee, 1832 [1803]), ii. 20, where he claimed to be following the mediaeval Welsh Triads, but as there is no such reference in Rachel Bromwich [ed.], *Trioedd Ynis Prydein: The Welsh Triads*, 2nd ed. (Cardiff: University of Wales Press, 1978) he may well have been referring to the somewhat creative edition of the Triads produced by Iolo Morganwg [Edward Williams] for whom SPT had a high regard. The theory of Ligurian origins (like much of Pughe's scholarship) is discredited today.

[33] This twelve mile journey took about 25 minute and was possibly one of SPT's earliest train journeys. The line from Leghorn to Pisa had only been open since 14 March 1844, *Hand-Book for Travellers in Northern Italy*, 3rd ed. (London: Murray, 1847), 441.

Three of the seven hills are almost wholly bare of habitation, and two others are almost as bare of houses as they.[34] All the remains of the old Rome are broken ruins, apart from the *Pantheon*, one bridge[35] and a few other things of less note. Most of the temples around the *Forum* are buried deep in the soil which has gathered over a long period; and the largest of all the ruins, the *Colosseum*, has fallen into such disrepair that it has been necessary to build great walls to support it from gradually falling to the ground.

Since I came here I have been pretty busy in various libraries, and also trying to gain admittance to see the *Vatican* manuscript, which is of the greatest importance. I have not yet succeeded in obtaining it to compare it, though I have looked at it several times and I have encountered more than a few difficulties with it. I had often heard of the idolatry of Rome, but before coming here and seeing for myself, I had not realized it existed to such an extent. There are in the city hundreds of churches and in every one carved figures and pictures of the saints (especially of the Virgin Mary) and even of the persons of the Trinity! In the great church of St Peter, there is an old ugly figure of brass which is now called "St Peter," and hundreds of people come every day to kiss its right foot! Some years ago it was necessary to restore its foot, because much of it had been kissed away; I saw people of all grades worshiping this idol, even the

[p.369]

Pope himself. The privileges of the churches are so great as to cause astonishment; there are indulgences in every one of them. In St John Lateran (the cathedral of Rome) there is to be seen a notice, which says that the indulgences of this church are so many that only God Almighty himself can count or remember them! I saw the Pope in public many times, and once I had a little conversation with him. The custom of Catholics is to kiss a cross on his right foot, but he does not expect such honour from Protestants.

And now let me tell you that I have had not a little difficulty regarding the object of my coming here. In fact after delays, expectations being held out to me, refusals, disappointments, promises etc, I have finally found

[34] The three "uninhabited" hills probably refer to the Aventine, Palatine and Caelian hills, and the other two ("almost as bare of houses as they") would have been the Viminal and Esquiline Hills, which only became residential districts when Rome became the capital of Italy in 1870, needing accommodation for the newly appointed civil servants. For a more thorough account of the seven hills, which must have benefited greatly from his observations in 1845–1846, see S.P. Tregelles, *Remarks on the Prophetic Visions in the Book of Daniel...*, new ed. (London: Bagster, 1852), 58n.

[35] The Pons Fabricius or possibly the Pons Aelius.

out today that they will not allow me to collate the manuscript, which I so particularly wished to examine. I have been detained upon this expectation, week after week, and, even when specific permission was granted me, by some in authority, some difficulty would be raised continually by those in charge of the Vatican library. And so things progressed until the permission itself was withdrawn finally and completely. I am not worried about the trouble I took, for I believe it to be particularly important that this manuscript be collated more fully; and any trouble taken regarding it could be as a service to the Lord. If He sees fit He can bring success to his servants' efforts; if not, He can teach them patience and humility. One thing fills the soul with joy amid many tribulations –"Jesus Christ the same yesterday, today and for ever." He is the same now in his love, exalted in glory, as he was when he laid down his life, bearing upon himself the weight of our sins; and He is as a good Shepherd forever watching and ready to comfort each one of his poor, needy and helpless sheep. And if we feel disorder and disappointment all round, it is but something to direct our souls more joyfully to the day when all these things will have gone by for ever, when Jesus shall reign as the Head of the new creation, and we shall reign with Him. The people of the Lord need to realize more and more, the worth of the person of Christ, as they rest in Him always. If we look on circumstances we shall constantly find something to try us and make us droop; but we are to remember that everything connected with us is known and present in the mind of God, before he gave Christ for us; and since he knew what would be the needs of each of us, he made provision for each of these needs. May he through the Holy Spirit, teach us so to rest in Jesus.

Amid the various sights of this city, I have often thought how much more pleasant it would be to be in C----g F----r [Clynog Fawr] far from these distractions. You have at least the opportunity to speak to sinners of Jesus Christ and of salvation through his blood; and also the opportunity to (enjoy) Christian society, which are not to be had here.

Perhaps you wish to know why I wanted to be introduced to the Pope. My only reason was this – that I thought it would not be right for me to leave untried any lawful means of achieving my object, and then, since an opportunity arose,

[p.370]

I made the best of it. The pope[36] looks a strong, active old man, of 81; his eyesight good enough to read writing without glasses, his voice strong and clear. He seems to be striving to entertain his visitors, by talking to them about a great variety of topics.

Now I expect I shall soon go to Florence to examine some manuscripts that are there. If you could write me a letter quite soon, addressed – *Poste Restante, Florence*, I should be very glad to receive it. I do not wish, however, to bear any of the expense of the postage, and I am sorry that I cannot prepay this [letter] beyond the borders of the Roman states.

There is something interesting, and at the same time sad, in being in this place, the city where the apostles preached and where they laid down their lives for Christ and for the testimony for his precious blood. Here St Paul wrote so many of those epistles which were moved by the Holy Spirit and which were kept on record for all future ages, and to the saints who were *once* in this place was addressed that epistle which gives the fullest explanation of the basic doctrine of salvation through faith. How have things changed by now! Everything reminds us that Rome has been the capital city of the popes for much longer than the whole space of time of all other governments. On all sides are to be seen the ruins of what *once* was; but its present glories and buildings have to do with what came to it in an ecclesiastical sense. Whatever manuscripts are to be found in the Vatican regarding the monastery of C[lynno]g F[aw]r, it is not easy to get to them because there is no proper index and the manuscripts have been placed by the thousand in cupboards. The long gallery of this library is a quarter of a mile long, full of cupboards; it is indeed one of the strangest places I have ever seen. The *Vatican* palace is extremely spacious, and stands next to the church of St Peter, it can be seen rising high, high into the sky. It is said to contain eleven thousand rooms, many of them extremely long. Apart from the rooms where the popes live in winter, it contains long galleries and rooms filled with old statues and carvings, the library, the Egyptian museum, the Etruscan museum, many rooms painted in fresco by Raphael, long galleries for the pope to take exercise in them, some rooms containing

[36] Gregory XVI was a very conservative Pope who despised modern inventions like gas-lighting as a step towards a more bourgeois and therefore liberal society. He condemned the railways with a French pun calling them *le chemin d'enfer* [the road to Hell]. Tregelles met him about seven months before his death in June 1846. He was born in September 1765, so in fact he was only 80 years old.

fifty valuable paintings. In spite of its wondrous size, the Church of St Peter seems small in comparison with this palace alongside.

A number of Englishmen were staying in Rome this winter, some pleasant friends, many of them in addition beautiful Christians. Mrs T[regelles] wishes to be remembered kindly to you and to your wife. Will you remember me to her too and to the other Christians in the neighbourhood whose company I enjoyed when I was with you eighteen months ago? I do not know when I can expect to see you again, but there are many in North Wales whom I should be happy to meet again. The climate makes this a very pleasant place to spend the winter, and many invalids come here for that purpose; but in the summer it is very
[p.371]
hot. The orange trees and the lemon trees are thick with fruit.

If the Lord ever allows us to meet again, perhaps I shall have much to tell you about Rome and her inhabitants. How are you getting on with searching the prophetic portions of scripture? I believe that the more we know about them, the more profitable, interesting and intelligible we shall find them.

I remain, dear friend, your brother in the Lord Jesus Christ.
S. Prideaux Tregelles

Signor E[benezer].T[homas].

LETTER 3
MS Letter from SPT to B.W. Newton
April 13th 1846, Florence
Transcribed [1962] and annotated by T.C.F. Stunt.
Formerly in the Fry Collection. The original is now accessible on line at
Mr Tom Chantry's website
https://www.brethrenarchive.org/manuscripts/letters-of-sp-tregelles/
four-page-letter-dated-apr-13-1846/

[p.1]

Florence Apr. 13. 1846

My very dear Brother,
In the midst of all the wearinesses of Rome I was very thankful to receive
your letter four days before setting out for this place. We were indeed glad
that thro' the Lord's loving kindness you were able to give a somewhat
improved account of Cousin Hannah[37]: we have felt for you in this trial
more than we can express, and should it please our God and Father again
to raise her up we shall indeed feel it to be a mercy from His hands. We have
had you much upon our hearts in prayer, both in connection with this and
with the trials amongst those who once met together at Plymouth. I know
comparatively little about how things are now; I ought to have written to
Mr Clulow[38] and so got an answer from him which would have kept me
better informed, only I have really not been able with varied occupation of
body, mind & time, to do this: - will you kindly tell him so, & I trust that
he will excuse the seeming negligence. Miss Pigeon has let us know a few
things; I am exceedingly thankful for the gracious way in which the minds
of those sisters at Clapham[39] have been kept simple and true in the midst
of so much opposition: - as soon as they saw what was involved in the
questions that were raised, it appeared to fix them as to the ground which
they must take, and the storms of opposition have indeed caused them to
make every point a matter not of mere intellectual apprehension, but of
conscience before God. I do believe that the cries and prayers of those who
humbly seek in these commotions to be true hearted to God & His truth,

---

[37] BWN's wife, Hannah (*née* Abbott) died the following month, 18 May, 1846.

[38] For Joseph Clulow (1797–1848), see Stunt, *Elusive Quest*, 173–74.

[39] Eliza Pigeon (1814–1898) lived with her sister Mary on the South side of Clapham
Common. She was later the second wife of Edward Steane, a Baptist minister, who was one
of the founders of the Evangelical Alliance.

will not be in vain; and tho' the consciousness of weakness will, I believe increase, yet there will be at the same time the conscious knowledge of the Spirit of God as leading both as to individual walk and in
[p.2]
any united service. Surely felt weakness is that which will continue until the Lord shall come, but what we have to seek is grace and wisdom to stand and act in each succeeding trial as it may arise.[40]

You speak of "Brethrenism with all its doctrinal and ministerial peculiarities," – this I think I understand; the Judaizing of a great portion of scripture so as to make it not Christian, and as to ministry the thought of unrestrainedness without the recognition of the responsibility of recognizing as teachers those whom the Lord has distinctly set as such, or of hindering the ministry which is without edification. Edward Foley[41] used to call the true thought in connection with ministry "stated ministry but not exclusive ministry"; meaning by stated ministry the distinct recognition that such and such are the persons who at such a place minister, and in fact whose ~~might~~ ministry may be expected; while at the same time there was no shut door so that any whom the Lord might fit for ministry should be prevented from exercising gifts so given. For my own part I believe that now gift is at a low ebb in the Church of God, and that nothing can be more outrageous than the thoughts and practices of some upon this subject. I cannot tell you how thankful I feel to the Lord for His gracious care in keeping together those who remain united at Plymouth; I do believe that the shaking will make not a few hold the truth of God with a more exercised and intelligent conscience, and that results in grace and service will be manifest.

For my own part it has felt strange to be out of these grievous contests, tho' probably it is better for those who cannot really be of service to be absent lest they should be hindrances to those who are fitted to contend. I hear a good deal rather unconnectedly about the reasons of those who

---

[40] Part of this paragraph appears to have been quoted selectively and inaccurately by B.W. Newton when referring to "A friend recently writing to me from abroad," in his letter to Alexander Rees, 14 May, 1846. Newton's letter was quoted at length by G.V. Wigram in his *Plain Evidence Concerning Ebrington Street, as to the Nature of the System Now Pursued Thereby* (Plymouth: J.B. Rowe; London, 1 Warwick Sq. [1847]), 14. The variations may have originated in the transcription of the letter by one or more of Newton's several female copyists.

[41] For Edward Foley (1807–1894) and some discussion of this paragraph, see Stunt, *The Elusive Quest* (2015), 201.

have separated but [al]most all is vague and unformed; the principle argument which they seem to use to shew the rightness of the step is the great alledged [sic] blessing which they have received since they took the step. They certainly have taken a good deal of pains in making Italy <u>swarm</u> with their letters & reasons. None however have [sic] been sent to me. A little before I left Rome I heard of someone who in passing thro' Naples put a copy of your "Thoughts on the Apocalypse"[42] into the English Library there; I was surprized [sic] at it & had

[p.3]

supposed mine to be the only copy in the place. Yesterday's post brought some introductions kindly sent by Miss Weston[43] and a few lines from Augusta[44]; she mentions the decease of M.E. Haydon,[45] an event at which we cannot be surprized [sic], after the mention which you made of her illness: - we do indeed feel <u>much</u> for the family.

After I had a positive and absolute refusal (or rather withdrawal of an express permission) from Cdl. Lambruschini,[46] I looked about me to see if any other means could be used: I had already seen the Pope and he had made no objection & I found that it would be useless to see him again; — I saw Cardinals Mai[47] & Mezzofante.[48] The former of these had a

---

[42] B.W. Newton, *Thoughts on the Apocalypse* (London: Hamilton, Adams; Plymouth: J.B. Rowe, 1844).

[43] Emily Weston (c.1821–?). In 1841 she was living in Plymouth in the household of James [Ebenezer] Batten but was later one of the English protestants (together with Eliza Browne and Charlotte Johnson) associated with the Brethren in Florence.

[44] Augusta Prideaux (1815–1900), a younger sister of Sarah Anna Tregelles.

[45] Mary Elizabeth Haydon (1814–1846), a daughter of Captain William Haydon (1779–1864) who was a member of the Brethren assembly at Plymouth.

[46] Cardinal Luigi Lambruschini (1776–1854).

[47] Cardinal Angelo Mai (1782–1854) the custodian of the Vatican Library and Secretary of the Sacred Congregation for the Propagation [*propaganda*] of the Faith.

[48] Cardinal Mezzofanti (1774–1849) is said to have been able to speak some forty languages and dialects. George Fox Tregelles, in his "Life of a Scholar" [S.P.T.] is referring to Mezzofanti when he claims that S.P.T "remembered that his eminence was reputed to know a marvellous variety of languages", so Tregelles addressed him in Welsh: —'Pa fodd yr ydwyt heddyw?' (How art thou today) to which the other replied: 'Yr ydw yn lled dda, diolch I ti' (I am very well thank thee.) Mezzofanti's knowledge of Welsh is confirmed in C.W. Russell, *The Life of Cardinal Mezzofanti with an Introductory Memoir of Eminent Linguists, Ancient and Modern* (London: Longman, Green, Longman, Roberts and Green, 1863), 320. A slightly different account of the encounter with SPT, in which Mezzofanti took the initiative, can be found in T. Mardy Rees, *A History of the Quakers in Wales and Their Emigration to North America*

permission to publish the text of the MS, but with regard to ~~which~~ this there are now some hindrances; this permission given to Mai had been used as a reason for acting in this slippery way about my application; — Mai was decided enough; he told me in civil words that he would never consent to any person using the MS but himself as long as he could help it; — it pleased me much more to have to do with a plain spoken person than with those who say one thing and mean another. Mezzofante could do nothing for me. I left Rome with any thing but pleasant feelings, for every thing there has discouraged me greatly about my work. The morning after I arrived in Florence[49] I went to the Medicean Library where that most important copy of the Vulgate, the Codex Amiatinus is kept. This requires to be collated accurately. After my annoyances at Rome I feared delays here; but on the contrary as soon as I had told my errand every facility was afforded me for doing all I want; the monstrous MS (so heavy that it takes two men to lift it) was brought to me, and my convenience about light, desk, &c consulted in a way that I never knew the like of in any library in England. As the especial object of my coming to Italy has so utterly failed I suppose that I had better do all that can be done with the materials, which are in themselves the less important. I propose going from this place to Modena (for about a week) then to Venice; at both these places there are ancient MSS very partially collated.[50] As the expense has been so much greater than I had at all contemplated, I think that I had better give up Milan and Turin (which are of <u>doubtful</u> importance) and return from Venice by Munich where there is now an important MS[51] about which Scholz[52] told

(Carmarthen: Spurrell and Son, 1925), 244 where the author also states that Mezzofanti was 'taught Welsh in exchange for Italian by a notable Welsh portrait painter, Thomas Brigstocke of Carmarthen, when an art student in Rome.'

[49] From SPT's entry in the *Album dei visitatori della Biblioteca Laurenziana*, ii, the date was 6 April 1846.

[50] The Codex Mutinensis at Modena is a ninth century uncial MS of the Acts. The Codex Nanianus in the Biblioteca di San Marco is a tenth century uncial MS of the Gospels. For SPT's published account of these visits, see Tregelles, *Account*, 158.

[51] The mutilated tenth century Codex Monacensis had previously been in the ancient university of Ingolstadt and had only recently (1827) arrived in Munich when the University was relocated there by King Ludwig I of Bavaria.

[52] Johann Martin Augustin Scholz (1794–1852) differed greatly from SPT in his approach to New Testament textual criticism, but SPT nevertheless always gave him credit for his readiness to share details of his discoveries with other scholars and acknowledged the help he had received from this Roman Catholic scholar; see Tregelles, *Account*, 92–97, 159.

me just before I left England; then Bâle where I am promised the use of the MSS at my lodging, and then back to England: — truly glad shall I be when the Lord brings us safe again amongst you.

In one sense I neither regret the time nor the expense of Rome (tho' it is disagreeable to be spending other people's money in such a way) – the attempt <u>ought</u> to have been made and I have learned <u>a great many</u> things in connection with my work and have got together various materials the existence even of which is utterly unknown

[p.4]

in England. But it troubles me that I am only like one learning how to do such a work as that I have before me. I should be thankful if some really competent Christian scholar were to take the thing in hand & then all my collations should be at his service most cheerfully; but I do not expect this: from 1838 to 1842 I tried by all the inquiries I could make to get someone to undertake this work but in vain. I can only look to the Lord for His blessing [,] and labour on tho' I think the result will be only an <u>approximation</u> to what I would desire. Indeed the more I know the Vatican MS the more persuaded I am that until it is properly collated we shall in many places be making rather <u>guesses</u> at readings that [*sc.* than] conclusions based upon known evidence. I am indeed thankful to those who kindly render pecuniary aid. I believe that I shall get on [*sc.* get by, financially] till my return with what you mention, for tho' I am now breaking in for living upon the money which I had kept for travelling, yet the expenses here are light when compared with Rome, in fact they would be light in England. I do not ask you to write to me, but will you tell Mr Clulow that I should be most glad to hear from him: — I do not know when I shall find time to write to him or to Lord Congleton which I wish to do: — many hours close work in a library in Italy do not leave me fit either in body or mind for much writing, and then there are many needful letters to be written. In thinking about returning to England I hope that I may be rightly guided as to my location; the two considerations are, where my N. Test. Work can be best carried on, and where I can be of any service in the present shattered and confused condition of things.

Very much love from both of us to Cousin Hannah and yourself. I trust that we may hear of the Lord continuing to care for you and bless you,

Most affectionately your brother in the Lord

S. Prideaux Tregelles

[postmark Apr 14 1846 Firenze…Plymouth Apr 24 Al Signor B W Newton, Gasking [Gascoigne] St, Plymouth

LETTER 4
MS Letter from SPT to B.W. Newton,
July 1st 1849, Paris
Transcribed [1962] and annotated by T.C.F. Stunt.
Formerly in the Fry Collection. The original is now accessible on line at
Mr Tom Chantry's website
http://www.brethrenarchive.org/manuscripts/letters-of-sp-tregelles/
three-page-letter-to-bwn-dated-1st-july-1849/

[p.1]

Paris   July 1, 1849

My beloved brother

We were very glad to receive your letter a few days ago, before we quit this place where we have indeed received many mercies from the Lord's hand, which we desire thankfully to acknowledge.

Our plan is to quit this place tomorrow at one by the railway for Amiens: — this is a journey of less than four hours; but tho' I am much better,[53] I do not think it well to try to do more, at least at first: we propose passing one or two nights at Amiens: this must depend on how I feel and how I bear journeying; then on to Boulogne, and cross to Folkstone, [sic] and so to London without any unnecessary delay. We expect to find a line from Lucy[54] for us at the Post Office at Folkstone to tell us about lodgings (if she knows of any) where we may be for the few days which we shall have to be in London before we go on to Plymouth; we are anxious to get there as soon as we can conveniently: — I am truly glad that we are likely to have some of your company there [presumably in Plymouth], and from what Miss Pigeon[55] wrote to Sarah Anna yesterday, it seems possible that we may see you in London before you go; but of course you will not let our coming at all influence your movements.

---

[53] SPT had fallen victim in Paris, to the cholera. His wife had come to care for him and to bring him home.

[54] Lucy Prideaux [1820–1896] was the very much younger sister of Sarah Anna Tregelles.

[55] Eliza Pigeon (1814–1898) of Clapham was later the second wife of Edward Steane, the Baptist minister, one of the founders of the Evangelical Alliance.

I got out to the little meeting at the de Tharon's[56] this morning; — this was some exertion to me, but I was glad to be there: — they have been diligently warned against me, and I did not go to their meeting until I was asked: the warnings which they have received have been so strong as to have the contrary effect to what was intended: the Lord shews us that he knows how to overrule such things: — they think that we have been treated very ill.

The present political condition of things in France[57] has given me a good deal of trouble about Passports; the number of places in which it was needful for me to be present in person and the annoyances have been almost as much as a convalescent can stand — however I have got thro' that part of my difficulties.

I am still very feeble in body and mind, and my limbs and body still feel the effects of the spasms and cramps: but I am not as weak as when I wrote [p.2] you last; that was only the second time that I had taken a pen in my hand: once before I wrote a few lines to my dear Mother: I knew that you would like to hear from me as soon as I could write.

I must have given you an imperfect impression as to what it is that Cardinal Mai[58] wishes to dispose of: it is not a MS transcript of the Vatican MS, but the text of the MS printed, not a facsimile edition; its value will depend greatly on Mai's accuracy: but still it is sure to be very valuable: I must inquire about [it] when in London. I doubt whether Chevalier

---

[56] Hippolyte Michel, Comte de Tharon (1786, Nantes–1863, Paris) in exile (with his father) during the French revolution, served in the British army in Europe and America, and was decorated in 1808 at the Battle of Vimeiro where Wellington defeated General Junot in Portugal. He married an Irish lady Elisabeth Hore Hatchell and had two sons (https://fr.wikipedia.org/wiki/Gabriel_Michel). For his death see SPT to BWN 23 October 1863 (Manchester, CBA 7181 [56]). He had been 'at Plymouth, many years ago.' 'We often saw him in Paris, the last time being in 1860.'

[57] In the wake of the 1848 revolution and the violence of the 'June days' the election of Louis Napoleon as President of the Republic gave rise to a great deal of administrative uncertainty, especially in Paris where, two weeks before this letter was written, an unsuccessful rising against Napoleon had put the city in a state of siege.

[58] Cardinal Angelo Mai (1782–1854) was the custodian of the Vatican Library and Secretary of the Sacred Congregation for the Propagation [*propaganda*] of the Faith (located to the SE of the Spanish steps). Mai's edition of the Codex Vaticanus was only published posthumously in 1860. SPT reviewed it in the *Edinburgh Review* (July 1860).

Bunsen[59] could do much now; the state of Prussian finances is not the most pleasant to their Ambassadors abroad.[60]

Whilst here I have at my leisure read through most part[s] of the Syriac version of the Gospels which has been recently discovered: I think I told you about it, and perhaps I shewed you the sheets which Mr Cureton[61] so kindly let me have: the MS which contains this version is of about the year 400; the places in which this text accords with the most ancient Greek copies are extremely numerous; it seems to be much the oldest Syriac translation. It is an important collateral witness for the more ancient text.

It seems as tho' we should find many of our friends absent from London when we ~~of~~ arrive: we shall be sorry to miss them tho' at the same time we could have seen but little of them. I feel much for Mr Egerton[62] in his long continued sufferings: may the Lord graciously deal with him and support those who are brought into trial and special sympathy on his account.

We shall feel in leaving this place where we have passed thro' a good deal, and where the loving kindness of the Lord has been markedly shewn in many ways: we little liked to be obliged to leave our former lodging, but here we had many, many conveniences and comforts in illness which we could not have had there; — the large airy rooms and pleasant garden have been indeed advantageous: — but especially we have to be thankful for the kindness of friends and attendants; our domestique, Julie Loyeau has been devoted in her service: we cannot but feel taking our leave of those from whom we have received so much kindness, and we desire to own the Lord's hand in it all. Mrs Erskine gave Julie a French New Test. about a month ago,

[p.3]

---

[59] Baron Christian Karl Josias von Bunsen (1791–1860), diplomat and evangelical theologian, had been the Prussian minister to the Vatican (1823–1838) and was the Prussian ambassador to the court of St James from 1842 to 1854.

[60] Clearly Tregelles had in mind the failure of the 1848 revolutions in Germany and the subsequent political uncertainty.

[61] William Cureton (1808–1864), assistant keeper of manuscripts in the British Museum, and Canon of Westminster. The MS of the Syriac gospels had been in the monastery of St Mary Deipara in the Nitrian desert in Egypt, where the Coptic scholar Henry Tattam [1788–1868] acquired it for the British Museum. Cureton's edition was not published until 1858 but he was privately circulating copies as early as 1848. For SPT's published account of his own work in 1849, see Tregelles, *Account*, 160–61.

[62] Probably the father of Jane Egerton, who, like Eliza Pigeon and Mary Boniface, was one of several unmarried admirers and *amanuenses* of B.W. Newton.

it has been very interesting to see with what eagerness she reads it, and the real delight which she finds in reading of the actions and teaching of our Lord when on earth; may she indeed be made wise unto salvation by the instruction of the scripture.

The cholera has greatly lessened in Paris, but the condition of many of the poorer convalescents is very sad: they are discharged from the hospitals where they have been <u>well</u> cared for, and they have no means of procuring the great quantity of nourishment which they need to recruit their debilitated frames. The <u>Maire</u> of this (the 1st) Arrondissement of Paris has put forth an appeal on behalf of these convalescents which is peculiarly touching. I must say that the authorities of this city have done more than could be expected in <u>personal</u> exertion with regard to the Cholera patients; the general destitution, however, of the poor of Paris is grievous.

Amiens. July 2. At this place by the blessing of the Lord we arrived comfortably at about 5 o'clock. M. & Mde de Tharon kindly saw us off: M. de Th. desires his Christian love and all other love to you: his kindly feeling is very marked.

We hope to get on to Boulogne tomorrow, — sleep at the Hôtel de Londres, — cross to Folkestone⁶³ Wednesday morng. leave by the train at 2 o'clock, getting to London bridge ¼ before 6. (I expect that we shall not be able to cross in time to leave Folkestone at 10 & get up to London at ¼ before 2 — we should like to do this if we can.)

Much love from both of us to those around you and to yourself
Your very affectionate brother in the Lord
                    S. Prideaux Tregelles

[p.4]

Amiens Juillet 2, PD JY 3 1849   Affranchie
À Monsieur B.W. Newton
11 Victoria Grove Terrace Bayswater
Londres

⁶³ Until the mid nineteenth century there was considerable uncertainty as to the spelling of Folk[e]stone. Interestingly SPT spells it with only one 'e' in the earlier part of this letter and with two 'e's in the last part.

LETTER 5
Letter from SPT to Eben Fardd
June 30 1860, Granada
Welsh/English original in *Y Traethodydd* 29 (July 1884), 292–93. [[Double bracketed text]] originally in Welsh, translated by Mrs Olwen Wonnacott.
Annotations by T.C.F. Stunt.

[p.292]   [[Granada
                                                  June 30, 1860
[[Dear Bard
    To have a letter from me in *Spain* will be probably something you did not expect, but in truth I am in this far-off land and in the seat of so many remains of the *Moors*. Granada was their principal city until its conquest in the year 1492. I have only a few books with me, but amongst them are *two* of Welsh poetry, one the work of Goronwy Owain,[64] the other 'Sonnets by Ebenezer Thomas, Clynnog'. Here within the stony shell of the *Alhambra* (a famous palace of the Moorish Kings) I read anew your epic on the destruction of Jerusalem and some other compositions of yours. It is probably very rare to find Welsh books being read in this land of Andalucia.]]
    I was very far from well, and I wanted some change and rest for my head and eyes; and as for many years we have been interested in Spain, we have come to visit some parts of the country in which Popery has so long reigned, but where now some testimony to the gospel of Christ is given. After crossing France by Railway to Bayonne, we there took the Diligence[65] for San Sebastian; we then visited Bilbao, and went to Madrid by way of Vitoria, Burgos, Valladolid (famous in the time of the Reformation for believers and sufferers). All the middle of Spain is dreary enough. Madrid is now a fine place, but with a very modern look. There are some there who know the gospel, but they are hardly acquainted one with another. We hope that our visit may tend to bring some of these together. My wife knows Spanish, and I can read it. We were for a day at Toledo to see the magnificent Cathedral; the walls and other ancient remains of that city are

---

[64] A week later, SPT wrote a letter from Seville to the editor of another Welsh magazine, *Y Brython* [*The Briton*] concerning errors and omission in this work of Goronwy Owain. His letter, which was written in Welsh, was published in *Y Brython* iii.2 (August 1860), 311–12.

[65] The French word for a Horsedrawn stage-coach.

very curious. Thence partly rail and partly by Diligence to Jaen, going thro'
La Mancha (Don Quixote's country) and by the pass of Sierra Morena.

[[At present we are resting a little *here*: but what must I tell about
Granada? I cannot rightly *describe* the Alhambra though it is easy to tell
you something about it. Over against the city of Granada lies the Sierra
Nevada, mountains of about 12000 feet height, the highest in Spain. The
city is partly on a hill and partly on the level and on one side the rising hill
of the Alhambra skirted around by ancient towers and walls. One slope of
the hill is well wooded and at the top, an old Moorish mansion with its
rooms, courts and such like: parts of it are well preserved, other parts of it
are just heaps of stones. I have never seen anything like it.

[[But what is more worthy of note in Granada is its Protestant Church; a
secret body of folk, those who by the mercy of God have received Christ into
their hearts. It would be dangerous to tell of them. We must give thanks
and pray for them. We are the first foreigners to visit them. It is necessary for
them to worship in secret (sometimes at night) and it is difficult for them to
obtain copies of the scriptures. One evening we attended a meeting of some
of them and heard a magnificent sermon (on Gal[ations].i.9) given by a
gifted young man, spiritual and humble. It would be difficult to forget such
a meeting, doors and windows shut and each one careful that no *zealous*
papist should know the time and place of their meeting. Persecution again
in Spain!
[p.293]

[[Seville. July 7th. After leaving Granada we went to Malaga for two
days. I hoped to get a steamer to Cadiz, but there was not one.[66] We met
some in Malaga professing faith in the Gospel; in the meeting (at night
time) there were about 80 of us. A young man preached the Gospel well
and clearly.[67] Our journey from Malaga was very *long*: 28 hours by coach,
and four by rail. We stayed two hours in Córdoba, where we saw yesterday
([July 6th] at 5 o'clock in the morning) the old *Mosque*, which is now the
Cathedral Church. I never saw anything like it: *eight hundred* low columns,
and arches from them, like some very thick forest.

---

[66] The River Guadalquivir is navigable from Seville to the Gulf of Cadiz.

[67] This must have been Manuel Matamoros, 'One of these meetings was witnessed by Dr.
and Mrs. Tregelles...' William Greene, *Manuel Matamoros: His Life and Death: A Narrative of the Late Persecution of Christians in Spain, Compiled from Original Letters and Other
Documents*, 3rd ed. (London: Alfred Holness, 1889), 11.

[[Seville is a magnificent city regarding its buildings; the Cathedral Church of tremendous size; its beautiful tower – the work of the Moors, and its *Alcazar* or royal palace. Originally for the Moors and later for the kings of Spain for about 250 years, who made Seville their capital city (until the time of Charles V[68]).

[[We have some places to see here before going on to Cadiz. There is far more of the Lord's work going on in this part of Spain than in other places. Our aim is to go from Cadiz in a steamer to *Valencia* and to *remain* there a little before returning home. Whatever friend chooses to be so kind as to write to us will have to write to us at *Valencia* without delay.]]

There is much in this country to make us value the privileges of our own land: here, in spite of all the danger and difficulty, many get the word of God and many more desire it: books are printed and circulated in secret by those who know that if discovered they would be subjected to cruel imprisonment: surely this will go on in the gathering out of more who shall learn to the blessing of their souls the difference between trusting in the blood of Christ alone for salvation, and that which is set forth in Romish observances. There was a person quite lately imprisoned in this city for his profession: I have not yet been able to find whether he has been liberated[69]: he certainly was not prudent, but still any one persecuted for the truth's sake calls for our sympathy and prayers. The people of Spain seem to be divided between fanatical Roman Catholics, and people altogether indifferent: but both agree in disliking and opposing the truth of the gospel.

It is now getting quite hot here, so that very little can be done except in the mornings and evenings quite late: the plants and trees form a great contrast to those of our country. Here we see orange and olive trees; vine-yards cover the hills, palms occasionally, while cactuses grow in profusion

---

[68] SPT refers to the *Emperor* Charles V who in fact was *King* Charles *the first* of Spain.

[69] Martin Escalante, a member of the Wesleyan Church at Gibraltar, sold copies of the Bible at fairs in Andalusia and was arrested on 3 May 1859. He was liberated sometime in 1860. (*The Bulwark or Reformation Journal* [1 October 1859], 95; [2 July 1860], 1.) A few years later SPT wrote: 'There is no ground for mixing up any of the Granada Protestants with poor Escalante: when I saw him at Gibraltar I was satisfied that he was at best a very poor weak creature: he [as a Methodist] was earnest in denouncing Protestants in general as "Calvinists", and Calvinism he said was far worse than Popery.' (SPT, Plymouth to B.W. Newton, 29 January 1864, [Manchester/JRUL/CBA 7181(62)]). From this we may deduce that SPT visited Gibraltar after his time in Seville. Escalante eventually rejoined the Roman Church; see Sue Jackson, 'The Bible in Spain and Gibraltar,' in S. Batalden, K. Cann, J. Dean, [eds.], *Sowing the Word: The Cultural Impact of the British and Foreign Bible Society 1804–2004* (Sheffield: Phoenix Press, 2004), 311.

and the aloes are in full blossom every where. This country is but little visited by travellers, forming in this respect a great contrast to France, Italy and Switzerland.

[[Now, dear Bard, I must close my letter; this may be the first time that Clynnog Fawr has been addressed from the banks of the River *Guadalquiver* [sic]; but I am happy to remember my friends wherever I am

With much Christian love from myself and my wife

I remain, dear Bard, yours sincerely

S.P. Tregelles]]

LETTER 6
Lost MS Letter from SPT to B.W. Newton[70]
July 17 1862, Vienna
Formerly in the Fry Collection, present location unknown.
Now only surviving in transcription made by T.C.F. Stunt in 1962

Vienna
July 17 1862

My dear Cousin

The best way of getting from Prague to Nuremberg and Erlangen seemed to be to get to this place by rail and then by steam up the Danube: this therefore is what we have partly accomplished.[71] I have been glad to see the ancient and very valuable Greek MSS in the imperial library here. Some of these I have often <u>wished</u> to see but it has always been out of my way to get here.[72] We had a beautiful journey thro' Bohemia and Moravia. The night before last we slept at Brünn,[73] the capital of the latter country: both it and Prague seem to be very Popish places: I was glad to hear a really good sermon however in the Protestant church in ~~the former place~~ Prague: but I suppose that the Protestants there are simply German residents; for I do not think there is any Protestant service in Bohemian at Prague.[74]

---

[70] This letter was written in the summer of 1862. It was preceded by at least two other letters (not reproduced here) concerning the Codex Sinaiticus which SPT examined in the home of Constantin Tischendorf—one from Leipzig (June 20) and another from Berlin (July 3). They were probably addressed to B.W. Newton and extracts from them (copied in two unknown hands) were in the Fry Collection in 1962. These were published in full (from my transcripts) in my 'Some Unpublished Letters of S.P. Tregelles Relating to the Codex Sinaiticus', in the *Evangelical Quarterly* 48 (January 1976): 19–20. Recently acquired by Mr. Tom Chantry, the original copies can be accessed on line at https://www.brethrenarchive. org/manuscripts/letters-of-sp-tregelles/. Letter 6 of this appendix was written two weeks later from Vienna.

[71] To go from Prague to Nuremburg via Vienna was a huge detour, but in 1862 there was no direct link by rail across the border between the Habsburg Empire and Bavaria.

[72] SPT's use of the phrase 'ancient and very valuable Greek MSS' is somewhat exaggerated here as there were few MSS in the Imperial library which qualified for such a description in SPT's customary use of those adjectives. He was probably thinking of the *Fragmenta Vindobonensa* which, with the Fragmenta Cottoniana in the British Museum were later identified as part of the seventh century Codex Petropolitanus Purpureus. The other important MSS preserved in Vienna were later minuscules.

[73] Known today, in the Czech Republic as Brno.

[74] Although Joseph II's *Toleranzedikt* (1782) had allowed Protestants to meet unobtrusively in the Habsburg Empire, it was only in 1861, the year before SPT's visit, that Franz Joseph's *Protestantenpatent* gave them a legally recognized identity.

We find occasional use for some of your tracts, so that we are truly thankful to have them with us.[75] In the railway carriage yesterday there was a poor convalescent lad going back from the hospital to his Mother: Sarah Anna and my sister were able to shew him some kindnesses and I asked him to accept a tract (Justification) as a remembrance of his English fellow travelers: the poor lad kissed our hands in token of thankfulness & he seemed to value the kindness shewn him: we found afterwards that the poor lad is a Jew: I trust that the tract may shew him that there are those who bear the name of Christians who are not idolaters like the mass whom he must be accustomed to see and to hear of. This led to a gentleman who was in the carriage reading your "Blood that saveth" thro' and putting it with his pocket book. We have met with some Spaniards who have gladly recd. what Sarah Anna could give them in their own language.

I shall be glad to know if you are likely to be in London in the middle of August when we hope to be again in England: for if you are we should be most glad to stay a few days: for it often seems as if there are many things in which I could like to converse with you, as to my own arrangements and other matters. My sister[76] (whom we have found a most efficient travelling companion) will separate from us when we reach England: for she will go to various friends of hers in and near London[77] before she returns to Devonshire.

I do not wish to lay on you any burden of writing: but if you could just inform me of this, it would be a means of making my plans more definite. If you are at home we should be glad to accept the kind invitation which you sent us some time ago.

If you write before Friday, July 25, will you address Poste Restante, Nuremberg, Bavaria: if a few days after at Erlangen, Bavaria.

I quite hope that by God's blessing I shall return fit for work, at last by taking things easy

---

[75] In a subsequent letter SPT explained that he had met Mr. Harry, 'the Independent Minister of Bournemouth' who had introduced him to Theodor Ritz, 'a good man in a suburb of Vienna' who had a considerable stock of tracts including Newton's *The blood that saveth* and *Acceptance with God* (SPT, Nuremberg, 28 July 1862, to B.W. Newton, Manchester/JRUL/CBA 7181 [24]).

[76] Anna Rebecca Tregelles [1811–1885] see above Chapter 12, Footnotes 51–52.

[77] These included SPT's (and her) uncle Nathanael Tregelles [1803-87] in Tottenham; see SPT (Trèves, 11 August 1862) to B.W. Newton (Manchester/JRUL/CBA7181 [26]).

Sarah Anna has written to Alonzo[78] a very faithful letter remonstrating with him as to his perverse conduct. I can only pray that God may graciously bring him to a humble mind before the Cross of Christ. I feel for you about the matter more deeply than I can tell.

With our united kind regards
I remain yours most truly
S.P. Tregelles
[envelope] B W Newton Esq.,
70 New Finchley Road
London
NW
[Postmark]   London   SW   JY21   1862

---

[78] Nicolas Alonzo, a Spanish Protestant; see above Chapter 8, Footnote 52.

LIST OF ARCHIVES

ARCHIVE MATERIALS CONSULTED

The following is a list of MS materials consulted and referred to in my footnotes. Exact quotations have only been made with permission.

Aberystwyth/NLW: National Library of Wales

Cwrtmawr Collection

Iolo Morganwg Papers
Undated letter from S P Tregelles to Taliesin ab Iolo (MS 21277E #770)
William Owen Pughe papers (formerly Mysevin MSS) Two letters from S P Tregelles to Aneurin Owen: July and Sept 1833 (MS 13232E #32-33)

(Quoted with permission)

Cambridge/CUL: Cambridge University Library

B. and F. Bible Society Archive

S P Tregelles (Plymouth, 29 Nov 1848) to the BFBS (CUL/BSA/D1/2 Tregelles 29/11/1848)

Westcott Papers

S P Tregelles (Leipzig, 25 Jun 1862) to B.F. Westcott (CUL/Add. 8317/1/215

(Quoted with grateful acknowledgement to the Syndics of the Cambridge University Library)

Cambridge MA /AHTL: Andover-Harvard Theological Library

Papers of Caspar Rene Gregory

Augusta Prideaux, 'Life of Dr S P Tregelles' (bMS560/125[7]) **[Prideaux, MS Life]**

(Quoted with permission)

Durham/Cathedral: Durham Cathedral Archives

Lightfoot Papers

S P Tregelles (Plymouth 8 May 1857) to J B Lightfoot (CJBL/B/1857/3.189)
S P Tregelles (Plymouth 25 Jun 1859) to J B Lightfoot (CJBL/B/1859/3.16)

(Quotation by kind permission of the Chapter of Durham Cathedral)

Florence/BML: Biblioteca Medicea Laurenziana, Florence

Album dei visitatori della Biblioteca Laurenziana vol 2 Registro dei studiosi 1826–1863

(Quoted with permission)

Florence/BNC: Biblioteca Nazionale Centrale, Florence

Carte del Furia 82 cccxliii, 2–4

Letters from S P Tregelles to Francesco del Furia (Sept–Nov 1852)

(Quoted with permission)

Glasgow /UGL: University of Glasgow Library

Special Collections

Tischendorf — Davidson papers
C Tischendorf (Leipzig, 2 Apr 1861) to S. Davidson (GB 247 MS Gen 527/1)

(Quoted with permission of University of Glasgow Library, Special Collections)

London/BL: British Library

Egerton MSS

Letters from S P Tregelles to Sir Frederick Madden Aug–Oct 1853; May 1855 (MSS 2845-2846)

(Quoted with permission of the British Library)

London/LPL: Lambeth Palace Library

Wordsworth Papers, 1848–1851

Letters from Tregelles to Christopher Wordsworth (MSS 2143-2144)

(Quoted with permission of the Library)

London/LSF: Library of the Society of Friends

Friends House, Printed Collections

'Dictionary of Quaker Biography' [DQB] typescript

(Quotations with permission)

Manchester/JRUL/CBA: John Rylands University Library, Manchester/Christian Brethren Archive

Fry Collection

Fry MS Book (CBA 7049)
SPT letter to unknown person (2 Sept 1843) (CBA Box 585, file 2)
Tregelles—Newton correspondence (1846–1875)
(CBA 7181 [1–119])
Wyatt MSS 4 (CBA 7059)
Wyatt MSS 8 (CBA 7062)

(With authorization for extensive quotation)

Oxford/Bod: Bodleian Library, Oxford

Department of Western MSS

S P Tregelles (7 Sept 1854) to J.D. Macbride (MS Eng. Lett. d.185)

Library Records

C Tischendorf to Bodleian Library, 6 May 1855, (b.43, fol.295, 297)

(Cited with permission)

Oxford/Magdalen: Magdalen College Archive, Oxford

Routh Papers

S P Tregelles (Plymouth, 3 Sept 1851) to M J Routh (MC:PR30/1/C4/6 f.346)

(Cited with permission)

Oxford/Pusey: Pusey House Archives, Oxford

Scott Papers, 1/39/2

> S P Tregelles (Kingsbridge, 15 July 1864) to R Scott

(Quotation with acknowledgments and thanks to the Principal and Chapter of Pusey House)

St Andrews /UA: University Archives of St Andrews, Scotland

Senatus Academicus Misc Papers

> S P Tregelles letter 13 April 1854 (UYUY459, Box B, File 4 1846–1858)

Truro/CRO: Cornwall County Record Office

Stephens of Ashfield, Papers

> Copy of Tregelles Marriage certificate (ST/874) Debts of Samuel Tregelles, 1820 (ST/882) Newspaper cuttings (ST/905)

Society of Friends, Archives

> Minutes of the West Cornwall Monthly Meeting, Nov 1801–Oct 1804 (SF/105)
> Minutes of the West Cornwall Monthly Meeting, Oct 1808–Mar 1813 (SF/108)
> Minutes of West Divisional Monthly Meeting of Cornwall 1824–29, 1829–34 (SF/113-114)

(Quoted by kind permission of the Archives and Cornish Studies Service, Kresen Kermow, Redruth, Cornwall, UK)

Bibliography

Where a work is cited more than once, the subsequent abbreviated version of the reference is indicated in the bibliography in square brackets.

Abbot, Ezra, 'The Late Dr Tregelles' reprinted from *The Independent* (1 July 1875) in *The Authorship of the Fourth Gospel, and Other Critical Essays* (Boston: G. H. Ellis, 1888), 175–83. [**Abbot, 'Tregelles'**]

Alford, F.O., *Life, Journals and Letters of Henry Alford, D.D.*, late Dean of Canterbury, edited by his widow 3rd ed. (London: Rivingtons, 1874).

Allgemeine Deutsche Biographie (Leipzig 1875–1912).

Alumni Cantabrigienses ... See Venn, J.A.

Alumni Oxonienses ... See Foster, Joseph.

Anonymous, *Hand-Book for Travellers in Northern Italy*, 3rd ed. (London: Murray, 1847).

———, 'The Italian Reform Movement,' *The American Quarterly Church Review and Ecclesiastical Register* 15 (July 1863): 235–71.

———, *Kingsbridge and Salcombe, with the Intermediate Estuary, Historically and Topographically Depicted: Embellished with Four Views* (Kingsbridge: R. Southwood, 1819). [**Anonymous, *Kingsbridge and Salcombe***]

———, *Panorama of Falmouth Containing: A History of the Origin, Progress, and Present State of the Port; Particulars of the Packet and Other Establishments; Directions to the Public Offices, Taverns, Lodging Houses, etc* (Falmouth: Philp, 1827). [**Anonymous, *Panorama of Falmouth***]

———, 'The Public Libraries of Paris and London,' *The British Review, and London Critical Journal* 20 (December 1822): 466–74.

© The Editor(s) (if applicable) and The Author(s),
under exclusive license to Springer Nature Switzerland AG 2020
T. C. F. Stunt, *The Life and Times of Samuel Prideaux Tregelles*,
Christianities in the Trans-Atlantic World,
https://doi.org/10.1007/978-3-030-32266-3

————, *A Retrospect of Events That Have Taken Place Amongst the Brethren* (London: Benjamin L Green, 1849). [**Anonymous, *Retrospect of Events***]

————, 'Tregelles on the Printed Text of the Greek New Testament,' *Bibliotheca Sacra and American Biblical Repository* 12 (July 1855): 645–46.

————, 'Works on Hebrew Literature,' *Churchman's Monthly Review and Chronicle* 5 (February 1847): 127–38.

Bachmann, E.T. [ed.], *Luther's Works*, Vol. 35: Word and Sacrament I (Philadelphia: Fortress Press, 1960).

Bainton, R.H., *Here I Stand: A Life of Martin Luther* (Nashville: Abingdon, 1978 [1950]).

————, *Studies on the Reformation* (London: Hodder and Stoughton, 1964).

Bengel, J. A., 'Prodromus Novi Testamenti recte cauteque ordinandi,' in *Ioannis Chrysostomi De Sacerdotio* (Stuttgart: Mezierum & Erhardum, 1725).

Bentley, James, *Secrets of Mount Sinai: The Story of the Codex Sinaiticus* (London: Orbis, 1985). [**Bentley, *Secrets***]

Bentley, Jerry H., 'Erasmus, Jean Le Clerc and the Principle of the Harder Reading,' *Renaissance Quarterly* 31 (Autumn 1978): 309–21.

Biagini, Eugenio F., 'Risorgimento e Protestanti,' in S. Maghenzani, G. Platone [eds.], *Riforma, Risorgimento e Risveglio: Il Protestantesimo italiano tra radici storiche e questioni contemporanee* (Turin: Claudiana, 2011), 77–96.

Boase, G.C., and W.P. Courtney [eds.], *Bibliotheca Cornubiensis: A Catalogue of the Writings, Both Manuscript and Printed, of Cornishmen, and of Works Relating to the County of Cornwall, with Biographical Memoranda and Copious Literary References* (London: Longmans, 1878). [***Bibl. Cornub.***]

Böttrich, C., 'Constantin von Tischendorf und der Transfer des Codex Sinaiticus nach St Petersburg,' in A. Gössner [ed.], *Die Theologische Fakultät der Universität Leipzig* (Leipzig: Evangelische Verlagsanstalt, 2005), 253–75.

Boutry, Philippe, *Souverain et Pontife: recherches prosopographiques sur la curie romaine à l'âge de la restauration: 1814–1846* (Rome: École française de Rome 2002). [**Boutry, *Souverain et Pontife***]

Bowersock, G.W., *Roman Arabia* (Cambridge MA: Harvard, 1983).

Bradley, T.H., 'The Fox Family of Falmouth: Their Contribution to Cornish Industrial History 1640–1860,' *Cornwall Association of Local Historians' News Magazine* 14 (October 1987): 9–17.

Braithwaite, R. [ed.], *The Life and Letters of Rev. William Pennefather* (London: John F. Shaw, 1878).

Bricka, C.F. [ed.], *Dansk Biografisk Lexikon* (Copenhagen: Hegel, 1887–1905).

Bromwich, Rachel [ed.], *Trioedd Ynis Prydein: The Welsh Triads*, 2nd ed. (Cardiff: University of Wales Press, 1978).

B[rooking]-R[owe], J[oshua], 'The Late S.P. Tregelles, LL.D,' *Journal of the Plymouth Institution* 5 (1876): 386–89. [**Brooking-Rowe, 'Tregelles'**]

Brown, J. Wood, *An Italian Campaign; Or the Evangelical Movement in Italy 1845–1887: From the Letters of the Late R.W. Stewart, D.D., of Leghorn* (London: Hodder and Stoughton, 1890). [**Brown, *Letters of Stewart***]

Brown, Virginia, 'Manuscripts of Caesar's *Gallic War*,' in Scuola speciale per archivisti e bibliotecari dell'Università di Roma [ed.], *Palaeographica diplomatica et archivistica : Studi in onore di Giulio Battelli* (Rome, 1979), 105–57.

Bruce, F.F., 'The Humanity of Jesus Christ,' *Journal of the Christian Brethren Research Fellowship* 24 (1973): 5–15.

Bunsen, C.C.J., *Hippolytus and His Age; Or the Doctrine and Practice of the Church of Rome Under Commodus and Alexander Severus: and Ancient and Modern Christianity and Divinity Compared*, 4 vols., i. The Critical Inquiry: in five letters to Archdeacon Hare (London: Longman, Brown, Green, and Longmans, 1852). [**Bunsen, *Hippolytus***]

Burckhardt, John Lewis, *Travels in Syria and the Holy Land*, ed. William Martin Leake (London: John Murray, 1822).

Burgon, J.W., *Lives of Twelve Good Men*, 2 vols. 3rd ed. (London: John Murray, 1889).

———, *The Revision Revised: Three Articles Reprinted from the 'Quarterly Review' … to Which Is Added a Reply to Bishop Ellicott's Pamphlet in Defence of the Revisers and Their Greek Text of the New Testament …* (London: Murray, 1881).

Burnham, J.D., *A Story of Conflict: The Controversial Relationship Between Benjamin Wills Newton and John Nelson Darby* (Carlisle: Paternoster Press, 2004).

Calvin, John, *Commentary on a Harmony of the Evangelists Matthew, Mark, and Luke*, trans. W. Pringle (Edinburgh: Calvin Translation Society, 1845).

———, *Commentary Upon the Acts of the Apostles*, trans. C. Fetherstone, ed. H. Beveridge (Edinburgh: Calvin Translation Society, 1844).

Carne, John, *Letters from the East* (London: H. Colburn, 1826).

Carpenter, C. H., *Self-Support, Illustrated in the History of the Bassein Karen Mission from 1840 to 1880* (Boston: Rand, Avery, 1883).

Carus, W., *Memoirs of the Life of Charles Simeon, with a Selection from His Writings and Correspondence* (London: Hatchard, 1847).

Cavendish, Richard, 'The Discovery of Petra,' *History Today* 42 (8 August 2012).

Chadwick, Owen, *The Victorian Church Part 1, 1829–1859*, 3rd ed. (London: A & C Black 1971 [1966]).

Charnell–White, C., *Bardic Circles: National, Regional and Personal Identity in the Bardic Vision of Iolo Morganwg* (Cardiff: University of Wales Press, 2007).

Ciampini, Raffaele, *Gian Pietro Vieusseux: i suoi viaggi, i suoi giornali, i suoi amici* (Turin: Einaudi, 1953).

Clarke, E.D., *Travels in Various Countries of Europe, Asia and Africa. Part the Second: Greece, Egypt and the Holy Land: Section the Second. Volume the Sixth*, 4th ed. (London: Cadell and Davies, 1814).

Coad, F. Roy, *A History of the Brethren Movement: Its Origins, Its Worldwide Development and Its Significance for the Present Day* (Exeter: Paternoster, 1968).

Coate, Mary, *Cornwall in the Great Civil War and Interregnum, 1642–1660: A Social and Political Study* (Oxford: Clarendon, 1933).

Compton Street Chapel, *Confession* see Evangelical Protestant Church, Compton Street …

Cooney, J.D., 'Major Macdonald, a Victorian Romantic,' *Journal of Egyptian Archæology* 58 (August 1972): 280–85.

Cowper, B.H., 'Extraordinary Discovery of a Biblical MS by Dr Tischendorf,' *JSL* 9 (July 1859): 392–94.

Crewdson, Ellen, *Our Childhood at Perran* and *Postscript to Mother's Diary* by F. Mary Broadrick (Liverpool: Private circulation [1926]).

Crewdson, H.A.F., *George Fox of Tredrea and His Three Daughters: A Century of Family History* (Slindon, Sussex: Privately printed, 1976).

Cule, John H., 'John Pughe, 1814–1874: A Scholar Surgeon's Operation on the Imperforate Anus in 1854,' *Annals of the Royal College of Surgeons of England* 37 (October 1965): 247–57.

Curzon, R., *Visits to Monasteries in the Levant* (London: Humphrey Milford, 1916 [1849]).

D[arby], J.N., *Letters of J.N.D.*, 3 vols (Kingston on Thames: Stowe Hill Bible and Tract Depot, n.d.).

———, 'The Righteousness of God,' in *Collected Writings, 7* [Doctrinal 2] (Kingston-on-Thames: Stowe Hill Tract Depot, n.d.), 302–48.

Davidson, A. J. [ed.], *The Autobiography and Diary of Samuel Davidson: With a Selection of Letters from English and German Divines, and an Account* [by James Allanson Picton] *of the Davidson Controversy of 1857* (Edinburgh: T. & T. Clark, 1899). [**Davidson,** *Autobiography*]

Davidson, S., *Facts, Statements and Explanations, Connected with the Publication of the Second Volume of the Tenth Edition of Horne's Introduction to the Study of the Holy Scriptures …* (London: Longmans, 1857).

———, *Introduction to the New Testament, Containing an Examination of the Most Important Questions Relating to the Authority, Interpretation, and Integrity of the Canonical Books, with Reference to the Latest Inquiries*, Vol. ii. *The Acts of the Apostles to the Second Epistle to the Thessalonians* (London: Samuel Bagster and Sons, 1849).

Davies, G., 'The Reception of Gesenius's Dictionary in England,' in S. Schorch, E–J. Waschke [eds.], *Biblische Exegese und hebräische Lexikographie: Das "Hebräisch-deutsche Handwörterbuch" von Wilhelm Gesenius als Spiegel und Quelle alttestamentlicher und hebräischer Forschung, 200 Jahre nach seiner ersten Auflage* (Berlin and Boston: Walter de Gruyter, 2013).

De Luc, J.A., *Histoire du passage des Alpes par Annibal: dans laquelle on détermine d'une manière précise la route de ce général, depuis Carthagène jusqu'au Tésin, d'après la narration de Polybe, comparée aux recherches faites sur les lieux …* (Geneva: Paschoud, 1818).

[Denny, Edward], *Some of the Firstfruits of the Harvest by One Who Has Sown in Tears* (n.p. [1861]).

Dessain, C.S. [ed.], *Letters and Diaries of John Henry Newman*, vols. xi–xii (London: Nelson, 1961).

Dictionary of Welsh Biography [*DWB*] see Lloyd J.E.

Dizionario Biografico degli Italiani (Rome: Istituto della Enciclopedia italiana, 1960–2018). [*DBI*]

Doddridge, P., 'A Dissertation on the Inspiration of the New Testament as Proved from the Facts Recorded in the Historical Books of It,' in *Works*, 10 vols (Leeds: Edward Baines, 1803) 4: 168–94.

Dyke, P.J., and E.P. Uphill, 'Major Charles Kerr Macdonald 1806–67,' *Journal of Egyptian Archæology* 49 (1983): 165–66.

Eadie, John, *Life of John Kitto, DD., FSA* (Edinburgh: Oliphant, 1857).

Eaton, G., *Joseph Tregelles Price, 1784–1854: Quaker Industrialist and Moral Crusader: A Portrait of His Life and Work* (Neath: Glamorgan Press, 1987).

Eaton, K., *Protestant Missionaries in Spain, 1869–1936: 'Shall the Papists Prevail?'* (Lanham, MA: Lexington Books, 2015). [**Eaton, *Protestant Missionaries***]

Ehrman, Bart D., and Michael W. Holmes [eds.], *The Text of the New Testament in Contemporary Research: Essays on the Status Quaestionis*, 2nd ed. [New Testament Tools, Studies and Documents 42.] (Leiden: Brill, 2013). [**Ehrman and Holmes, *The Text***]

Elliott, J.K., *Codex Sinaiticus and the Simonides Affair* (Thessaloniki: Patriarchal Institute for Patristic Studies, 1982).

Evangelical Protestant Church, Compton Street Chapel, Plymouth, *Confession of Faith and Other Papers Connected with the Settlement of the Rev. William Elliott as Pastor; Addressed to the Pastors of Christ's Churches* (London: Houlston and Wright, 1863). [**Compton St Chapel, *Confession***]

Falcetta, Alessandro, *The Daily Discoveries of a Bible Scholar and Manuscript Hunter: A Biography of James Rendel Harris (1852–1941)* (Edinburgh: T & T Clark, 2018).

Fardd, Eben, *Cyff Beuno: sef awdl ar adgyweiriad eglwys Clynnog Fawr, yng nghyd a nodiadau hynafol, achyddiaeth y plwyf, rhestr o'r beirdd a'r llenorion* (Tremadog: R.I. Jones, 1863). [**Fardd, *Cyff Beuno***]

Farrer, J.A., *Literary Forgeries* (London: Longman, Green, 1907).

Felisini, Daniela, *Alessandro Torlonia: the Pope's Banker* (Cham, Switzerland: Palgrave Macmillan, 2016).

Ferretti, S., 'La mia conversione,' *L'Eco di Savonarola* 1 (1847): 158–61, 213–15, 241–46.

Fisher, G.W., and J.S. Hill [eds.], *Annals of Shrewsbury School* (London: Methuen, 1899).

Flint, J.P., *Great Britain and the Holy See: The Diplomatic Relations Question 1846–1852* (Washington, DC: Catholic University of America Press, 2003).

Foster, Joseph, *Alumni Oxonienses: The Members of the University of Oxford, 1715–1886*, 4 vols (London: Foster, 1887). [*Al. Oxon.*]

Fox, Sarah E. [ed.], *Edwin Octavius Tregelles: Civil Engineer and Minister of the Gospel* (London: Hodder and Stoughton, 1892).

Fromow, G.H. [ed.], *Teachers of the Faith and the Future: The Life and Works of B.W. Newton and Dr. S.P. Tregelles* (London: Sovereign Grace Advent Testimony, n.d.).

Gabbrielli, Veronica [ed.], *Carteggio: Gino Capponi – Raffaello Lambruschini (1828–1873)* (Florence: Spadolini–Le Monnier, 1996).

——— [ed.], *Carteggio: Lambruschini—Vieusseux I (1826–1834)* (Florence: Spadolini–Le Monnier, 1998).

Gale, Thomas, *Historiae Anglicanae Scriptores Veteres* (Oxford: E Theatro Sheldoniano, 1687).

Gay, Susan, *Old Falmouth: The Story of the Town from the Days of the Killigrews to The Earliest Part of the Nineteenth Century* (London: Headley Brothers, 1903).

Gesenius, William, *A Hebrew and English Lexicon of the Old Testament, Including the Biblical Chaldee*, trans. from the Latin by Edward Robinson (Boston: Crocker and Brewster, 1836).

Giannini, Pier Gio[vanni]. Vincenzo, *Notizie istoriche sopra la miracolosa imagine di Gesù Bambino che si venera nella ven. chiesa presbiterale di S. Maria in Aracœli di Roma: con alcuni divoti esercizi per conseguire le grazie che si domandono: coll'aggiunta di varie notizie, e savie riflessioni sopra la nascita del medesimo divin redentore* (Rome: Puccinelli, 1797).

Giorgi, Lorenza, and Massimo Rubboli [eds.], *Piero Guicciardini, 1808–86: Un Riformatore religioso nell'Europa dell'Ottocento* (Florence: Olschki, 1988).

Gorman, W. Gordon, *Converts to Rome: A List of About Four Thousand Protestants Who Have Recently Become Roman Catholics*, 2nd ed. (London: W Swan Sonnenschein, 1885).

Grass, Tim, *Gathering to His Name: The Story of Open Brethren in Britain and Ireland* (Milton Keynes: Paternoster, 2006). [**Grass, *Gathering***]

Greene, William, *Manuel Matamoros: His Life and Death. A Narrative of the Late Persecution of Christians in Spain, Compiled from Original Letters and Other Documents*, 3rd ed. (London: Alfred Holness, 1889). [**Greene, *Matamoros***]

Griesbach, J.J., *Symbolae Criticae ad supplendas et corrigendas variarum N.T. Lectionum collectiones ...*, 2 vols. (Halle: Curtius, 1793).

Grosse, Christian, *Les rituels de la cène: le culte eucharistique réformé à Genève* (Geneva: Droz, 2008).

Guinness, Grace, see Septima.

Hall, P.F., *To the Christians Who Heard ... Mr Venn's Sermon, Preached at Hereford, December 9th, 1838* (Leominster: Chilcott, 1839).

[Hanna, R.M.], 'Protestantism in Italy,' *The North British Review* 20 (November 1853): 37–80.

Haydon, C., *Anti-Catholicism in Eighteenth-Century England, c.1714–80: A Political and Social Study* (Manchester: University Press, 1993).

Head, Peter M., 'Additional Greek Witnesses to the New Testament (Ostraca, Amulets, Inscriptions and Other Sources),' in B.D. Ehrman and M.W. Holmes [eds.], *The Text of the New Testament in Contemporary Research: Essays on the Status Quaestionis*, 2nd ed. (Leiden: Brill, 2013), 429–60.

———, 'Reading in the Wren Library,' in *Evangelical Textual Criticism* blogspot (7 September 2015).

Hilgert, Earl, 'Two Unpublished Letters Regarding Tregelles' Canon Muratorianus,' *Andrews University Seminary Studies* 5 (July 1967): 122–30.

Holmes, M.W. [ed.], *The Greek New Testament*: SBL edition (Atlanta GA: Society of Biblical Literature, 2010).

Horne, Thomas Hartwell, *An Introduction to the Critical Study and Knowledge of the Holy Scriptures*, 6th ed. (London: T. Cadell, 1828).

———, *An Introduction to the Critical Study and Knowledge of the Holy Scriptures*. 10th ed., revised, corrected, and brought down to the present time. Edited by the Rev. T. Hartwell Horne, B.D. (the Author;) the Rev. S. Davidson, D.D., of the University of Halle, and LL.D.; and S. P. Tregelles, LL.D., 4 vols. (London: Longman, 1856).

Hort, A.F., *Life and Letters of Fenton John Anthony Hort*, 2 vols. (London: Macmillan, 1896). [**Hort, *Life and Letters***]

H[ort], F.J.A., 'Notices of New Books,' *Journal of Classical and Sacred Philology* 4 (1858): 201–11.

Howard, J.E., 'The Druids and Their Religion,' *Journal of the Transactions of the Victoria Institute* 14 (1881): 87–130.

Howard, J.J., and F.A. Crisp [eds.], *Visitation of England and Wales*, Vol. 15 (priv. printed, 1908). [**Howard, Crisp, *Visitation***]

Hug, Io[hann]. Leonardus, *De Antiquitate Codicis Vaticani commentatio qua Albertinae Magni Ducatus Zahringo Badensis* (Freiburg: Herder, 1810).

Ince, Laurence, *Neath Abbey and the Industrial Revolution* (Stroud: Tempus, 2001).

Irby, C.L., and J. Mangles, *Travels in Egypt and Nubia, Syria and Asia Minor During the Years 1817 and 1818* (London: T. White and Co, 1823).

Isaacson, Charles S., *The Story of the English Cardinals* (London: Elliot Stock, 1907).

Jacini, Stefano, *Un Riformatore Toscano dell'Epoca del Risorgimento: Il Conte Piero Guicciardini (1808–1886)* (Florence: Sansoni, 1940). [**Jacini, *Riformatore***]

Jackson, Sue, 'The Bible in Spain and Gibraltar,' in S. Batalden, K. Cann, J. Dean [eds.], *Sowing the Word: The Cultural Impact of the British and Foreign Bible Society 1804–2004* (Sheffield: Phoenix Press, 2004), 305–15.

Jarratt, F., 'Dean Alford and Dr Tregelles,' *Notes and Queries* 8 (28 September 1895): 246.

Jenkins, Geraint H. [ed.], *A Rattleskull Genius: The Many Faces of Iolo Morganwg* (Cardiff: University of Wales Press, 2005).

Jones, Ieuan Gwynedd [ed.], *The Religious Census of 1851: A Calendar of the Returns Relating to Wales, Vol. II, North Wales* (Cardiff: University of Wales, 1981).

Jongkind, D., and P.J. Williams [eds.], *Tyndale House Greek New Testament* (Cambridge: Crossway, 2018).

Keith, Alexander, *Evidence of the Truth of the Christian Religion Derived from the Literal Fulfilment of Prophecy; Particularly as Illustrated by the History of the Jews, and by the Discoveries of Recent Travellers* (Edinburgh: Waugh & Innes, 1826).

Kenyon, F.G., *Handbook to the Textual Criticism of the New Testament*, 2nd ed. (London: Macmillan, 1926).

Kerr, Ian, *John Henry Newman: A Biography* (Oxford: Oxford University Press, 2009 [1988]).

Kidd, W., *Joseph Kidd 1824–1918: Limerick, London, Blackheath: A Memoir* (priv. printed, 1920).

Knox, R. Buick, 'The Irish Contribution to English Presbyterianism,' *JURCHS* 4:1 (October 1987): 22–35.

Langdon, W.C. 'The Possibilities of Italian Reform,' *Andover Review* 5:26 (February 1886): 168–79.

Lauch, Erhard, 'Nichts gegen Tischendorf,' in E.H. Amberg and U. Kühn [eds.], *Bekenntnis zur Kirche: Festgabe für Ernst Sommerlath zum 70. Geburtstag* (Berlin: Evangelische Verlagsanstalt, 1960), 15–24.

Lewis, J. Vernon, 'S.P. Tregelles ac Eben Fardd,' *Y Dysgedydd* (March 1933): 68–71.

Lichtenwalner, Shawna, *Claiming Cambria: Invoking the Welsh in the Romantic Era* (Newark, DE: University of Delaware Press, 2008).

Lloyd, J., *The Early History of the Old South Wales Iron Works (1760 to 1840)* (London: Bedford Press, 1906).

Lloyd, J.E., and R.T. Jenkins [eds.], *Dictionary of Welsh Biography Down to 1940* [*DWB*] (London: Society of Cymmrodorion, 1959).

Luther, Martin, *Works...* see Bachmann, E.T; and see Pelikan, J.

Macmillan, Hugh, *Roman Mosaics, or Studies in Rome and Its Neighbourhood* (London: Macmillan, 1888).

Madan, B. [ed.], *Spencer and Waterloo: The Letters of Spencer Madan, 1814–1816* (London: Literary Serices, 1970).

Madan, Falconer [ed.], *A Summary Catalogue of Western Manuscripts in the Bodleian Library at Oxford, Vol. V, Collections Received During the Second Half of the 19th Century and Miscellaneous MSS Acquired Between 1695 and 1890* (Oxford: Clarendon Press, 1905).

Maghenzani, S., and G. Platone [eds.], *Riforma, Risorgimento e Risveglio: Il Protestantesimo italiano tra radici storiche e questioni contemporanee* (Turin: Claudiana, 2011). [**Maghenzani, *Riforma***]

Maier, Adalbert, *Gedächtnisrede auf Johann Leonhard Hug bei dessen akademischer Todtenfeier in der Universitäts-Kirche zu Freiburg am 11 März 1847 gehalten* (Freiburg: Poppen, 1847).

Mallery, Ann. *Crossing the Line: Women and the Railway Mission 1881–1901* (Sheffield: Sheffield Hallam University Research Archive, 2018)

Marsh, Catherine, *English Hearts and English Hands or The Railway and the Trenches* (London: Nisbet, 1857).

Maselli, Domenico, *Tra Risveglio e Millennio: Storia delle Chiese Cristiane dei Fratelli, 1836–1886* (Turin: Claudiana, 1974). [**Maselli, *Tra Risveglio***]

Masinelli, Antonio, *Notizie intorno alla vita ed alle opere del conte commendatore Giovanni Galvani di Modena* (Modena: Tipografia pontificia ed arcivescovile, 1874).

Matthew, H. Colin G., and Brian Harrison [eds.], *Oxford Dictionary of National Biography* [**ODNB**], 61 vols. (Oxford: University Press, 2004).

McGrath, Alister E., *Luther's Theology of the Cross: Martin Luther's Theological Breakthrough* (Oxford: Blackwell, 1990).

McNair, Philip, 'Benedetto da Mantova, Marcantonio Flaminio, and the *Beneficio di Cristo*: A Developing Twentieth Century Debate Reviewed,' *Modern Language Review* 82 (July 1987): 614–24.

Meille, J.P., 'Prospects of the Gospel in Italy,' in E. Steane [ed.], *The Religious Condition of Christendom, Exhibited in a Series of Papers ... Read at the Conference Held in Paris, 1855* (London: Evangelical Alliance, 1857).

Mendell, Clarence W., *Tacitus: The Man and His Work* (New Haven: Yale University Press, 1957).

The Mildmay Conference, 1894: Reports of the Addresses, Corrected by the Speakers (London: Shaw, 1894).

Miller, John, *Popery and Politics in England 1660–88* (Cambridge: University Press, 1973).

Milligan, William, 'Tischendorf and Tregelles as Editors of the Greek New Testament,' *The British and Foreign Evangelical Review* 25 (January 1876): 119–52.

Millward, E.G., 'Eben Fardd a Samuel Prideaux Tregelles,' *National Library of Wales Journal* 7 (Winter 1952): 58–61. [**Millward, *Fardd a Tregelles***]

Milne, H.J.M., and T.C. Skeat, *Scribes and Correctors of the Codex Sinaiticus* (London: British Museum, 1938).

The Myvyrian Archaiology of Wales Being a Collection of Historical Documents from Ancient Manuscript, ed. Owen Jones, Edward Williams, William Owen, 3 vols. (London: Rousseau, 1801–1807).

Neatby, W.B., *A History of the Plymouth Brethren*, 2nd ed. (London: Hodder and Stoughton, 1902).

Newlin, M., *Memoir of Mary Anne Longstreth by an Old Pupil* (Philadelphia: J.P.Lippincott, 1886).

Newman, J.H., *Letters* ... see Dessain, C.S.

Newton, B.W., *Thoughts on the Apocalypse* (London: Hamilton, Adams; Plymouth: J.B. Rowe, 1844).

Nicholas, Thomas, *Dr. Davidson's removal from the Professorship of Biblical Literature in the Lancashire Independent College, Manchester, on Account of Alleged Error in Doctrine: A Statement of Facts, with Documents; Together with Remarks and Criticisms* (London and Edinburgh: Williams and Norgate, 1860).

Nichols, John, *Literary Anecdotes of the Eighteenth Century, Containing Biographical Memoirs* ..., 9 vols. (London: Nichols, 1815).

Oxford Dictionary of National Biography [*ODNB*] see Matthew, H.G.C.

Paget, Catesby, *A Letter to Dr Tregelles on Vicarious Law Fulfilling* (London: Yapp, [1863]).

P[akenham], F.J., *Life Lines; Or God's Work in a Human Being* (London: Wertheim, Macintosh and Hunt, 1862). [**Pakenham,** *Life Lines*]

Parker, David C., 'The Development of the Critical Text of the Epistle of James: From Lachmann to the *Editio Critica Maior*,' in *Manuscripts, Texts, Theology: Collected Papers 1977–2007* (Berlin: W. de Gruyter, 2009).

Patrick, G., *F.J.A. Hort: Eminent Victorian* (London: Bloomsbury, 2015 [1987]).

Paz, D.G., *Popular Anti-Catholicism in Mid-Victorian England* (Stanford: University Press, 1992).

Pecchioli, Alessandra, 'Giulia Baldelli: Una prima breve panoramica delle famiglie Walker, Baldelli e Tommasi,' in A. Pecchioli [ed.], *La Chiesa 'degli italiani': All'origine del Evangelismo risvegliato in Italia* (Rome: GBU, 2010), 207–22.

Peddie, Mrs. Robert, *The Dawn of the Second Reformation in Spain: Being the Story of Its Rise and Progress from the Year 1852* (London: S. W. Partridge, 1871). [**Peddie,** *Second Reformation*]

Peile, J.A. [ed.], *Biographical Register of Christ's College, 1505–1905* ..., 2 vols (Cambridge: Cambridge University Press, 1913).

Pelikan, J. [ed.], *Luther's Works, Vol. 1: Lectures on Genesis Chapters 1–5* (Saint Louis, MO: Concordia, 1958).

Peterson, M.D., 'Tischendorf and the Codex Sinaiticus: The Saga Continues,' *Greek Orthodox Theological Review* 53 (2008): 125–39.

Phillips, D. Rhys, *The History of the Vale of Neath* (Swansea: Phillips, 1925). [**Philips.** *Vale of Neath*]

Pickering, H. [ed.], *Chief Men Among the Brethren*, 2nd ed. (London: Pickering and Inglis [1931]).

Picton, James Allanson, see Davidson, A. J.

Piggott, T.C., and T. Durley, *Life and Letters of Henry James Piggott of Rome* (London: Epworth, 1921).

Pinto, P.M., 'Simonides in England: A Forger's Progress,' in A.E. Müller, L. Diamantopoulou, C. Gastgeber and A. Katsiakiori- Rankl [eds.], *Die getäuschte Wissenschaft: Ein Genie betrügt Europa – Konstantinos Simonides* (Vienna: Vienna University Press, 2017).

Ponchon, Henri, *L'Incroyable Saga des Torlonia: des monts du Forez aux palais romains* (Olliergues: Les Éditions de la Montmarie, 2005).

Porter, John Scott, *Principles of Textual Criticism, with Their Application to the Old and the New Testaments* (London: Simms and M'Intyre, 1848).

Porter, S.E., *Constantine Tischendorf: The Life and Work of a 19th Century Bible Hunter* (London: Bloomsbury, 2015). [**Porter, *Tischendorf***]

P[rideaux], F[rances]. A[sh]., *In Memoriam F[rederick]. P[rideaux]*. (Privately printed, 1891).

Prideaux, Frederick, *The Hand-Book of Precedents in Conveyancing, Adapted to Modern Law and Practice with Notes* (London: Wildy and Sons, 1852).

Prideaux, R.M., *Prideaux, a West Country Clan* (Chichester: Phillimore, 1989).

Pritchard, John, *Methodists and Their Missionary Societies* (London: Routledge, 2013).

Pughe, John [trans.], and John Williams Ab Ithel [ed.], *The Physicians of Myddvai; Meddygon Myddfai* (Llandovery: D.J. Roderic, 1860).

Pughe, W. Owen, *A Dictionary of the Welsh Language Explained in English with Numerous Illustrations, from the Literary Remains and from the Living Speech of the Cymmry*, 2nd ed. (Denbigh: Thomas Gee, 1832 [1803]).

Railton, Nicholas M., *No North Sea: The Anglo-German Evangelical Network in the Middle of the Nineteenth Century* [Studies in Christian Mission XXIV] (Leiden: Brill, 1999).

[Rathbone, W.], *A Narrative of Events, That Have Lately Taken Place in Ireland Among the Society Called Quakers, with Corresponding Documents and Occasional Observations* (London: Johnson, 1804).

Rees, T. Mardy, *A History of the Quakers in Wales and Their Emigration to North America* (Carmarthen: Spurrell and Son, 1925).

Religious Liberty in Tuscany in 1851: Or Documents Relative to the Trial and Incarceration of Count Pietro Guicciardini and Others, Exiled from Tuscany by Decree of 17 May, 1851. Translated from the Italian (London: James Nisbet, [1851]). [*Religious Liberty*]

[Reynolds, H.R.], 'The Great Vatican MS of the New Testament,' *British Quarterly Review* 47 (April 1868): 345–65.

Robinson, M.A. and W.G. Pierpont [eds.], *The New Testament in the Original Greek: Byzantine Textform* (Southborough, MA: Chilton Book Publishing, 2005).

Rogerson, J.W., *W.M.L de Wette, Founder of Modern Biblical Criticism: An Intellectual Biography* (Sheffield: JSOT, 1992). [**Rogerson, *de Wette***]

Ronco, D.D., *La fede e l'opera di Matilde Calandrini (dalle lettere a Gian Pietro Vieusseux)* (Bangor: Privately Printed, Central Print Unit, University of Wales, c.1995).

——, *'Per me, vivere e Cristo': La vita e l'opera del Conte Piero Guicciardini nel centenario della sua morte 1808–1886* (Fondi, Italy: Unione Cristiana Edizioni Bibliche, 1986).

——, *Risorgimento and the Free Italian Churches, Now Churches of the Brethren* (Bangor: University of Wales, 1996).

Rossetti, T. Pietrocòla, *Biografià di Rosa Madiai* (Florence: G Pellas, 1871).

Rowdon, H.H., *The Origins of the Brethren, 1825–1850* (London: Pickering and Inglis, 1967). [**Rowdon, Origins**]

Russell, C.W., *The Life of Cardinal Mezzofanti with an Introductory Memoir of Eminent Linguists, Ancient and Modern* (London: Longman, Green, Longman, Roberts and Green, 1863).

Salmond, S.D.F., 'Franz Delitzsch,' *The Expositor* 3 (1886): 456–71.

Santini, Luigi. *The Protestant cemetery of Florence, called 'The English Cemetery'* (Florence: K.S. Printing House, 1981).

Scholz, J.M.A., *Travels in the Countries Between Alexandria and Parætonium, The Lybian Desert, Siwa, Egypt, Palestine, and Syria, in 1821* (London: Phillips, 1822).

Scio de San Miguel, Phelipe, *La Biblia Vulgata Latina traducida en Español, y anotada conforme al sentido de los santos Padres y expositores Cathólicos* (Valencia: Joseph and Thomas de Orga, 1790).

Scrivener, F.H.[A.], *A Full Collation of the Codex Sinaiticus, with the Received Text of the New Testament, to Which Is Prefixed a Critical Introduction* (Cambridge: Deighton, Bell and Co, 1864).

——, *A Plain Introduction to the Criticism of the New Testament for the Use of Biblical Students,* 4th ed., 2 vols ed. by Edward Miller (London: George Bell, 1894). [**Scrivener, Plain Introduction**]

——, *Six Lectures on the Text of the New Testament and the Ancient Manuscripts Which Contain It: Chiefly Addressed to Those Who Do Not Read Greek* (Cambridge: Deighton, Bell and Co, 1875).

[Senhouse, Sarah [ed.], *Letters of the Madiai and Visits to Their Prisons by the Misses Senhouse* (London: Nisbet, 1853).

Septima [Grace Guinness], *Peculiar People* (London: Heath Cranton, 1935).

Ševčenko, Ihor, 'New Documents on Constantine Tischendorf and the Codex Sinaiticus,' *Scriptorium* 18 (1964): 55–80.

Sheehan, Jonathan, *The Enlightenment Bible: Translation, Scholarship, Culture* (Princeton: University Press, 2005).

Shipton, Anna, *The Upper Springs and the Nether Springs; Or, Life Hid with Christ in God* (London: James Nisbet, 1882).

Smith, R.A.H., 'Department of Manuscripts: Acquisitions January–December 1980,' *The British Library Journal* (1982): 222.

Soltau, H.W., and J.E. Batten, W.B. Dyer, and J. Clulow, *Remonstrance Addressed to the Saints at Rawstorne Street, London, Respecting Their Late Act of Excluding Mr. Newton, from the Lord's Table, and Protest Against It* (Plymouth: Tract Depot, 1846).

Soltau. W., 'The Story of the Madiai,' *Sunday at Home* (1904): 446–53. [**Soltau, Story of Madiai**]

Southall, Hannah, 'The Price Family of Neath,' *Friends' Intelligencer and Journal* [Philadelphia] (September 1894): 601–602, 619–20.

———, 'The Price Family of Neath,' *Friends Quarterly Examiner* 28 (1894): 189–203.

Spini, Giorgio, 'Nuovi documenti sugli Evangelici toscani del Risorgimento,' *Bolletino della Società di Studi Valdesi* 78 (December 1960): 79–92.

———, *Risorgimento e Protestanti* (Naples: Edizioni scientifiche Italiane, 1956).

Spon, I., *History of the City and State of Geneva, from Its First Foundation to This Present Time* (London: White, 1687).

Stone, R. C., *The Language of the Latin Text of Codex Bezae: With an Index Verborum* (Eugene, OR: Wipf and Stock, 2009).

Strivens, Robert, *Philip Doddridge and the Shaping of Evangelical Dissent* [Ashgate Studies in Evangelicalism] (London: Routledge, 2016).

Stunt, Timothy C. F., *The Elusive Quest of the Spiritual Malcontent: Some Early Nineteenth Century Ecclesiastical Mavericks* (Eugene, OR: Wipf and Stock, 2015). [**Stunt, Elusive Quest**]

———, *From Awakening to Secession: Radical Evangelicals in Switzerland and Britain, 1815–35* (Edinburgh: T and T Clark, 2000). [**Stunt, From Awakening**]

———, 'L'influenza del *réveil* svizzero prima dell'Unità d'Italia,' in S. Maghenzani and G. Platone [eds.], *Riforma, Risorgimento e Risveglio: Il Protestantesimo italiano tra radici storiche e questioni contemporanee* (Turin: Claudiana, 2011): 105–13.

———, 'Some Unpublished Letters of S. P. Tregelles Relating to the Codex Sinaiticus,' *EQ* 48 (January 1976): 15–26. [**Stunt, 'Some Unpublished letters'**]

———, 'Trinity College, John Darby and the Powerscourt *milieu*,' in J. Searle and K.G.C. Newport [eds.], *Beyond the End: The Future of Millennial Studies* (Sheffield: Sheffield Phoenix Press, 2012): 47–74.

———, 'Understanding the Past in the city of Florence,' *Harvester* (September 1983): 6–8.

Tayler, W. Elfe [ed.], *Passages from the Diary and Letters of Henry Craik of Bristol* (London: J. F. Shaw, [1866]).

Taylor, J., *Petra and the Lost Kingdom of the Nabataeans* (Cambridge, MA: Harvard University Press, 2002).

Thomas, R., *History and Description of the Town and Harbour of Falmouth* (Falmouth: J. Trathan, 1827).

Tischendorf, Aenotheus [Lobegott] Fridericus Constantinus, *Notitia editionis codicis Bibliorum Sinaitici: auspiciis imperatoris Alexandri II susceptae; accedit catalogus codicum nuper ex Oriente Petropolin perlatorum* ... (Leipzig: Brockhaus 1860).

——, 'New Testament Critics: Tischendorf Versus Tregelles [Extracts from Introduction to Tischendorf's NT (7th ed.) anonymously translated into English by Samuel Davidson],' *JSL* 1 (July 1862): 369–76.

—— [ed.], *Novum Testamentum Graece ad antiquos testes denuo recensuit cumque apparatu critico et prolegomenis* ..., 7th ed. (Leipzig: Adolphus Winter, 1859). [**Tischendorf, *Novum Testamentum* (1859)**]

——, *Travels in the East* (London: Longman, 1847).

——, *Wann wurden unsere Evangelien verfasst?* (Leipzig: Hinrichs 1865).

Tomlin, Jacob, *Critical Remarks on Dr Tregelles' Greek Text of the Revelation and His Two English Versions Compared with the Received Text and Authorised Translation Showing the Great Superiority of the Latter, by a Close and Candid Examination of His Various Readings, Tested by the Context, Parallel Places, and General Analogy of Scripture* (Liverpool: Arthur Newling, 1865).

Tomline, George, *Elements of Christian Theology: Proofs of the Authenticity and Inspiration of the Holy Scriptures* ..., 2 vols., 9th ed. (London: T Cadell and W. Davies, 1812).

[Tregelles, Anna Rebecca], *The Ways of the Line, a Monograph on Excavators* (Edinburgh: Oliphant; London: Hamilton Adams, 1858).

Tregelles, George Fox, 'The Life of a Scholar,' *Friends Quarterly Examiner* (October 1897): 449–60. [**Tregelles, G.F., '*Life of a Scholar*'**]

Tregelles, Samuel Prideaux, *An Account of the Printed Text of the Greek New Testament, with Remarks on Its Revision Upon Critical Principles* ... (London: Bagster, 1854). [**Tregelles, *Account***]

[——], 'Babylon,' *Christian Witness* 3 (July 1836): 277–87.

[——], 'The Blood of the Lamb and the Union of Saints,' *The Inquirer*, 3 (January 1840): 1–10. Later published as a tract (London: Central Tract Depôt, n.d.).

——, *The Book of Revelation in Greek Edited from Ancient Authorities* ... (London: Bagster, 1844). [**Tregelles, *Book of Revelation* (1844)**]

——, *The Book of Revelation Translated from the Ancient Greek Text. With an Historical Sketch of the Printed Text of the Greek New Testament, etc. A new edition, with a notice of a Palimpsest MS. hitherto unused* (London: Bagster, 1859). [**Tregelles, *Book of Revelation* (1859)**]

———, 'A Brief Account of Mr. Newton's Paper on the Doctrines of the Church in Newman Street' [November 1847] included as an appendix to B.W. Newton, *Statement and Acknowledgement Respecting Certain Doctrinal Errors* (Plymouth, 1847), 8–10.

——— [ed.], *Canon Muratorianus: The Earliest Catalogue of the Books of the New Testament* … (Oxford: Clarendon Press, 1867). [**Tregelles,** *Canon Muratorianus*]

[———], 'Cardinal Mai's Edition of the Vatican Codex,' *Edinburgh Review* 112 (July 1860): 256–65.

———, 'Codex Mayerianus and Simonides,' *Notes and Queries,* 4th S. 3 (24 April 1869): 369.

——— [ed.], *Codex Zacynthius* Ξ : *Greek Palimpsest Fragments of the Gospel of Saint Luke, Obtained in the Island of Zante, by the Late General Colin Macaulay and Now in the Library of the British and Foreign Bible Society* (London: Bagster, 1861). [**Tregelles,** *Codex Zacynthius*]

[———], 'Davidson's Introduction to the New Testament,' *JSL* 4 (October 1849): 343–55.

———, 'Definitions of Miracles,' *JSL* 5 (April 1850): 511–12.

[———], 'Dr Cureton's Syriac Gospels,' *Edinburgh Review* 110 (July 1859): 168–90.

———, 'Dr S. Davidson and Horne's Introduction,' *JSL* 4 (January 1857): 424–39.

[———], 'Edom,' *Christian Witness* 4 (April 1837): 101–22.

———, 'A Few Notes on Codex Reuchlini of the Apocalypse, Together with a Collation of its Text with the Common Editions,' in *Handschriftliche Funde von Franz Delitzsch,* Vol. 2 (Leipzig: Dörffling und Franke, 1862), 1–16. [**Tregelles,** '**A Few Notes**']

———, *Five Letters to the Editor of 'The Record,' on Recent Denials of Our Lord's Vicarious Life,* 2nd ed. ([reprinted] London: Hunt, Barnard & Co, 1910 [1864]). [**Tregelles,** *Five Letters*]

——— [trans. and ed.], *Gesenius's Hebrew and Chaldee Lexicon to the Old Testament Scriptures, with Additions and Corrections from the Author's Thesaurus and Other Works* (London: Bagster, 1847). [**Tregelles,** *Gesenius's Lexicon*]

———, *The Greek New Testament: Edited from Ancient Authorities, with Their Various Readings in Full, and the Latin Version of Jerome,* 7 vols (London: Bagster, 1857–79). [**Tregelles,** *Greek New Testament*]

———, *The Historic Evidence of the Authorship and Transmission of the Books of the New Testament: A Lecture Delivered Before the Plymouth Young Men's Christian Association, October 14th 1851* (London: Bagster, 1852). [**Tregelles,** *Historic Evidence*]

————, *The Hope of Christ's Second Coming: How Is It Taught in Scripture? And Why?* 2nd ed. with Appendix by C.Y Biss (London: Bagster, 1886 [1864].
[**Tregelles,** *The Hope*]

————, *An Introduction* [originally by T H Horne] *to the Textual Criticism of the New Testament, with Analyses, of the Respective Books, and a Bibliographical List of Editions of the Scriptures in the Original Texts and the Ancient Versions* (London: Longmans, 1856). [**Tregelles,** *Introduction*]

————, 'The Jansenists and Their Remnant in Holland, a Chapter in Church History,' *JLS* 7 (January 1851): 34–82. (Later in 1851 published as a book by Bagsters).

————, *Letter [from] Mr. Tregelles to Mr. Gough Relative to the Exclusion of Mr. Newton from the Lord's Table in Rawstorne Street, London, Published by Request* (London: I.K. Campbell, 1847).

————, 'Letters Concerning Cesare Magrini,' *News of the Churches* 8 (1 April 1861): 88–89 and (18 June 1861): 174.

————, 'Letters from the Continent,' *JSL* 12 (October 1850): 451–59. [**Tregelles, 'Letters from the Continent'**]

————, Letters 'On the Vatican Codex,' *JSL* 5 (April 1857): 162–63 and 8 (January 1859): 458–60, and 460–61.

————, 'Letter to Professor Samuel Lee,' *Churchman's Monthly Review* (April 1847): 312–16.

————, 'Letter to the Editor,' *Churchman's Monthly Review* (August 1847): 648.

————, 'Letter to the Editor,' *JSL* (27 August 1862): 178–79.

————, 'Letter to the Editor of the Record (1858) concerning Horne's *Introduction*,' *Quarterly Journal of Prophecy* 9 (January 1857): 66–67.

————, 'Llythyrau Dr Tregelles at Eben Fardd,' *Y Traethodydd* 29 (July 1884): 283–94.

[————], 'The Man of Sin,' *The Inquirer* 3 (June 1840): 241–56.

————, 'Matthew xvi.18,' *Christian Annotator* 1 (8 July 1854): 174.

————, 'The Nitrian Palimpsest of St Luke's Gospel,' *JSL* 4 (January 1856): 451–52. [**Tregelles, 'Nitrian Palimpsest'**]

————, *Notes of a Tour in Brittany* (Edinburgh: Johnstone and Hunter [1881]). [**Tregelles,** *Notes of a Tour*]

[————,] *On Eternal Life and Those Who Receive It*, signed S.P.T, September 17, 1845 (n.p., n. d. [Copy in BL]).

————, 'On the Original Language of St Matthew's Gospel, with Particular Reference to Dr Davidson's Introduction to the New Testament,' *JSL* 6 (January 1850): 151–86. [**Tregelles,** *Original Language*]

————, 'Passages in the Book of Revelation Connected with the Old Testament' 3 Parts, *CW*, 3 (January, April, October 1836): 55–86, 182–214, 317–59.

————, *Pastoral Relations* in five parts (London: Houlston and Wright, 1862–63).

———— [ed.], *Prisoners of Hope: Being Letters from Florence Relative to the Persecution of Francesco and Rosa Madiai, Sentenced to Solitary Confinement and Hard Labour for Reading the Word of God and Professing the Gospel of Jesus Christ,* edited with an introduction by S.P. Tregelles, LL.D, with an abstract of the trial, 2nd ed. with an appendix of recent information (London: Partridge and Oakey, 1852). [**Tregelles, *Prisoners***]

————, *A Prospectus of a Critical Edition of the Greek New Testament, Now in Preparation, with an Historical Sketch of the Printed Text* (Plymouth: Jenkin Thomas, printer, 1848).

————, *Remarks on the Prophetic Visions in the Book of Daniel, a New Edition and Greatly Enlarged with Notes on Prophetic Interpretation in Connection with Popery and a Defence of the Authenticity of the Book of Daniel* (London: Bagster, 1852). [**Tregelles, *Remarks on Daniel***]

[————,] L.M, 'Review of *Religious Liberty,*' *JSL* (January 1852): 464–468. [[**S.P.T.**], '**Review of *Religious Liberty***']

————, 'Tischendorf's Greek Testament,' *JSL* 4 (October 1849) and 5 (January 1850): 197–216. [**Tregelles, 'Tischendorf' Greek Testament'**]

————, *Three Letters to the Author of 'A Retrospect of Events That Have Taken Place Among the Brethren',* 2nd ed. (London: Houlston and sons, [1849] 1894). [**Tregelles, *Three Letters***]

[————,] *Valera's Spanish Bible of 1602: Appeal to Protestant Christians Respecting the Reprinting of This Version,* prefatory note signed B.W.N[ewton] (London: Houlston and Stoneman, 1856).

————, *The Versions of Scripture for Roman Catholic Countries: An Appeal to the British and Foreign Bible Society* (London: Wertheim and Macintosh; Plymouth: W. Brendon, 1856).

[Trollope, T.A.], 'Giampietro Vieusseux, The Florentine Bookseller,' *The Saint Pauls Magazine* 2 (1868): 727–35.

Venn, J. A., *Alumni Cantabrigienses: A Biographical List of All Known Students, Graduates and Holders of Office at the University of Cambridge from the Earliest Times to 1900.* 2 pts., 10 vols. (Cambridge: Cambridge University Press, 1922–54). [**Al. Cantab**]

Vercellone, Carlo, *Variae lectiones Vulgatae Latinae editionis Bibliorum editionis quas Carolus Vercellone sodalis Barnabites digessit,* Vol. I, Complectens pentateuchum (Roma: Iosephum Spithöver, 1860).

Vossius, Gerardus Ioannis, *De Historicis Latinis, Libri Tres* (Leyden: Maire, 1627).

Walker, Norman L., *Chapters from the History of the Free Church of Scotland* (Edinburgh: Oliphant, Anderson & Ferrier [1895]).

Waring, Elijah, *Recollections and Anecdotes of Edward Williams, the Bard of Glamorgan, or Iolo Morganwg, B.B.D.* (London: Charles Gilpin 1850) [**Waring, Recollections of Iolo Morganwg**]

The Wesleyan Missionary Notices Relatiang Principally to the Foreign Missions under the direction of the Methodist conference, 3rd series 2 (October 1855).

West, Gerald T. *From Friends to Brethren: The Howards of Tottenham, Quakers, Brethren and Evangelicals* [Studies in Brethren History, Subsidia] (Troon: BAHN, 2016).

Whetter, James, *The History of Falmouth* (Redruth: Truran, 1981) [Wigram, G.V. (ed.)], *The Englishman's Greek Concordance of the New Testament; Being an Attempt at a Verbal Connexion Between the Greek and the English Texts* (London: Central Tract Depot, 1839).

[Wigram, G.V. (ed.)], *The Englishman's Hebrew and Chaldee Concordance of the Old Testament, Being an Attempt at a Verbal Connexion Between the Original and the English Translation* (London: Longmans, 1843).

Wigram, G.V., *Plain Evidence Concerning Ebrington Street, as to the Nature of the System Now Pursued Thereby* (Plymouth: J.B. Rowe; London, 1 Warwick Sq., [1847]).

Williams, J.G. *The Times and Life of Edward Robinson: Connecticut Yankee in King Solomon's Court* (Atlanta, GA: Soc. Biblical Lit., 1999).

Williams, Taliesin (ab Iolo), *Coelbren Y Beirdd; a Welsh Essay on the Bardic Alphabet* (Llandovery: W. Rees, 1840).

Wiseman, [Nicholas Patrick] Cardinal, *Recollections of the Last Four Popes and of Rome in Their Times* (London: Hurst and Blackett, 1858). [**Wiseman, Recollections**]

Woide, C.G., *Appendix Ad Editionem Novi Testamenti Græci e Codice MS. Alexandrino …. quibus subjicitur Codicis Vaticani Collatio* (Oxford, 1799).

[Wordsworth, Christopher, ed.], *Correspondence of Richard Bentley, Master of Trinity College, Cambridge* (London: Murray, 1842).

———, *The New Testament of Our Lord and Saviour Jesus Christ, in the Original Greek*: With Notes and Introductions: The Four Gospels (London: Rivingtons, 1859).

Worth, R. N., 'A Cornish Valhalla', lecture delivered 13 September 1881 [in the Polytechnic Hall, Falmouth] in *The Royal Cornwall Polytechnic Society, 49th Annual Report* (Falmouth; Truro, 1881), 216–31.

Periodicals

American Quarterly Church Review and Ecclesiastical Register,
Andover Review
Andrews University Seminary Studies
Baptist Handbook
Bible Treasury
Bibliotheca Sacra and American Biblical Repository
Bolletino della Società di Studi Valdesi

The Bookseller
The British and Foreign Evangelical Review
British Library Journal
British Quarterly Review
The British Review, and London Critical Journal
The Bulwark or Reformation Journal
Christian Annotator
Christian Witness [CW]
Christian World: Magazine of the American & Foreign Christian Union
Churchman's Monthly Review
L'Eco di Savonarola
Edinburgh Review
Evangelical Christendom (formerly *News of the Churches*)
Evangelical Quarterly [EQ]
The Expositor
The Friend
Friends' Intelligencer and Journal (Philadelphia)
Friends Quarterly Examiner [FQE]
Gospel Magazine
Greek Orthodox Theological Review
Harvester
Journal of Classical and Sacred Philology
Journal of Sacred Literature [JSL]
Journal of the United Reformed Church History Society [JURCHS]
National Library of Wales Journal
News of the Churches (later *Evangelical Christendom*)
The North British Review
Notes and Queries
Quarterly Journal of Prophecy
Renaissance Quarterly
Scriptorium
Sunday at Home
Wesleyan Missionary Notices
Y Brython
Y Dysgedydd
Y Traethodydd

INDEX

British Museum, 58, 65, 66, 81, 145,
151–153, 171, 174, 229
purchase of Tischendorf's MSS, 152,
153, 171
reading room, 174
Brittany, 18, 190, 191
Brown, William Thomas (1821–99)
Wesleyan missionary in Plymouth
and Barcelona, 111
Browne, Eliza (died 1881) English
evangelical in Tuscany, 86, 87,
91–94, 105, 224
Bulteel, Henry Bellenden (1800–66)
evangelical teacher in Plymouth,
178
Bunsen, Baron Christian von (1791–
1860) scholar and diplomat,
167
Burckhardt, Jean Louis (1784–1817)
Swiss traveller, 24
Burgess, Henry (1808–86), priest;
second (1853–61) editor of *JSL*,
122, 150
Burgh, William (de) (1801–66)
Hebrew scholar, 29, 30, 45
Burgon, John William (1813–88) Dean
of Chichester, 167, 200, 201, 205

C
Caesar, Julius (100–44BC) Roman
general, historian and dictator, 53,
54, 215
Calandrini, Mathilde (1794–1866)
Swiss Protestant in Tuscany, 103
Calvin, Jean (1509–64) Genevan
pastor, 27, 120
Campbell, Sir Alexander Cockburn
(1804–71) Plymouth Brother, 45
Caradoc of Llancarfan (fl. 1135.) Welsh
biographer of Gildas, 16, 17
Carne, John (1789–1844) Traveller, 26

Carus, William (1804–91) Dean of
Trinity, Cambridge, 168
Castlereagh, Robert Stewart, Viscount
(1769–1822) politician, 66
Cathcart, Rev Nassau (c.1828–1911+)
Vicar of Holy Trinity, Guernsey,
185
Catholic Emancipation Act (1829), 38,
97
Ceriani, Antonio Maria (1828–1907)
Prefect of the Ambrosian Library,
164, 166, 192
Chalk, William (1814–78) SPT's Friend
and proof-reader, 195–197, 203
Chapman, Robert Cleaver (1803–
1902) early Plymouth Brother,
109
Cholera, 38, 81, 82, 227, 230
Christian Annotator, 72, 76, 138, 139
Cisneros, Francisco Jiménez de
(1436–1517) Spanish Cardinal,
55
Clarke, Edward Daniel (1769–1822)
traveller, 144, 145
Clement X, Pope (Emilio Altieri)
(1590–1676), 74, 75
Clulow, Joseph (1797–1848) Plymouth
Brethren leader, 41, 222, 226
Codices
Alexandrinus (A) London British
Museum, 58, 65, 66
Amiatinus (vgA) Florence, Lauren-
tian Library, 78, 87, 117, 151,
225
Angelica (L) Rome, Augustinian
library (codex Passionei), 77
Augiensis (F) Cambridge, Trinity
College Library, 168
Basiliensis (E) Basel, University
Library, 79

Price, Joseph Tregelles (1784–1854)
Iron master, son of Peter Price,
12, 13
Price, Peter (1739–1821) iron master,
married Anna Tregelles, 9, 12
Prideaux, Augusta (1815–1900), SPT's
sister-in-law and biographer, 6,
172, 177, 198, 204, 224, 240
Prideaux, Charles (1809–93), SPT's
brother-in-law, 177
Prideaux, Dorothy. See Tregelles,
Dorothy
Prideaux, Eliza (née Abbott) (c.1801–
1856) wife of C. Prideaux and
sister-in-law of Benjamin Newton,
177
Prideaux, Elizabeth (née Ball) (1786–
1866) mother-in-law of SPT,
32
Prideaux, Frances (Fanny) Ash (née
Ball) (1826–1894) wife of
Frederick Prideaux, 32
Prideaux, Frederick (1817–91) cousin
and brother-in-law of SPT, 32, 33,
36, 44
Prideaux, George (1744–1815) of
Kingsbridge, 4
Prideaux, Joseph Hingston (1823–40)
drowned off Plymouth Hoe, 33,
36
Prideaux, Lucy (1820–96) cousin and
sister-in-law of SPT, 177, 227
Prideaux, Sarah Anna. See Tregelles,
Sarah Anna
Prideaux, Sarah Elizabeth Ball (1786–
1867), mother of Sarah Anna and
mother in law of SPT, 177
Prideaux, Walter (1779–1832) Uncle
of SPT; banker, 32, 36, 176
Printing revolution, 55
Prisoners of Hope, 91, 106

Prophecy, biblical, 24, 25, 28, 39, 125,
186. See also Millennium
concerning Babylon and Edom,
24–26, 28, 119
futurism, 25, 186
historicism, 24, 25, 119
pre- and post-millennialism, 125
social uncertainty increases interest,
38
SPT's attitude, 22, 107, 109, 119,
120
Protestant Alliance, 113
Protestantism, 85, 93, 94, 109
attitude to scripture, 96, 99, 120
influence on SPT, 102, 114
in Spain, 106, 111, 113, 114
in Tuscany, 85, 88, 91, 94–96, 102,
104, 213
Pughe, David William (Dafydd ab Hu
Feddyg) (1821–62) surgeon, 47
Pughe, John (Ioan ab Hu Feddyg)
(1814–1874) Aberdovey surgeon
and Brethren leader, 47, 49
Pughe, John Elliot Howard (1845–80),
48

Q
Quakers
Almshouses in Falmouth, 4
attitude to Roman Catholicism and
ritual, 12, 99
attitude to scripture, 21, 22, 119
Beaconite crisis, 23
belief in Inner Light, 21, 22
commercial probity, 2
divisions among, 21
in Falmouth, 2–5, 13, 22, 23
Howard family leave Quakers, 47
in Neath, 12, 13
pacifism, 2
SPT's abandonment, 27, 35
view of the sacraments, 21, 99

Printed by Printforce, United Kingdom